OP 12

Society and Bureaucracy in Contemporary Ghana

Society and Bureaucracy in Contemporary Ghana

ROBERT M. PRICE

UNIVERSITY OF CALIFORNIA PRESS
Berkeley   Los Angeles   London

University of California Press
Berkeley and Los Angeles, California

University of California Press, Ltd.
London, England

ISBN 0-520-02811-2

Library of Congress Catalog Card Number: 74-81439

Printed in the United States of America

For my wife, Miriam,
and for my father; and
to the memory of my mother,
Anne Gordon Price.

Contents

Tables and Figures

TABLES

ix

FIGURES

Acknowledgments

Since this book developed out of my doctoral dissertation, the intellectual influences that stimulated and shaped it are many.

The writings of Fred W. Riggs, Philip Selznick, and Franz Schurmann were particularly influential, informing much of my perspective on the relationship of organization building and political development. The teaching and scholarship of Carl Rosberg and K. W. J. Post stimulated and maintained my interest in African politics; that of David Apter and Chalmers Johnson developed in me a concern for approaching the substantive material of Area Studies from the perspective of comparative social and political theory. Richard Hamilton, now of McGill University, taught me the importance of linking social theory to systematic empirical investigation. I also owe an intellectual debt to an extraordinary group of graduate students who shared with me that incredibly exciting politico-social environment that was Berkeley during the middle sixties. There are many that could be mentioned, but those that stand out are Robert Jervis, Donal Cruise O'Brien, Andrew MacFarland, Karl Boggs, Joseph Paff, and Fred DuBow. To my good friend and colleague Ken Jowitt my intellectual debt is immeasurable; he has been a constant source of stimulation and insight.

The Ghanaians who aided this research in one form or another literally number close to one thousand. But special acknowledgment is due a group of University of Ghana students who befriended me during my stay in their country, who provided me with invaluable insight into Ghanaian society and culture, and who helped me with the interview stage of my field research: Laddie Nylander, Gloria Mate-Kole, Duke Danquah, Elinor Torto, and, especially, Victor Nanka-Bruce. Yaw Twumasi, of the political science faculty of the

University of Ghana, graciously offered his time, assistance, and access to his keen intellect. Mr. B. D. G. Folson, then chairman of the Political Science Department at Legon, also provided a great deal of assistance at crucial junctures of my field work. And to Armstrong Folie I owe an especially large debt of gratitude. A young man of little education and social standing, but with deep human sensitivity and insight, he taught me more about Ghana than any book I have read or person I have met.

The Foreign Area Fellowship Program provided generous support for a year of field work in Ghana, and for part of the writing phase of the project. The Institute of International Studies of the University of California, Berkeley, provided funds for keypunching and interview coding, as did the Survey Research Center, through its International Data Library and Reference Service. The assistance of Mrs. Heidi Nebel of the International Data Library was invaluable in the coding and data-processing stages of the study.

Jon Kraus read the book manuscript in its entirety, commenting in great detail and with extraordinary insight and intellectual power.

And finally, without the support of my wife, Mimi, who endured a great deal directly attributable to this project and who, along with Erik and Matty, accepted my absences, sometimes at extremely trying periods, this study could not have been completed.

Introduction

Social science scholarship on African political systems has witnessed, within the last decade and a half, a perceptible shift in underlying perspective and in the designation of crucial problems. In the late 1950s and early 1960s, caught up in the heady atmosphere of newly won African independence, academic observers viewed developments in Africa in terms of the expansion of opportunities, and the related increasing potential for meaningful political choice, that is, in terms of freedom. Fifteen years later, however, the limitations have become more visible than the opportunities, and constraint has replaced choice as the underlying orienting concept for many scholarly observers.[1] The realities of political and economic change in Africa during this period have convinced most observers that the formal sovereignty obtained earlier meant less in the way of opportunity for autonomously defined choices than was once believed. If, from the perspective of the polity, choice involves the capacity of the political system to influence its environment in a purposeful direction, then there are few observers of Africa who have not been impressed with the apparent limits of choice under present circumstances.

Much of the discussion of constraint has focused on matters related

[1] See, for example, Michael F. Lofchie, "Political Constraints on African development," pp. 9-18; see also Immanuel Wallerstein, "The Range of Choice: Constraints on the Policies of Governments of Contemporary Independent States," in M. Lofchie, ed., *The State of the Nations*, pp. 19-36; and Henry Bretton, *Patron-Client Relations: Middle Africa and the Powers* (General Learning Press, 1971); and Reginald Green, "Political Independence and the National Economy: An Essay in the Political Economy of Decolonisation," in C. Allen and R. W. Johnson, eds., *African Perspectives* (Cambridge, 1970), pp. 273-324. [Most footnote citations will be abbreviated. Complete citations can be found in the Bibliography.]

1

to the economic position of the African countries vis-à-vis the industrialized states: on international dependency or "neocolonialism."[2] Without minimizing the significance of external factors in limiting the options open to African political leaders, it is also important to look internally for constraining elements. Here the analysis of public bureaucracy in contemporary African states deserves high priority. In any complex political system governmental administrative institutions are crucially important. It is these that translate into action community goals as they are expressed in policy decisions. But in the new states of the contemporary world public bureaucracies take on a special significance because their operation greatly affects the ability of postcolonial states to overcome two of their most pressing problems—economic underdevelopment and political malintegration. Most new states lack an indigenous entrepreneurial group with the resources necessary to play an economic role functionally equivalent to that of the capitalist bourgeoisie in Western history, so the governments have taken on major responsibility in economic matters. Consequently, the ability of these countries to translate economic develoment goals into reality is directly related to the effectiveness of public bureaucracies.

Beyond this central role in economic development, in most new states the legitimacy and stability of the political system itself will be directly affected by the operation of governmental administrative organizations. In states with recent origins the normal process of cultural socialization is unlikely to generate orientations of positive affect or legitimacy toward the political community and regime. They are therefore unlikely to receive from their citizens what David Easton has called "diffuse support," that slack or "reservoir of goodwill" which prevents short-term citizen dissatisfaction from being translated into general alienation from the political system.[3] When there is little diffuse support, the quality of contacts between citizens and agents of the regime, and the availability of short-term material payoffs, are major factors in determining the allegiance of citizens on a day-to-day basis, as well as in determining whether enduring affective commitments to existing institutions will be developed. Public bureaucracy plays a crucial role in both cases. Obviously, the effectiveness and efficiency that government administrative organizations display in the carrying out of economic policy will be an important

---

[2] See Green, "Political Independence"; Reginald Green and Ann Seidman, *Unity or Poverty* (Baltimore, 1968); and G. Arrighi and J. S. Saul, "Socialism and Economic Development in Tropical Africa"; and Bretton, *Patron-Client Relations*.

[3] David Easton, *A Systems Analysis of Political Life*, pp. 273-347.

element in determining the ability of a political system to make short-term material payoffs. Moreover, the experiences clients have with public bureaucrats will be one of the few bases on which citizens can shape their orientations toward the political system; and with support being calculative rather than expressive, negative experiences are likely to produce an alienated orientation.

New states, then, can be seen to be more vulnerable to deficiencies in public administration than the older and more established states of the West. Because the "functional load" carried by public bureaucracy in new states is so large,[4] and because these states tend to lack a cushion of political legitimacy to soften the immediate impact of governmental breakdowns, ineffective administrative organizations pose a threat not only to the achievement of community goals but also to the very survival of regime and political community. In short, the level of operational effectiveness of public bureaucracy can be a constraining factor of enormous significance within the political system of contemporary new states.

Theoretical considerations alone do not suggest the importance of public bureaucracy in the process of politico-economic change. A recurring theme in the empirical literature on politics in contemporary "low income" countries, as well as in the public statements of politicians within such countries, involves the limitations on political and economic choice that are produced by the organizational weakness of existing agencies of public administration. Comments on the phenomena of administrative corruption, nepotism, ritualism, and mismanagement abound. Rather than stimulating and encouraging developmental change, as is suggested by the widespread use of the phrase "development administration," public bureaucracies in newly emergent states have often appeared to be obstacles to change.[5] Merle Fainsod has noted:

Anyone who has traveled in underdeveloped countries and talked with those responsible for development programs soon runs into a familiar complaint. Over and over again he is told: "We know what needs doing: the real problem

[4] For a discussion of the concept of "functional load" and an analysis of its importance in the study of postindependence African political systems, see James Coleman and Carl Rosberg, eds., *Political Parties and National Integration in Tropical Africa*, pp. 655-669.

[5] The designers of Pakistan's First Five-Year Plan went so far as to observe in the text of the Plan: "The most serious limitations on the feasibility of the programme are to be found in the area of organization and administration. . . . In a real sense, the first requisite for the success of a development programme . . . is a substantial reform and improvement in governmental organization and administration." Quoted in I. Swerdlow, "Economics as Part of Development Administration," p. 108.

is how to get it done." Planners talk eloquently of goals and objectives, but administrative implementation tends to be neglected in favor of resounding policy directives which carry no executive bite.[6]

What has been said about administrative performance in "developing" countries generally applies with equal force to Africa, although this is coming to be recognized only slowly. In the scholarly literature on political institutions in contemporary sub-Saharan Africa, public bureaucracy clearly has been the "poor relation."[7] This neglect stems in part from the greater political visibility of other institutions—political parties and military organizations—but probably also from a general assumption during the early years of independence that public bureaucracy was simply not a "problem" area.[8] The inherited civil service organizations were generally viewed as highly professional and "development" oriented; their personnel were considered central members of a "modernizing elite."[9]

Recently there has been a slow growth in scholarly attention to the public bureaucracies of sub-Saharan African states. This growth coincides with an emerging awareness that the civil service organizations in at least some African countries countries are not quite what they were once thought to be.[10] Thus in the case of Ghana, the empirical focus of this study, a weak public-sector bureaucracy has now come to be viewed as a serious element in the problems that have faced each of the country's successive political regimes.

As a consequence of the particular approach that was adopted toward economic and political change, this weakness was perhaps most acutely felt during the Nkrumah period. The strategy of transformation opted for by the Nkrumah regime necessitated placing

[6] Merle Fainsod, "The Structure of Development Administration," p. 1.
[7] See Nelson Kasfir, "Towards the Construction of Theories of Administrative Behavior in Developing Countries," p. 155.
[8] This offers a striking contrast to the study of the Asian area, where the problem of deficient performance of public bureaucracy has received major attention and generated a voluminous literature. See, for example, Fred W. Riggs, *Administration in Developing Countries*, and *Thailand: The Modernization of a Bureaucratic Polity*; William J. Siffin, *The Thai Bureaucracy*; Lucian W. Pye, *Politics, Personality, and Nation-Building*; Richard Taub, *Bureaucrats Under Stress*; Gayl D. Ness, *Bureaucracy and Rural Development in Malaysia*; James Scott, *Political Ideology in Malaysia; Jose Abueva, "Administrative Doctrines Diffused in Emerging States: The Filipino Response."*
[9] Cf. J. Donald Kingsley, "Bureaucracy and Political Development, with Particular Reference to Nigeria," p. 301.
[10] For example, Dennis Dresang, "Entrepreneurialism and Development Administration in Zambia"; Goran Hyden, "Social Structure, Bureaucracy, and Development Administration in Kenya"; and also the collection of essays, *Development Administration, The Kenyan Experience*, ed. by Goran Hyden, Robert Jackson, and John Okumu.

the management of newly created state-owned enterprises as well as the overall control of the economy in the hands of public bureaucracies. But the coordination and control demanded by such a strategy never materialized. State-run corporations, plagued by corruption, mismanagement, and a shortage of raw materials and spare parts, operated at a fraction of capacity, failed to show a return on the public capital invested in them, and often required further government subsidies just to remain in operation.[11] Administrative organs set up to implement rationally conceived monetary, fiscal, and import policies often performed so poorly that bottlenecks of unmanageable proportions were created in the economy. Administrative infrastructure, established to solve economic problems, served instead to create additional obstacles to economic success. A classic example of this was provided by the administration of Ghana's import licensing system, set up to limit the importation of luxuries and thus conserve foreign reserves for needed capital goods imports. Official government commissions have examined the Ministry of Trade's handling of import licensing, have exposed the haphazard, inconsistent, and often corrupt manner in which the system was administered, and have commented on the direct economic consequences of such administrative performance.[12] For example, an official report issued in 1964 commented on severe commodity shortages that had been experienced in the previous year.

Among the immediate causes of the shortages were first and foremost the non-issuing of import licenses in a rational manner. Even when licenses were issued in values adequate for a year, delays in their actual issue inevitably meant a shortage of specific commodities in the market for a period. [And this] slap-dash attitude has also led to such undesirable situations as the importation of machines ahead of the readiness of civil engineering structures; and [the prolongation of construction of factories] because the Ministry of Trade would not issue licenses to import paint to protect steel structures.[13]

The direct consequences of the Ministry of Trade's inadequate implementation of import licensing—critical shortages of industrial

[11] Douglas Rimmer, "The Crises in the Ghana Economy," p. 26.
[12] The Akainyah Commission, *Report of Commission of Enquiry into Alleged Irregularities and Malpractices in Connection with the Issue of Import Licences* (Accra, 1963); The Abraham Commission, *Report on the Commission of Enquiry into Trade Malpractices in Ghana* (Accra, 1964); The Ollennu Commission, *Report of the Commission of Enquiry into Irregularities and Malpractices in the Grant of Import Licences* (Accra, 1967).
[13] Akainyah Commission, *Report*, p. 17.

raw materials and consumer necessities—had significant indirect ramifications on the Ghanaian economy. These shortages adversely affected the utilization of productive capacity and contributed to rapid inflation in the cost of living, since imported foods were increasingly in short supply, and locally grown produce could not be moved to market because of the lack of spare parts to maintain transportation facilities.[14]

With the performance of the Ministry of Trade being replicated throughout the Ghanaian public bureaucracy,[15] it is not difficult to understand why practically every postmortem analysis of the Nkrumah period mentions administrative inadequacy as one significant variable in the complex of factors that produced the economic breakdown of the Nkrumah regime.[16]

Since economic breakdown deprived the regime of the resources necessary to maintain its political support, administrative weakness can also be seen to have contributed indirectly to the political breakdown of the system. Moreover, there is evidence to suggest that the performance of public bureaucracy played a direct part in alienating Ghanaian citizens from the new postcolonial polity. For example, in 1966 an official inquiry was held into the operation of the agency through which government "buying-agents" purchased cocoa from thousands of Ghanaian farmers for resale on the world market.[17] The Commission of Inquiry reported that the performance of the cocoa-purchasing system was characterized by mismanagement, corruption, and the virtual tyranny of buying-agents over farmers.[18] The catastrophic effect this had for the Nkrumah govern-

[14] See Rimmer, "The Crises in the Ghana Economy," p. 27; and Robert W. Norris, "On Inflation to Ghana," p. 104.

[15] An observer of the Ghana Civil Service's implementation of foreign aid concludes: "Even allowing for the faults directly attributable to donors and for the difficulties to be expected, the performance of Ghana's bureaucracy in handling aid was in general dismal. The civil service included many men of intelligence and dedication. Yet somehow the bureaucracy managed to turn Herculean tasks into Sisyphaen labors" (Norman T. Uphoff, "African Bureaucracy and the 'Absorptive Capacity' for Foreign Development Aid: Analysis and Suggestions, with Consideration of the Case of Ghana," paper presented to the Social Science Research Council Conference on the Development of African Bureaucracies, Belmont, Maryland, March 6-9, 1974, p. 36).

[16] See, for example, Tony Killick, Development Economics in Action: A Study of Economic Policies in Ghana (London, 1975), Chapter 12.

[17] In 1961 the Nkrumah government removed the cocoa trade from the auspices of private expatriate business firms, who had employed their own buying-agents.

[18] Ghana, Commission of Enquiry on the Local Purchasing of Cocoa (Accra, 1967), pp. 15-17. In fairness it should be noted that this commission was appointed by and reported to the governing military-police council that had overthrown Nkrumah, and therefore had reason to want to discredit him. But it should also be noted that the findings of this commission coincide, in general, with other observations of the govern-

ment's effort to build a sense of commitment to the new Ghanaian nation and an orientation of legitimacy toward new state institutions is attested to in the commission's report.

> The overwhelming majority of farmers who appeared before us favoured the return of expatriate Buying Agents. . . . Farmers often associated the shortage of many essential commodities with the absence of expatriates from the buying field. . . . Throughout our tour, we were given the feeling that the farmer's confidence in his fellow Ghanaian and indeed in his fellow African had been seriously undermined. . . . And he saw the re-introduction of the white faces in the cocoa business as the surest hope for honesty and prosperity.[19]

It appears quite clear that Ghana's external economic environment, and particularly her major dependence on an international cocoa market over which she had no control, presented economic and political difficulties of extraordinary magnitude; but I would argue that an administrative infrastructure inadequate to the strategy employed to overcome these difficulties must also be taken into account if we are to understand the ultimate political breakdown of the Nkrumah regime.

This brief discussion has concerned the Nkrumah period of Ghanaian political history because it was in that period that the consequences of administrative malfunctioning were the most dramatic. But the problem has persisted, plaguing successor regimes and defying efforts at reform. Neither the military regime that overthrew Nkrumah nor the civilian one that replaced the soldiers was able to reform the public bureaucracy so as to eliminate the type of abuses and breakdowns experienced during the Nkrumah years. Thus in 1972, Tony Killick, an economist with long experience within the Ghanaian public bureaucracy, found that, despite substantial increases in the number of technically trained personnel, "the performance [of the Finance Ministry's Planning Division] remained indifferent because of poor leadership, inadequate personnel policies, low morale and weak motivation." Killick's observations outside the Planning Division suggested "this type of malaise to be rather general in the public service."[20] Pointed commentary on administrative weakness has also

---

ment-operated cocoa-buying system, both during and after the Nkrumah era, and that its findings have not been contested as have those of other similar commissions of enquiry (most notably the enquiry into Nkrumah's personal financial situation). See "Ghana's Cocoa Buying Problem," *West Africa*, No. 2854 (February 25, 1972), p. 213.

[19] Ghana, *Commission of Enquiry on the Local Purchasing of Cocoa, Report*, p. 33.

[20] Killick, *Development Economics in Action*, chapter 12, pp. 25-26. Killick had been

come from Ghanaian officials. In 1970, J. H. Mensah, the then minister of finance, opened an official report with these frank, indeed anguished, comments:

When one watches the cruel ineffectiveness with which so much expensively-acquired equipment is operated in Ghana, when one realises the inability of most parts of our administrative and managerial machinery to deliver the high quality performance which is required for a more rapid pace of national progress, then one realises that Ghana may possess an articulate and polished elite ... but she does not yet possess the managerial resources for running a fully modernized country.[21]

Most recently the head of the current military government indicated that administrative weakness continues to persist, when he confided to a respected British journalist that "more than eighteen months after taking over the leadership ... the great problem is less to find the right policies than to get them implemented."[22]

In summary, administrative weakness seems to have characterized each of the regimes of postcolonial Ghana, whatever the institutional base or ideological predisposition of the particular governing elite.

Theories of Administrative Weakness

Given the apparent and often observed inadequacies of public bureaucracy in developing countries, it is natural that "organization building" should become a major focus of attention for students of modernization, and that theoretical explanations of ubiquitous organizational weakness should be sought. A number of theoretical approaches can be found in the literature. These can be placed under two general rubrics—psychological and ecological.[23] Psychological

---

a participant within various economic ministries of the Ghanaian government both during and after the Nkrumah regime.

[21] J. H. Mensah, *The State of the Economy and the External Debts Problem* (Accra, 1970), p. 1.

[22] "Matchet's Diary," *West Africa*, No. 2935 (September 10, 1973), p. 1259; at about the same time the head of the civil service, in a speech to a conference of civil servants, remarked that "their Service was notorious for lack of a sense of urgency and of dispatch in carrying out decisions" (ibid).

[23] There is a third approach, which, strictly speaking, is not theoretical. Here problems with organizational performance are viewed simply as a consequence of a deficiency in the supply of skilled manpower. The problem then is defined as technical, to be remedied through a combination of educational policy, training programs, and stopgap technical assistance. The persistence of administrative problems which third-world polities experience suggests strongly, however, that more fundamental reasons must be sought for organizational weakness.

approaches focus on individual actors in transitional organizations and find their behavior to be nonrational or "distorted" because of unsuccessful or incomplete psychological adjustment to the reality of social change. "There is no questioning," writes Lucian Pye, "the extent to which the acculturation process in transitional societies twists and warps people's motivations and their capacities to strive effectively for any goals which they are able to articulate."[24] Although psychological approaches have in common the assumption that organizational problems are a consequence of individual malad-justment in an environment of socio-cultural change, they can be differentiated depending on whether this maladjustment is viewed as a function of personality disorder or as a function of psychic stress. In the former case, most closely associated with the work of Lucian Pye, bureaucrats in developing countries are viewed as possessing malintegrated personalities as a consequence of discontinuities in their process of socialization (primary socialization taking place within traditional social structures, and secondary socialization within co-lonially introduced modern bureaucratic institutions). The individual "identity crisis" so produced is believed to render the transitional bureaucrat lacking in commitment, insecure in action, suspicious in interpersonal behavior, dominated by anxiety, and generally ineffec-tual in the "art of associating together."[25]

The second variant of the psychological explanation for ubiquitous organizational weakness in transitional polities focuses on malinte-gration at the level of the bureaucrat's system of attitudes, beliefs, and values. The image presented in this model is of the transitional actor attempting to operate in terms of the secular norms of the formal organization but being constantly pulled in another direction by the internalized sacred values and primordial sentiments of his traditional background. "Caught between two worlds" and unable to come to grips with conflicts between the traditional and the modern, the transitional bureaucrat, it is proposed, engages in wildly erratic anomic type behavior, or is overcome by inertia, or retreats from the situation behind a façade of bureaucratic ritualism. Such behavior is viewed as characteristic of incomplete adaptation to social change, as nonrational, or in the words of Hahn-Been Lee, as a "distorted response to the pressure and tension of change."[26]

There are at least three reasons why I feel the psychological

[24] Lucian W. Pye, *Politics, Personality, and Nation-Building*, p. 50.
[25] Ibid., p. 53.
[26] Hahn-Been Lee, "Developmentalist Time and Leadership in Developing Coun-tries," p. 5.

approach to organizational weakness in "third world" societies lacks persuasiveness. First, it attributes to general psychological states behavior which occurs only in specific social arenas. If bureaucrats perform poorly beause they suffer from personality or psychic malintegration, we would expect such malintegration to affect their behavior in all arenas—in the "traditional" extended family as well as in the "modern" bureau. But clearly this is not the case, for the seeming maladjustment does not appear to carry beyond the context of the formal bureaucratic organization. I would draw the inference that whatever behavior is displayed within the bureaucratic context cannot be attributed to generalized psychological states.

Second, there is reason to believe that the psychological approach is based on a dubious theoretical assumption. The notion that malintegrated belief and personality systems must inevitably produce psychic stress and maladjustment has recently been disputed by scholars in both political science and social psychology. These scholars argue that, rather than a highly integrated and consistent set of beliefs and values, most people have belief systems containing "a proliferation of clusters of ideas among which little constraint is felt, even, quite often, in instances of sheer logical constraint."[27] And, the individual can deal with such incompatibilities in his value or belief constellation without appreciable psychological tension because all the aspects of the constellation are seldom operative at the same time. As researchers in the area of reference group identification have been able to demonstrate experimentally, attitudes are situationally specific; elements in any given situation trigger only a portion of a person's attitudes, and the individual behaves in terms of those attitudes whose salience has thus been heightened.[28] Therefore, the fact that transitional bureaucrats hold values that appear contradictory need not, by itself, have adverse behavioral consequences.

The third difficulty with the psychological approach to organizational weakness is its failure to acknowledge that behaviors that appear nonrational from the vantage point of the organization may very well be rational from the vantage point of the individual. What in the psychological approach appear to be maladjusted, "distorted,"

[27] Philip E. Converse, "The Nature of Belief Systems in Mass Publics," p. 213.

[28] See W. W. Charters and T. M. Newcomb, "Some Attitudinal Effects of Experimentally Increased Salience of a Membership Group," in E. E. Maccoby et al., eds., *Readings in Social Psychology* (New York, 1958), pp. 276-281; see also Harold H. Kelly, "Salience of Membership and Resistance to Change of Group Anchored Attitudes"; and C. Sherif, M. Sherif, and R. E. Nebergall, *Attitude and Attitude Change: The Social Judgment-Involvement Approach* (Philadelphia, 1965), pp. 350-358; Lewis M. Killian, "The Significance of Multiple-Group Memberships in Disaster."

or nonrational responses to socio-cultural change may, from another angle, appear to be quite pragmatic and rational adjustments to the social, economic, political, and cultural reality of the transitional environment. Such an assessment, however, demands that we go beyond arguments about what is assumed to be happening in the psyche of "transitional" man to an analysis of the social environment in which he must act. The various approaches which attempt this are generally referred to as ecological.

The ecological approach to organizational behavior in transitional societies has at its base the assumption common in most studies of institutional development in Europe and America—but not often found in studies of the less industrialized portion of the world—that institutions are shaped by their socio-cultural environment.[29] Fred W. Riggs, who has offered the most detailed and carefully worked out presentation of this point of view in his theory of the "prismatic society," states the basic perspective this way: "The new formal apparatus, like the administrative bureau, gives an illusory impression of autonomousness, whereas in fact it is deeply enmeshed in, and cross-influenced by remnants of older traditional social, economic, religious, and political systems."[30] The major thrust of Riggs's explanation for administrative weakness in transitional societies lies in the idea that organizations whose formal aspects have been transplanted from highly industrial societies, and which therefore appear to the observer as "modern" social structures, are in reality penetrated by aspects of the indigenous ("traditional") social system, and that this produces hybrid institutions, many of whose features are dysfunctional to successful achievement of organizational goals. Riggs refers to this socio-cultural hybrid as "poly-normativism."[31]

[29] For example, in the early 1960s Lucian Pye wrote, "When we turn to the newly emergent countries this model [that the dynamics of the system lie within the society and that it is the institutions which must be responsive] no longer seems appropriate. For in these societies the historical pattern has been the introduction of institutions from outside, with a minimum concession to the values and behavior of the people. . . . Rather than responding to indigenous values they have often proved to be the dominant factor in stimulating further changes throughout society" ("Armies in the Process of Modernization," p. 73).

[30] Fred W. Riggs, *Administration in Developing Countries*, p. 15.

[31] Riggs's explanation of endemic administrative weakness in what he terms prismatic societies actually has two aspects, only one of which involves poly-normativism. The other is overweaning bureaucratic power. Riggs argues that public bureaucracy will be dependable and efficient only when it is subject to external political control, and that the weakness of political structures external to the administrative bureaucracy in most third-world polities accounts in part for the lack of dependability and inefficiency of administrative agencies. The "bureaucratic power" aspect of Riggs's theory has been strongly criticized, leading in many cases to its rejection. In our view, the poly-normative aspect of prismatism is more central to the theory, and is of interest

Underlying all these features of the sala [prismatic bureaucracy] is the phenomenon we have called poly-normativism. The diffracted [modern] office presupposes a set of "ground rules" or a "formula" which is generally accepted by all participants, the officials in the bureau as well as the clienteles served or regulated. . . .

In the prismatic model, however, these conditions do not exist. Here a new set or norms, political formulas, and myths, based on foreign experience, are superimposed on a social order which continues to adhere, in large measure, to older traditional norms, formulas, and myths. The result is naturally dissensus, poly-normativism, and normlessness. The administrative implications of these orientations may be traced in the behavior of both sala officials and the public.[32]

What is especially important in this approach is that, unlike many other conceptions of the development process, social change is not viewed in zero-sum terms, where society is divided into traditional and modern compartments and an expansion in one necessarily means a commensurate reduction in the other.[33] The zero-sum perspective on social change follows logically from the common conception of traditional and modern sectors as concretely, as well as analytically, separate. In contrast, in Riggs's "prismatic model" traditional and modern elements are concretely merged in the same social structures and formal organizations. Hence an increase in one sector need not produce an equal and opposite reduction in the other. Yet this mixture of traditional and modern within the same social structure is not viewed as necessarily producing integration or synthesis. On the contrary, it is the interpenetration of traditional and modern elements without their integration that is seen to produce the *seemingly* nonrational, inconsistent, and chaotic behavior which underlies administrative weakness in transitional societies.[34]

---

and utility independently of one's judgment on the validity of the bureaucratic power hypothesis. The intellectual influence that prismatic theory has exercised over this study relates entirely to this poly-normative aspect. For a fuller discussion of the relationship between bureaucratic power and poly-normativism in Fred Riggs's theory of the prismatic society, see my doctoral dissertation, "The Social Basis of Administrative Behavior in a Transitional Polity: The Case of Ghana," University of California, Berkeley, 1971, pp. 32-37.

[32] Riggs, *Administration in Developing Countries*, p. 277.

[33] In this respect Riggs's prismatic model shares the perspective of many critics of the modernization literature, such as Whitaker, Gusfield, and the Rudolphs, in that social change is viewed as occurring "dysrhythmically" rather than "eurhythmically." See C. S. Whitaker, Jr., "A Dysrhythmic Process of Political Change"; Joseph Gusfield, "Tradition and Modernity: Misplaced Polarities in the Study of Social Change"; L. I. and S. H. Rudolph, "The Political Role of India's Caste Associations."

[34] Here Riggs parts company with the critics of the tradition-modernity dichotomy, who seem to argue that the mixture of elements is a matter of indifference, and that therefore the analytic distinction between modern and traditional elements is of little

If the core of Riggs's approach is seen to be his notion of the interpenetration of traditional and modern forms within a single enduring organization, then its approximation of reality is clearly established in the recent literature. In Africa, especially, the tenacity of indigenous social systems, and their ability to penetrate and transform structures that are emulative of the industrialized part of the world, have emerged as important aspects of contemporary social and political affairs. Thus Aristide Zolberg, in a general overview of the area, refers to contemporary African social and political systems as "syncretic" and uses the concept in a way that closely parallels the "poly-normative" aspect of Riggs's prismatic society.

If we conceive the original African societies as sets of values, norms, and structures, it is evident that they survived to a significant extent everywhere. ... Furthermore, the new set of values, norms, and structures, which constituted an incipient national center, did not necessarily grow at the expense of the older ones. ... Although many individuals left the country for new towns, they did not necessarily leave one society to enter a new one.[35]

In Ghana this "syncretic" or "prismatic" poly-normativism is clearly revealed by the research findings of the past decade. For example, Philip Foster, writing on social change, states the following:

A considerable body of evidence points to the persistence of elements of traditional social structure even within the most "modern" sectors of Ghanaian society. Ethnic background, kinship affiliation and traditional residence patterns still play a role even within the urban context and indeed may provide the basis for organizations which appear at first sight to be essentially western in nature.[36]

In this study I shall elaborate an ecological theory of bureaucratic behavior in transitional-type societies, particularly those with a recent colonial past, and shall offer an empirical analysis of the civil service of one such society, the West African state of Ghana, in terms of that theoretical model. Although I have found the theory of the prismatic society as developed by Fred Riggs extremely useful in

---

utility. Riggs in contrast views the mixture as empirically possible, indeed likely, but functionally consequential.

[35] Aristide Zolberg, "The Structure of Political Conflict in the New States of Tropical Africa," p. 71.

[36] Philip Foster, *Education and Social Change in Ghana*, p. 301. For a similar view see David Brokensha, *Social Change at Larteh, Ghana*.

informing my understanding of the relationship between colonially introduced bureaucratic structures and the social systems in which they have been embedded, I have had to look elsewhere for an analytic framework which could link a theoretical understanding of this relationship between structure and system to an empirically testable explanation of the behavior of individuals. There is a need to reveal the *process* aspect of the relationship between structure and system, a need for a bridge to link the macro-level concern with poly-normativism to a micro-level concern with the actual behavior of transitional bureaucrats. It is my belief that the concept of social role provides such a bridge, mediating between formal structures and the society of which they are a part, and allowing for an empirical focus on the behavior of individuals as role incumbents.[37] Consequently, the theory and analysis that will be presented in this work will rely heavily on the conceptual framework of social role theory. It is important at the outset, therefore, that the reader have a clear understanding of the particular definitions and the theoretical assumptions that underlie the role concepts that will figure centrally in the analysis that follows.

Role Theory and Group Theory

Social systems can be conceived of as clusters of social interaction, usually termed *groups*. The clusters of social interaction which are enduring, which continue in a similarly structured way over time, are accorded common recognition by members of a social system—for example, family, school, government bureaucracy, business corporation, church, and so forth—and are usually referred to by social analysts as *institutions*. Individuals can be located within a social system by the *positions* they occupy in these social institutions. Positions have two analytically distinct aspects, *status* and *role*. The status aspect of position is the esteem and prestige conferred on the individual by virtue of his occupation of a given position, and the social expectations directed toward him regarding the personal appearance and "character" that are relevant for a person granted such prestige.[38] Role is the action component of a position. Its content is determined by the expectations that members of the social system

[37] For an elaboration of this view of the social role concept, see Ralph Dahrendorf, *Essays in the Theory of Society* (Stanford, 1968), pp. 38-44.

[38] Conventionally, the term *status* is used as a synonym for position. But since the concept of status usually connotes esteem or prestige, it seems analytically appropriate to distinguish it from position, which then becomes a purely locational concept.

have about the way occupants of given positions will behave. Both roles and statuses, therefore, are culturally prescribed patterns of attitude and behavior tied to specific positions in the social system.[39] The two can be distinguished by the fact that in the case of roles these cultural prescriptions are related to the *performance* of positions; while in the case of statuses, to their *prestige*.

Roles are manifest in actual behavior because positions are structural locations in interacting social groups. The significance of this is clearly established in the experimental literature of social psychology, which has demonstrated that the behavior of the individual is largely a function of the beliefs and expectations of those with whom he socially interacts and psychologically identifies. For a variety of reasons—the need for social validation of personal belief, a desire to obtain tangible resources controlled by the group, as well as a concern for the intangible rewards of group membership, such as affection, affiliation, security, esteem, and identity—the individual will tend to mold his behavior to the norms of the group.[40] Thus the personal beliefs held by an individual are only one element influencing his behavior; ultimately a given behavior is a consequence of the vector of social pressure placed on the individual by his "significnt others"— those with whom he identifies or interacts. In role theory terms we can say that the role behavior of an individual will be influenced by (1) his cognition of the proper behavior for a person occupying his position: his *role orientation*; (2) his perception of expectations that others hold for him as a role occupant: his perceived *role*

[39] Confusion has resulted in the role theory literature from the use of the role concept to refer to individual styles of behavior engaged in by incumbents of positions, as well as to refer to the more general cultural prescriptions which define the parameters of behavior for an occupant of a given position. Thus, for example, Wahlke and his associates in their study of legislative behavior classify legislators according to whether they play trustee, delegate, or politico "roles." But these distinct roles are all attached to the same social structural position; they are personal adjustments to the culturally prescribed obligations attached to the position of legislator. Clarity in role analysis demands conceptual separation of *social or cultural roles*, the culturally prescribed pattern of behavior attached to specific social positions, and *personal roles*, the variety of styles that are permissible within this pattern. In this study we are concerned with the former definition of the role concept. See John C. Wahlke et al., *The Legislative System*, and Roland L. Warren, "Social Disorganization and the Interrelationship of Cultural Roles," p. 83.

[40] See George Homans, *The Human Group*, passim, and p. 294; S. E. Asch, "Effects of Group Pressure upon the Modification and Distortion of Judgments," pp. 393-401; S. E. Asch, *Social Psychology*, pp. 450-464; Muzafir Sherif, *The Psychology of Social Norms*, passim; R. S. Crutchfield, "Conformity and Character"; Leon Festinger, "Informal Social Communication"; L. Festinger, S. Schachter, and K. Back, *Social Pressures in Informal Groups*, pp. 166-168; J. M. Jackson and H. D. Saltzstein, "The Effect of Person-Group Relationships and Conformity Processes"; Stanley Schachter, "Deviation, Rejection, and Communication."

obligations; and (3) the sanctions he fears will be forthcoming in the event he deviates from these expectations: his perceived *role pressures*.

Since any single role is only one aspect of a larger system of social interaction, roles must be complementary if they are to be operational. That is, unless ego and alter define their roles in a reciprocal manner, interactions will break down. A physician cannot perform in his role unless those who occupy related positions in the interaction system of medical practice—such as nurse, patient, pharmacist—perform properly in their roles. The same statement can be made from the point of view of the patient, the nurse, the pharmacist. All members of a *role-set*, incumbents of related positions in a system of interaction, are dependent on reciprocal behavior from their role "partners" for the proper performance of their own roles. It is the complementarity of roles in a role-set that provides the coordinated effort, or "teamwork," which is the hallmark of effectively organized endeavor. If the unit of analysis moves from the organization to the social system, role complementarity is another term for social integration. Social integration can be said to exist to the degree that roles are organized into sets of complementary and reciprocal interactions, and to the degree that there is complementarity and reciprocity between role-sets. The first aspect of social integration, the internal coherence of role-sets, involves the problem of *role congruency*. The second aspect, coherence between role-sets, involves what is termed *role conflict*.

Role congruency exists when an actor as an incumbent of a position receives role pressures from the members of his role-set which are mutually reinforcing and consistent with his own perception of his role obligations. Thus, to utilize an example from the classic study in role theory of Gross, McEachern, and Mason, if a school superintendent perceived that his teachers, principals, school board, and students all expected him to handle a disciplinary problem in the same way, a situation of role congruency would exist. But, if teachers and principals had expectations for his behavior in dealing with a curriculum problem that were incompatible, then there would exist a situation of role incongruity.[41] Role incongruity is, then, the absence to some degree of reciprocity and complementarity *within* a given role-set.[42] Gross and his associates, as well as other practitioners of

[41] See N. C. Gross, W. S. Mason, and A. W. McEachern, *Explorations in Role Analysis: Studies of the School Superintendency Role.*

[42] The position of foreman within industrial organizations has been widely commented on as inevitably involving role incongruity because of the contradictory pressures and expectations that the foreman receives from management and worker members of his role-set.

role theory, refer to this type of situation as one of role conflict.[43] I prefer, however, to make an analytic distinction between role incongruency and role conflict, the former referring to incompatibilities within a role-set, the latter involving incompatibilities between an individual's roles in two or more role-sets. Thus, a potential for role conflict would exist if our school superintendent had a role obligation to promote to principal those teachers with the highest scores on a promotion examination, and if his daughter was one of the teachers who took the examination but failed to rank among the highest. The potential role conflict would become real if the superintendent or members of his family felt that it was his obligation as a father to promote his daughter despite her low scores. Here incompatibility exists because of the actor's membership in two role-sets with competing claims on him. The distinction between role incongruity and role conflict is not merely analytic; one can exist empirically without the other.

In complex societies, because of the multiple positions occupied by social actors, the potential for role conflict is ubiquitous, but when such societies are integrated, there exist institutionalized mechanisms to prevent this potential conflict from becoming real. These mechanisms, combining cultural norms and structural arrangements, segregate or compartmentalize each of the individual's multiple roles in distinct spheres of social interaction. Such role compartmentalization is most clearly evident in the separation of occupational and family roles within a modern society such as our own. The spatial separation of office and home, and the temporal sequence in which occupation and family role playing occur, obviously prevent potential role conflicts from becoming real. Locational cues (office or home) provide a clear definition of which role is appropriate, and the clear division of the day into working and nonworking hours allows for sequential rather than simultaneous role playing. Perhaps more important than these structural arrangements in preventing role conflict is the existence of cultural norms that define in what type of situation a given role-set is relevant. Thus, in an integrated social system, role-sets that may place incompatible obligations on an individual with common membership (such as occupation and family) will be culturally defined as belonging to distinct social spheres—that is, a role-set that is a reference group in one situation may be defined as irrelevant in another. To the degree that there is agreement among social actors about the role-set that is relevant in a given situation,

[43] N. Gross, A. McEachern, and W. S. Mason, "Role Conflict and Its Resolution," p. 288.

the individual role player will not be subject to incompatible role pressures from his significant others.[44] Thus, for example, in our school superintendent scenario it is likely that there would be agreement between both school system and family role-sets that the superintendent had *not* abrogated his father role when he denied promotion to his daughter because she failed to qualify. Members of both role-sets, as well as other interested observers, would be likely to agree that in making decisions about career promotions the relevant and thus controlling reference group or role-set should be the school system, and that the family role-set and father role are inappropriate in such a context.

Traditional and Modern Defined

In the course of this book I shall refer to particular social organizations and role obligations as traditional or modern. Because of the considerable controversy that has surrounded the "tradition-modernity dichotomy" during the past several years,[45] it is important that the reader understand how I am using these classifications, and the implications of such use. I believe it is most useful to view the tradition-modernity dichotomy that derives from nineteenth-century social theorists such as Toennies, Durkheim, and Weber, and is most succinctly summarized in Talcott Parsons' pattern-variables, as specifying mutually exclusive *principles* of social organization. These principles represent contrasting modes of integrating behavior (roles). Thus, to use as an example the pattern variable that is central to this study, in some social organizations interpersonal behavior is governed by particularistic norms—these relate behavior to the total social "personality" of the actors involved; in other social organizations the norms that integrate behavior are universalistic—these relate interpersonal interaction to the functional needs of the organization by defining as illegitimate the taking into account of an actor's total social "personality."[46] The former type of organization and supporting

---

[44] For an experimental validation of this proposition, see Jackson Toby, "Some Variables in Role Conflict Analysis," p. 288.

[45] See Gusfield, "Tradition and Modernity"; Whitaker, "A Dysrhythmic Process"; L. and S. Rudolph, "The Political Role"; Samuel Huntington, "Change to Change," *Comparative Politics*, III, 3 (April 1971), pp. 283-322; Reinhard Bendix, "Tradition and Modernity Reconsidered"; Rajni Kothari, "Tradition and Modernity Revisited."

[46] Parsons defines five pattern variables: particularism vs. universalism, specificity vs. diffuseness, ascription vs. achievement, affectivity vs. affective neutrality, self-orientation vs. collective orientation. I believe the first three have been the most central to the modernization literature. In this study the first is the most relevant.

norms are termed traditional and the latter modern. Such a classification derives from the observation that one major aspect of the change
accompanying industrialization is the emergence of very large social
organizations that are functionally specialized and structurally independent (differentiated), and that come to perform functions that
had previously been carried out by smaller, usually face-to-face,
multifunctional social units.[47] The size and functional specialization
of these differentiated organizations preclude the utilization of particularistic norms as an *effective* mechanism of integration. Since such
differentiated organizations are "partial" social institutions (they
occupy only a portion of their members' social space), and since
members come to them from a multiplicity of external social affiliations, the members' total social "personalities" do not provide a basis
for the integration of their behavior within the organization; effective
integration demands that members act, while within the differentiated
organization, as if they had no additional social memberships, identi-
fications, and obligations. Such is the function of universalistic norms
of behavior; they provide a criterion of choice that ignores those
aspects of actors' social "personalities" that fall outside the "partial,"
differentiated organization.

At the outset I stated that the distinction between traditional and
modern involved the specification of mutually exclusive *principles*
of social organization. Since what is meant by mutually exclusive
in this context is generally misunderstood, a few comments are
necessary. First, to say that we are dealing with mutually exclusive
principles should not be taken to imply that empirically any given
social unit cannot contain elements of both, although with important
consequences for the integration and thus performance of the unit.
For example, such a formulation in no way precludes the possibility
that in any formally bureaucratic organization particularistic forms
of behavior may actually occur, or even predominate. It does alert
us, however, to the likelihood that in such a structurally differentiated
organization the presence of particularistically oriented behavior will
have serious consequences for role coordination and control and
therefore for organizational efficiency and effectiveness.

Second, the formulation in terms of contrasting principles in no
way implies that any given individual is incapable of behaving on

[47] Although contemporary theorists have often attempted to define modernity as
something distinct from industrialism, such efforts lack a persuasive rationale for their
acceptance. Linking modernity to industrialism, as the fundamental principles of social
and cultural organization that accompany an industrial economic order either as
prerequisite or consequence, provides the basis for such a rationale.

the basis of both types of principle. Rather, incompatibility in the empirical sense exists only as far as a single "behavior-event" is concerned. Thus, although on simple logical grounds, a person cannot engage in role behavior which is at the same time both universalistic and particularistic, he could behave universalistically in one event and particularistically in another.

Third, the formulation suggested here does not preclude the existence of modern and traditional social units within the same social system. Nevertheless, such a system could be classified as modern or traditional if one or the other type of social organization predominates. Thus, although I would classify American society as modern, because of the predominance of bureaucratic forms of organization, I would also maintain that the American family continues to exhibit important elements of a traditional social unit (role relationships between members of the unit are characterized largely by particularism, ascription, and affectivity, for example).[48]

Fourth, the formulation in terms of contrasting principles does not suggest that traditional social units are fixed and unchanging entities, something that is often attributed to the modernity-tradition dichotomy. Since classification of a social unit as traditional is based on an assessment that role behavior is structured on the principles of particularism, ascription, and so forth, changes that take place without altering this assessment should not affect the classification. Thus it is entirely possible that a traditional kinship group might move from a situation of subsistence to commercial agriculture and, as a result, find its economic, social, and political position considerably altered; but until and unless these alterations affect the predominately particularistic and ascriptive basis on which behavior within the kin group is structured, we can legitimately classify it as traditional. It is in this sense that we can call African kinship groups traditional and at the same time recognize that they have undergone a considerable transformation during the last century.

With the above concepts in mind we can now tackle the main issue—the creation of effective organizations in the historical context of institutional transfer from industrial to nonindustrial societies. Chapter 1 provides a theoretical elaboration of the problem of institutional transfer and organizational effectiveness, and chapter 2 describes the research instrument that was utilized to obtain the

[48] Bureaucratic forms of organizations can be said to predominate in the sense that most social functions are performed by them, and in the sense that most social interactions occur within them.

data for the related empirical portion of this study. Although my theoretical framework was shaped in part by a year of field experience in Ghana, and most of the data were obtained during that time, I intend my analysis to be applicable in its fundamental aspects to so-called transitional societies generally.

I

The Social Basis of Administrative Behavior in Transitional Societies: A Theory

Organizational theorists Daniel Katz and Robert Kahn have suggested that there are two behavioral requirements for the achievement of organizational effectiveness.[1] The first is dependability of role performance. Since organized behavior involves patterned activity of a cooperative and interdependent nature, that is, teamwork, personnel must carry out their assigned roles at some minimal level of quantity and quality if there is to be organizational accomplishment. Otherwise, the existence of interdependence results in confusion and chaos, not in the coordination and cooperation in which the superiority of organized activity lies. The second behavioral requirement of organizational effectiveness is some measure of innovative and spontaneous action to facilitate the accomplishment of organizational goals. No matter how perfect role dependability may be, no organizational plan can accurately anticipate all possible contingencies, and so the successful carrying out of organizational functions requires that at least some individuals perform beyond the routine requirements of their role and direct this nonroutine behavior toward organizational goal achievement.

[1] Daniel Katz and Robert Kahn, *The Social Psychology of Organizations*, pp. 336-340.

Both of these behavioral requirements of organizational effectiveness can be usefully seen as directly related to two general analytic constructs that link organizations to their socio-cultural environment—integration and institutionalization. Integration implies the absence of role conflict in the relationship between organizational and extraorganizational role-sets. Integration can be said to exist when the social pressure on members from role-sets external to the organization does not impinge on their carrying out of organizationally prescribed roles. It involves effective boundary maintenance between role-sets or between the organization and its surrounding social environment. Obviously, then, integration is directly linked to role dependability, and thus is crucial in the building of new organizations, whether they develop endogamously, or are exogenously introduced as in institutional transfer.

Institutionalization, following the work of Philip Selznick, refers to the process whereby a social system comes to place moral or consummatory value in an organization and its constituent roles.[2] Institutionalization, like integration, contributes to role dependability, since by linking roles to transcendental individual and social goals it provides both internalized motivation and social support for the carrying out of organizational roles. The mere absence of competing roles will not lead to high levels of role performance unless the individual is motivated to invest energy in his role, and the amount of energy so invested is related at least in part to the extent of institutionalization. Institutionalization also provides the motivational source and the basis in social support for innovative and spontaneous behavior in the pursuit of organizational goals. Unless the individual's assigned role is linked to some value which he himself adheres to or whose achievement is socially rewarded, he is likely to behave in only the most perfunctory manner and to perform only those tasks routinely prescribed by the formal rules governing his role. Thus in the absence of institutionalization as defined here, the resources of people for innovation and spontaneous cooperation, which are vital to organizational effectiveness, are not likely to be placed in the service of organizational goals.[3]

[2] See Philip Selznick, *Leadership in Administration*, p. 151.

[3] Instrumental rewards could be used to create the motivation to peform organizational roles, but such rewards are more costly and less effective than the internalized, expressively based motivation created through institutionalization. Furthermore, the effective use of a structure of instrumental rewards presupposes a leadership cadre willing and able to distribute rewards so as to create incentives directed toward

It is the basic thesis of this study that within public bureaucracy in Ghana the two behavioral requirements of organizational effectiveness—dependable role performance and spontaneous behavior in the service of organizational goals—are largely lacking because of the manner in which this bureaucracy has been institutionalized, and because the socio-cultural environment into which it has been transferred inhibits integration.

The Integration of Organization and Society

In the new states of Asia and Africa, that is, those with a recent colonial heritage, most institutions at the national level—legislatures, administrative agencies, government business corporations, universities—can be considered exogenous. They have been introduced into Asian and African societies as a consequence of the colonial relationship or under the guidance of postcolonial political elites. They are emulative of organizations found in the highly industrial countries, and have been set up to fulfill similar functional needs.

Within the industrialized countries these institutions are products of a lengthy period of social and cultural change. As most of the sociological literature on this period has noted, a central aspect of this change process was the differentiation of social structures. Structural differentiation involved not only the development of new structures to perform social functions that had previously been performed by kinship units, but also the creation of a cultural basis of legitimacy for the segregation of these new structural positions and their related role-sets into specific social spheres. As Parsons and Shils have noted, most of the new role structures that characterized modernization, and particularly those of a bureaucratic nature, depended for their proper functioning on universalistic rather than particularistic role expectations.[4] That is, in order for these structures to function effectively, the behavior of actors within them had to be based on standards defined in completely abstract and generalized terms, rather than on the specific personal relationship that might exist between the actors outside of the given organizational context. For the purposes of this study, the most significant thing

---

organizational success. The existence of such a leadership group itself entails a degree of integration and institutionalization. For a discussion of the effectiveness of instrumental as compared with expressive rewards in organizations, see Amatai Etzioni, *A Comparative Analysis of Complex Organization*, pp. 3-22; and pages 167-168 of this book.

[4] Talcott Parsons and Edward Shils, eds., *Toward a General Theory of Action*, p. 82.

about this requirement for universalistic behavior is that, if it is to occur, the actor must be able to separate his official role from all of his other social roles. In other words, the operative role-set must be only that one which is relevant to organizational functioning. If such a separation of roles and role-sets is to occur regularly, it must be culturally sanctioned, so that it becomes part of the role expectations of most actors in a social system, and thus is socially permissible. The emergence of a culture that legitimates the separation or compartmentalization of roles, and is thus congruent with structural differentiation, can be viewed as a crucial aspect of the process of modernization.

In the former colonial countries generally, and the African countries particularly, there have occurred few of the socio-cultural changes that accompanied the development of complex bureaucratic organizations in the West. Thus the existence of congruity between exogenous role structures and the role orientations, obligations, and expectations sanctioned by the culture in which they are embedded is highly problematic. It is true that contact with the technologically advanced societies of the West has begun a process of social change in the nonindustrial countries similar to that which occurred earlier elsewhere. However, that contact is, in most cases, relatively recent, and until the last few decades was of rather low intensity in most areas. Colonial rule was established in Africa only at the end of the nineteenth century; its impact on the societies it dominated was gradually felt and was generally of low intensity until the 1940s. It is not surprising, then, that in the last decade research on African societies has revealed the contemporary importance and viablity of the relatively undifferentiated traditional African social systems, and particularly the continued strength of the corporate kinship structures on which these systems are based. Despite the very real changes that have taken place, most observers would agree that "the lineage system remains a primary focus of cohesion and source of stability and control."[5]

Many scholars, especially in the field of economics, have pointed to traditional kinship systems as inhibitors of modernization. They usually have in mind the scope of kin relationships in extended families and lineages. The economists point out that the nuclear family, with its much smaller membership and thus narrower range of dependent kin, is more likely than the extended family to permit entrepreneurs to accumulate capital for productive investment. Stu-

[5] William B. Schwab, "Oshogbo—An Urban Community," p. 104. See also chapter 3 in this book.

dents of bureaucracy argue that the great number of individuals related through extended kinship makes it more likely that bureaucrats will be faced with particularistic demands than when the smaller nuclear family is the predominate kinship unit.[6] These arguments fail to take sufficient note of the importance of the separation of role-sets into distinct social spheres as a systemic means to avoid such role conflicts. If there exists a cultural consensus on the legitimacy of role segregation, and if there is agreement that the occupational role-set is appropriate within the bureaucratic sphere, then it would make very little difference how many relatives bureaucrats have. I would argue that it is the corporate nature of kinship units, rather than the extent of their membership, that places strain on bureaucratic organizations within African societies.

When, as in traditional Africa, society is organized on the basis of corporate groups, social and political rights, obligations, and identities reside in the group, not, as in the comtemporary West, in the individual. Society is perceived by its members as a collectivity of groups; individuals are viewed as extensions of their corporate groups—they have no autonomous existence and identity outside of their group membership.[7] Thus, interaction can be conceived of as taking place not between individual social actors but rather between

[6] See Lloyd A. Fallers, *Bantu Bureaucracy*, p. 231; this is only one aspect of Fallers' analysis of bureaucracy and extended kinship.

[7] Contemporary African thinkers and Western scholars both have commented on this central distinction between African and contemporary Western social organization. For example, Leopold Senghor argues that there exists a fundamental difference between even the socialist European societies—that is, those that have a "collectivist" orientation—and traditional African society. He writes: *"The collectivist society [in Europe] inevitably places the emphasis on the individual, on his original activity and his needs.* In this respect the debate between 'to each according to his labor' and 'to each according to his needs' is significant. Negro-African society puts more stress on the group than on the individual, more on solidarity than on the activity and needs of the individual, more on the communion of persons than on their autonomy" (*On African Socialism*, pp. 93-94 [emphasis added]). P. C. Lloyd, the British social anthropologist, makes a similar point in a discussion of descent groups as the social basis of even contemporary African social systems: "Descent groups ... are the antithesis of the nuclear family upon which industrial society is so often based; they stress group loyalty rather than individual independence" (*Africa in Social Change*, p. 30).

Actually, the emphasis on group solidarity rather than individual autonomy is not something peculiarly African. Western sociological theory since the nineteenth century has generally recognized it to be a characteristic of preindustrial societies, wherever they happen to be located. Thus, for example, Sir Henry Sumner Maine wrote in his classic *Ancient Law* that "the movement of the progressive societies has been uniform in one respect. Through all its course it has been distinguished by the gradual dissolution of family dependency and the growth of individual obligation in its place. The individual is steadily substituted for the family, as the unit of which civil laws take account" (in Parsons et al., eds., *Theories of Society*, p. 138).

representatives of corporate groups. As Martin Kilson has pointed out, "Traditionally in African society, a person contracts ties beyond his primary unit more as a member of the primary collectivity than as an individual, thereby continuing basic allegiance to the primary unit and its needs and obligations. ... In other words, the primary collectivity itself mediates one's wider social relations."[8]

This predominance of group over individual identity in African cultures is manifest in a wide variety of social institutions. In marriage, for example, the commonly practiced levirate and sororate forms, whereby a widow marries the brother of her deceased husband or a widower marries the sister of his deceased wife, mark marriage as basically the joining of two corporate groups rather than two individuals.[9] Practices relating to debt repayment similarly illustrate the corporate, as opposed to individual, definition of obligation and responsibility. In many African societies a creditor who has trouble obtaining payment of a debt may make claims on the property of any member of the debtor's descent group.[10] A dramatic illustration is the manner in which many segmentary lineage systems settle cases of homicide: the group of the murdered individual may kill any member of the murderer's descent group; or a transfer payment is made, from the group of the murderer to that of the murdered, consisting of either a person or enough goods for the obtaining of a wife. Thus a just and equitable solution is defined in group rather than individual terms; justice has been done when the relative size of the two groups has been restored.[11]

The corporate definition of individual existence can be seen to make the separation of the individual's roles into distinct role-sets extremely difficult, if not impossible. Compartmentalization of roles cannot occur unless a culture legitimates some degree of individual autonomy from group memberships. Only if the individual can be conceived of as existing apart from his group is there a context in which he can behave in a manner free from his group obligations. When bureaucratic organizations are embedded in social systems based on corporate descent groups, the kinship group will tend to appropriate to itself any bureaucratic positions held by its members. Just as an

[8] Martin Kilson, *Political Change in a West African State*, p. 262.

[9] For a discussion of African marriage practices, see Paul Bohannan, *African Outline*, pp. 151-160.

[10] See Lloyd, *Africa in Social Change*, pp. 31-32.

[11] Ibid. These practices have been referred to as particular social arrangements that illustrate the corporate principle of social organization in traditional African cultures. No suggestion is being made that all or any of these practices are as widely in use today as they were a number of decades ago.

individual's debts or crimes are conceived of as group obligations and responsibilities, so his possession of a post in a governmental institution is viewed as a group possession. The jurisdiction of the kinship role-set penetrates the bureaucratic organization.

In such a situation the demands placed on the bureaucrat by his significant others—that is, by members of his corporate group—will be shaped by corporate group interests rather than by the formal obligations of his organizational role. This means that not only will the bureaucrat be expected to behave in the correct particularistic fashion when he encounters a member of his extended kinship group in the bureaucratic setting, but in general he will be expected to use his office in a manner that will enhance the wealth, status, and influence of his group. Thus as a representative of his descent group he would be expected to provide special treatment for members of groups that have a traditional relationship with his own—nonkin residents of the village in which his lineage makes its home, for example. He may be expected to use his office to repay the investment his lineage made in his education, and to find employment for unemployed kin. To refuse demands of this type by giving precedence to one's identity as a bureaucrat and one's commitment to the universalistic norms of the bureaucratic role would be tantamount to defining oneself as outside the corporate group. And as long as the corporate group remains important for the individual in terms of his personal sense of social identity and his psychological and material security, as most authorities maintain it still is in Africa, he is unlikely to do so.[12]

[12] The logic of this argument suggests that those aspects of Western liberalism that relate to the value placed on the autonomous individual as a social actor should to some extent be viewed as an aspect of modernization, rather than as an aspect of Westernization, as is usually the case. I am arguing that some degree of individualism within a culture is a prerequisite to the development of modern social institutions, and not a cultural trait peculiar to a geographic area. In this light it is interesting to note C. K. Yang's study of changes in marriage and family patterns that have been introduced by the Chinese communists. Yang notes that a revolution has occurred in Chinese marriage practices under the communist regime, with the government, through reforms in marriage law, prohibiting marriage based on corporate group obligations and establishing the individual commitment of the bride and groom as the only legal basis for marriage. The new wedding ceremony "has the effect of dramatizing the role of the marrying couple and dwarfs the importance of both the parents and the kinship system since it focuses public attention on the marrying individuals and not on the kinship group. . . . The new form of marriage based on the free choice of partners has an obviously disintegrating effect on the structure of the traditional family." The significance of Yang's study for the purposes of this work is that it illustrates how a modernizing regime not generally seen to be in the Western liberal tradition has introduced the notion of individual rights and personal will as a basic part of its attempt to alter a traditional system based on corporate kinship

There is a second, related feature of traditional African socio-cultural systems which undermines the integration of modern bureaucratic roles—a focus on the personal aspect in social interaction. Like most other "traditional" social systems, those in Africa tend to be oriented *toward persons not toward rules*. Of course rules exist, but these are tied to specific persons. "Within the sphere of traditional values," writes social anthropologist Ronald Cohen, "moral prescriptions are clearly focused on *interpersonal* relations."[13] Rather than stressing abstract moral principles such as "Honesty is the best policy," norms of behavior are related to direct interaction with other people—"So and so must be treated in such and such a manner," "You may say that to your mother's brother but not to your father's brother," and so forth. "Literally dozens of specific prescriptions about interpersonal behavior are drilled into children at a very early age."[14] The consequences of this type of socialization have been summed up by Cohen:

> If a person is continually made to feel that his obligations to other people are the most important part of his life, then his anxieties, his personal goals, and his security must derive primarily from these relationships. In our society it is possible for a career-oriented bachelor novelist to find satisfaction and even to achieve status in his individualistic relationship to his work. In traditional African society an individual would not be likely to seek such isolation from institutionalized personal relationships, and *certainly the approval and support of the society would be withheld from any member who did wish to pursue a solitary or individualistic occupation.*[15]

It should be clear that the central normative focus on interpersonal relationships is closely tied to the corporate family basis of African societies. If the person-to-person relationship is viewed as primary, then obligations to the kinship group will likely be honored, since traditionally most personal ties had a basis in kinship.

In the contemporary period the traditional stress on the primacy of the person-to-person relationship confronts "transplant" bureaucratic structures with major difficulties. The design of these structures is a system based on abstract rules, not persons. As much of the criticism of modern bureaucracy indicates, universalism in role be-

---

groups. Cf. C. K. Yang, *Chinese Communist Society: The Family and the Village*, (Cambridge, Mass., 1950) chap. 2, passim, and pp. 41-44.

[13] Ronald Cohen, "Traditional Society in Africa," p. 40. Emphasis added.

[14] Ibid., p. 41.

[15] Ibid. Emphasis added.

havior is by necessity impersonal. This impersonality need not include rudeness or discourtesy—when these occur they should be considered pathologies—but it does include the demand that, in his interaction with other bureaucrats or with clients, the bureaucrat act without consideration for the personal ties or feelings he may have toward them. This bureaucratic form of behavior, I would suggest, is in direct opposition to the central ethos of African socio-cultural systems, where "individual actors in their traditional society are strongly oriented to their fellow actors, not to some abstract notion of conscience."[16] Consequently, I would hypothesize that when actors in African societies play bureaucratic roles, either as bureaucrats or as clients in recently "transplanted" structures, they tend to expect personal considerations to dominate; that is, there will be a consensus that an extra-organizational role-set will be dominant within the bureaucratic setting. Indeed, when no preexisting personal connection links bureaucrat and client, both actors may feel it necessary to establish one. Creating such a personal tie may be one of the social functions performed by the West African institution of "dash" (often misleadingly translated as bribery), and one of the reasons why the practice of giving dash is so difficult for contemporary political elites to eliminate.[17]

To summarize this discussion of African cultures as social environments for the integration of bureaucratic organizations: I am arguing that the corporate nature of these cultures creates a situation in which the role pressures placed on officials in bureaucratic organizations by members of their social system are overwhelmingly particularistic. Social pressure in such societies, rather than permitting the separation of personal roles from official roles, demands that particularistic or personal criteria enter into the performance of official roles. Pressures of this kind come not only from the individual bureaucrat's extended kinship group, which is likely to view his official position as an extension of his kinship role, but also from other members of his society, whose interaction with him is shaped by generalized personalistic expectations founded in the corporate nature of their society and culture. In such a context particularistic behavior on the part of the bureaucrat is, from a personal point of view, highly rational, since to violate social expectations in a society where social relations are centrally valued and in which individual existence outside of group membership is practically unthinkable, would be to court social, psychological, and even material disaster.

[16] Ibid., p. 42.
[17] See the discussion in chapter 4, pp. 116-121.

I am not suggesting that particularism, group loyalties, and social pressures do not exist in the Western societies in which bureaucratic organization originally developed, as the earlier discussion of conformity pressure and role theory should make clear.[18] But an important distinction can be made between modern Western cultural systems and those found in contemporary Africa. Within the former there exist certain values that permit the generation of social support for behavior that, in the name of abstract ideals and universalistic standards, ignores, or if need be, sacrifices, personal social relationships. The emphasis that Western culture gives to the values of individualism and nonconformity is crucial here.[19] In Western social myth the man who is admired and who receives respect is the man who resists social pressures and behaves according to an individual commitment to abstract principle. Such a man is a "profile in courage."[20]

Although individualism and nonconformity exist as values in Western culture, these societies are obviously not committed to such behavior in all contexts and in all forms. But the existence of such values does permit the cultural legitimation of the sacrifice of certain social relationships in specific contexts. The values of individualism and nonconformity make it possible for social support to exist for the bureaucrat or politician who resists the demands of his personal relationships in the name of commitment to abstract principles and

[18] See the Introduction, pp. 14-18.

[19] The use of the concept of individualism here should be clearly distinguished from the notion of "rugged individualism" often associated with American culture. While the latter infers interpersonal competitiveness and an anticollectivist orientation, the usage here refers only to the cultural understanding of the individual as the basic unit of social organization, with intrinsic significance beyond any of his social memberships. As such, individualism is not necessarily antithetical to a collectivist orientation. See quote from Leopold Senghor, n. 7 above; and n. 12 above.

[20] Among the role models presented by the mass media to children in the United States are characters whose ability to function at their important jobs is directly and explicitly related to their avoiding the encumbrance of social ties. Superman, Batman, Robin, the Lone Ranger—each dons a disguise so as to prevent personal social ties from interfering with his important work (the Lone Ranger's Indian companion Tonto has no need for a disguise, since his ethnic background precludes the establishment of such ties). The Lone Ranger is so fanatical about his freedom from the encumbrance of "extraorganizational," nonfunctionally specific, personal relations that after completing a mission he sneaks off without a farewell to those he has helped—a major motif of this "folk-hero." These childhood role models point up the sharp contrast between Western cultural orientations toward social relations and those of Africa. In Africa such behavior would probably be considered deviant and antisocial, not heroic. Among the Kanuri of Nigeria, for example, "the man who lives alone is called *ngudi*, or unfortunate, and he is not to be trusted because his lack of social ties indicates that he may not be bound by the moral precepts of his own society." See Ronald Cohen, "Traditional Society in Africa," p. 42.

universalistic standards. In addition, the cultural conception of the autonomous individual places a narrow limit on the repercussions that may follow the violation of a personal relationship. If negative affect is generated by the application of universalistic rules, it is not likely to flow much beyond the dyadic relationship between the two interacting individuals, bureaucrat and client for example. In a corporate-based society, however, there is no such mechanism for the limitation of repercussions. The violation of a particularistic expectation is likely to draw hostility not only to the bureaucrat himself but to his entire corporate group; and since the client is also a member of a corporate group, the social slight that has been committed is likely to be interpreted not only as an attack on him, but as an act against his corporate group as a whole. In this way the violation of particularistic expectations in corporate-based societies can have wide social ramifications. And when social status is determined by the extent of one's positive social relations, as is true in most African societies, only with great trepidation can a bureaucrat risk the application of universalistic standards when these are in conflict with particularistic expectations.

The Institutionalization of Bureaucratic Organizations in Africa

In discussing the creation of effective bureaucratic organizations in terms of the need for congruity between formal structural differentiation and the role differentiation permitted and encouraged by the cultural system in which the bureaucratic organization is embedded, it has been my thesis that certain cultural arrangements make possible the generation of social support for the types of role behavior demanded by the technical organization of bureaucracy, and that others tend to inhibit it. However, even if a cultural environment sanctions role differentiation, that is, role compartmentalization, social support is not likely to be generated for the roles of a formal organization unless those roles and the structures which they constitute are positively valued by organizational members and their significant others. If an actor is to be bound by role obligations, then he and those he interacts with and cares about, must perceive these obligations as having moral force. We can say that the organization must become a reference group for its members and their significant others if the formally defined organizational role-set is to become operative in the actual process of social interaction. Students of organization theory, especially those utilizing the "human relations" approach, have long recognized this, as is attested to by the importance they place in organizational identification as a variable affecting role performance and the achievement of organizational goals. Organizational identification or loyalty, according to Chester I. Barnard, creates the "willingness of persons to contribute efforts to the cooperative system" and thus is "recognized as an essential condition of organization."[21] When organizational identification on the part of members is paralleled by positive affect toward the organization on the part of those in society who are outside it, then the conditions exist for social pressure to "encourage" members to contribute to the cooperative system. In such a situation social rewards and punishments will be so arranged that it is in the interests of individuals to act in accordance with the rules prescribed for their organizational positions, and to make critical innovative decisions to further organizational goals in situations where routine regulations are inapplicable. An organization with this type of relationship to its social environment can be considered institutionalized.

For an understanding of the means by which formal organizations and their constituent roles become institutionalized—that is, come to be regarded with positive affect by members of a society—Franz Schurmann's discussion of pure and practical ideology provides a useful starting place.[22] Both types of ideology are present, according to Schurmann, in an effectively functioning organization.

The ideas of pure ideology state values: moral and ethical conceptions about right and wrong. . . . The ideas of practical ideology state norms: rules which prescribe behavior and thus are expected to have direct action consequences.[23]

The values of the ideology are designed to bring about a moral and psychological transformation of the individual. *By acquiring a pure ideology and internalizing its values, the individual develops commitment to the organization.* . . . By acquiring a practical ideology and learning its norms, the individual becomes an effective actor in the organization.[24]

Practical ideology in a bureaucratic organization can be viewed as corresponding roughly to a combination of the formal rules governing behavior in specific positions and the general norm of universalism governing organizationally relevant role expectations. The signifi-

[21] Chester I. Barnard, "The Theory of Formal Organization," p. 34.
[22] Franz Schurmann, *Ideology and Organization in Communist China*, pp. 23-53.
[23] Ibid., p. 38.
[24] Ibid., pp. 45-46. Emphasis added.

cance of pure ideology is that it legitimizes or institutionalizes the specific role behavior called for by the practical ideology through linking it to the goals of the organization and then tying the latter to some transcendent social value or "cause." In an organization without a pure ideology, or what Selznick terms a "socially integrating myth,"[25] members will have little commitment to their roles or to the performance goals of the organization. This will be revealed in role performances that are characterized by ritualism, and in a willingness in the case of conflict to give priority to other roles, roles that *are* tied to a morally binding set of values.[26]

The pure ideology of an organization will oftentimes involve nationalism; at other times it will involve some aspect of a social philosophy (Marxism, "the American Business Creed," and so forth); and at still other times, some combination of the two. Nationalism is a particularly important aspect of the pure ideology of public bureaucracy, because usually such organizations and their constituent roles are portrayed as elements in a legitimate political order. Since nations have the character of terminal communities, the linking of public service roles to community goals is a particularly powerful means of establishing the priority of organizational roles over all others. When, on the contrary, public roles are not tied into a "moral

---

[25] See Philip Selznick, *Leadership in Administration*, p. 151.

[26] Discussions of bureaucracy and politics have often suggested that, because universalism implies "neutrality" in role behavior, the politicization of bureaucracy is ipso facto damaging to bureaucratic performance. As my discussion of ideology and organizational commitment suggest, I do not share this view. Indeed, I would maintain that in certain circumstances the reverse will be the case. The source of confusion is the inference that universalism and ideological commitment are mutually exclusive. But if universalism is viewed as a "practical" ideology—a technical means—to achieve goals sanctioned in a "pure" ideology, then commitment to the latter does not preclude universalistic role behavior. Rather, personnel committed to both types of ideology are likely to be more effective organizational performers—to be more highly motivated in their role behavior, and to apply universalistic standards in a manner that is more rational in relation to organizational purposes—than are personnel whose commitment is merely to the practical ideology of bureaucracy. Moreover, in the context of rapid change, political ideology may be an important means available to leadership for introducing universalism into a situation that would otherwise sanction particularism. In such a situation the recruitment or promotion of personnel based on political criteria might well enhance organizational performance. Such recruitment techniques should not necessarily be viewed as a violation of achievement norms, but rather might well be an instance of their application, achievement norms being technically defined as criteria which "give priority to . . . [the actor's] actual or expected performances, and to . . . attributes only as directly relevant to these performances" (Parsons and Shils, p. 83). If individuals with a particular political affiliation or set of beliefs are more likely than others to share the goals of a given organization, then this would be an attribute relevant to performance, and thus in such a situation the utilization of political criteria in recruitment and promotion would be consistent with criteria of achievement.

community," they are likely to be utilized as vehicles for private plunder rather than for public service.

This is at the crux of the problems facing exogenously introduced public organizations in the African states. The legitimacy of the regimes to which these exogenous structures are linked is highly problematic in all African states, as is the existence of a strong sense of national identity among a large proportion of citizens. As a consequence, public organizations lack an effective "pure ideology" to link them with a set of values and goals that are collectively held by members of the societies they "serve." The Nigerian novelist Chinua Achebe has beautifully captured this aspect of contemporary African political systems in his novel *Man of the People*. To explain why African politicians are able to engage in corrupt practices without apparently suffering public disapproval, he relates a parable about a dishonest village trader who, by his actions, raises the wrath of the village population and is driven out of business. At the end of the parable Achebe draws the following moral: "[When] the owner was the village, and the village had a mind, it could say no to sacrilege. But in the affairs of the nation there was no owner, the laws of the village became powerless."[27]

When there is little commitment to organizational roles and related performance goals on the part of both members and the general public, administrative performance suffers from ritualism as well as from particularism. Paradoxically, these two forms of behavior involve opposite orientations toward bureaucratic rules: particularism involves the violation of such rules in favor of personal obligations, and ritualism involves their rigid application. This paradox can be resolved, however, within the terms of the role model we have been developing. Ritualism shares with particularism one important feature; it is behavior that is not oriented toward the achievement of organizational goals. The application of bureaucratic regulations are ends in themselves, regardless of the relationship between a specific application of a regulation and the goal that the regulation was designed to serve. The ritualistic adherence to rules in a bureaucratic organization is often a mechanism for shirking work and avoiding risks. "Red tape" is used by bureaucrats to deny services to clients and to avoid making decisions that might expose them to sanctions. This use of ritualism is endemic to bureaucratic organizations, and it is particularly pervasive in transitional bureaucracies, where bureaucratic roles are not linked through a "pure ideology" to a set

[27] Chinua Achebe, *A Man of the People*, (London, 1966), p. 167.

of shared community goals. When the commitment of members to organizational goals is low, they are likely to seek means to minimize the amount of risk and energy they direct toward goal-related performance. Since in transitional societies social approval is given to those individuals who manifest commitment to personal ties and obligations, it is to the enhancement of these that their efforts are directed, and ritualism permits the avoidance of work and risk in those situations in which no personal relationships are activated. Ritualism, then, will be the dominant mode of behavior when the only relationship between bureaucrat and client, or between two bureaucrats, is official; particularism will be the dominant mode of behavior when the two actors are linked by some personal tie.

Although the lack of political integration in most African states makes unlikely the existence within public bureaucracies of effective "pure ideology," the positions within these organizations are highly valued in African society. Indeed, the desire for access to the so-called "European" posts in the colonial civil service was a major source of grievance against colonial rule. Today, positions within exogenously introduced organizations are strenuously sought after, for they represent an important channel of upward social mobility in contemporary African societies. A post at one of the top rungs of the civil service hierarchy, a seat in Parliament, a professorship at a university, and the like, are generally recognized as embodying elite social status. What is interesting, in the context of this discussion, about this orientation toward "transplant" organizations is that greater value has been placed on certain aspects of the newly introduced positions than on other aspects.

Students of culture change generally hold the view that change induced by culture-contact occurs selectively rather than in toto. Members and groups within the host culture tend to adopt those aspects of the impinging culture that appear, on the manifest level, to be of instrumental value from their own point of view, and to resist those aspects that appear threatening. This insight is useful in understanding institutional transfer under colonialism, when we recall the earlier distinction that was drawn between the status and role aspects of organizational or group positions.[28] I have already argued at length that the role demands of exogenously introduced positions are incongruent wih fundamental elements of traditional African culture, and thus one would expect the role or performance aspects of these positions to be unvalued as long as those elements

[28] See discussion in the Introduction, pp. 14-15.

of traditional culture retain their importance. There is no similar problem of incongruity in 'regard to the status aspect of these positions. On the contrary, occupancy of such positions brings economic benefit and social status, not only to its incumbent but to his corporate group as well. Thus positions within "transplant" organizations have come to be valued as important economic and social assets for traditionally based corporate groups.[29] The adoption of this new mode of status attainment does not necessarily imply change in the basic patterns of social behavior. For example, Simon Ottenberg, in an observation about social change under colonialism among the Ibo of Nigeria, states, "Basic patterns of social behavior, of interpersonal relationships, have changed little, though new symbols of success replace old ones and new goals appear."[30] One arena in which this process can clearly be seen in operation is the response of African society to the introduction by Europeans of Western-type education. Bruce Grindal, writing about the Sisala of northern Ghana, provides a lucid description of this response:

Parents felt that education was an investment which would enhance the family's prestige by producing a young adult who stood in an ingratiating relationship to the white man. As the literate member of the community, the schoolboy was regarded as a liaison between his elder men and the colonial government. ... Beyond this, education was perceived as meaningless, and the school boy was expected to conform to the same ... moral conduct as his illiterate brothers. ...

The older educated often say that they ... attended school because their parents desired them to do so, and it was always their goal to serve their families. As one man put it, "Every family has its people who hunt and its people who farm. In the same way every family has its educated people.[31]

To summarize: I have been arguing that exogenously introduced bureaucratic organizations and their constituent positions have been

[29] Cultural traits that appear on the manifest level to be nonthreatening may, of course, have latent functions that lead to alteration in the social system. The fact that the status aspects of bureaucratic positions are positively valued because they are integrated into a traditionally based system of motivation does not mean that the utilization of these new status elements will not have latent functions that are disturbing to the traditional system. For an insightful critique of what the merger of "modern" status elements with traditional social organization has done to contemporary African social systems see the novel *Fragments*, written by the Ghanaian novelist Ayi Kwai Armah. For a discussion of the distinction between manifest and latent functions of social structures, see Robert Merton, *Social Theory and Social Structure*, pp. 60-82.

[30] Simon Ottenberg, "Ibo Receptivity of Change," in William Bascom and Melville Herskovits, eds., *Continuity and Change in African Cultures* (Chicago, 1959), p. 142.

[31] Bruce Grindal, *Growing Up in Two Worlds: Education and Transition among the Sisala of Northern Ghana* (New York, 1972), p. 74.

institutionalized in their status but not their role aspects. In the process of institutional transfer those aspects of differentiated bureaucratic structures that could be utilized to instrumentally enhance the well-being of traditionally defined social units came to be valued by the host society, and those aspects whose definition ran counter to the solidarity of these traditionally defined social units were not valued, or at least not to the same extent. Thus it is incorrect to ascribe the problems of public bureaucracy in contemporary African states to the fact that transferred bureaucratic structures lack institutionalization. Rather, the problem, as I see it, lies in what has been institutionalized, and what has not.

The placing of social value in the status but not the role aspects of organizational positions is likely to have serious consequences for the behavior of organization members. There will probably be social pressure on the incumbent to utilize his position for the status benefit of his corporate group, without regard for the norms that define the role aspect of his position. A senior civil servant, for example, by virtue of the position he holds, may be expected to make large contributions to the social and economic welfare of his extended family; school fees for nieces and nephews must be paid, community improvement projects in his home village must be financially supported, monetary contributions must be made on special family occasions such as funerals, weddings, and "outdoorings," and jobs must be found for unemployed kinsmen. He will also be expected to possess those material objects that are outward symbols of his high social status and thus, by indirection, that of his corporate descent group. For him to fail to own an automobile, expensive imported clothing, and a European-style house would be to deny to his family the public verification of their status. Such abstinence would likely be interpreted as the act of an ingrate who refuses to repay the great investment made by his family in his upbringing and education. This combination of demands is likely to exceed the resources available from a civil service salary, and thus the need to find means to augment income is created. Consequently, corrupt practices become the means to maintain the social approval of the civil servant's significant others.

It should be noted, however, that when deviance from the norms of the official role endangers the status interests of the individual and his group, as when discipline from a superior is likely to be forthcoming, conformity to organizational norms will receive social support. Thus the institutionalization of status aspects of a bureaucratic position can, under certain circumstances, provide an instrumental commitment to its performance aspects. Such a situation is likely to occur rarely, however, since superiors, being part of the same socio-cultural system as their subordinates, are subject to similar role expectations and are likely to accept, as normal behavior in their societies, the violation of official norms to satisfy particularistic obligations. The supervisor who is too zealous in his demands for conformity to formal role obligations would likely become the object of social hostility. With little social support for his behavior, he would place himself in the position of alienating important social ties on which he and his extended family depend for their status and security. Thus it is likely that such zeal would be rare.

From this perspective an interesting insight can be gained into the oft observed effectiveness of expatriate European managers in upgrading administrative performance. The success of these few Europeans should be seen as lying less in the skill they bring to their jobs than in the fact that they are not members of the local society and thus are not subject to the same social pressures as are African senior personnel.[32] As such they are relatively free to demand "proper" organizational role performance from administrative personnel, and to use negative sanctions in the case of "deviance." In this type of situation the satisfaction of traditional corporate group interests would dictate conformity to the obligations of the official role, since only then can the status perquisites of the position be maintained. It should be noted that administrative capacity created by this type of "technical assistance" does not necessarily represent genuine or self-sustaining change, since its effect is likely to be only temporary. With the departure of the expatriate managers the traditional socio-cultural environment once more will control behavior of organization members. It might be said that technical assistance thus leads to "growth without development" in the administrative sphere.[33]

[32] The utility of being "outside" of local society for the performance of nontraditional activities is recognized by Yoruba migrants to Ghana. This group of Nigerians erects barriers to intermarriage with local people and insists that a man marry only a "homelander." Ronald Cohen and John Middleton explain that this practice is dictated by the functional position of women within the migrant Yoruba community: "Yoruba wives must serve as traders, and the fewer connections they have to the local population, the greater their ability to escape noncommercial obligations for the economic support of relatives" (*From Tribe to Nation in Africa* (Scranton, Penn., 1970), p. 21).

[33] The concept of "growth without development" was created with reference to the economic sector by Robert Clower and his associates in a study of the Liberian economy. See Robert Clower et al., *Growth Without Development, An Economic Survey of Liberia* (Evanston, 1960).

Summary

In the industrialized states of the West, public bureaucracies, as products of a lengthy process of socio-cultural change, are constituent parts of legitimate national political systems and are embedded in cultures that are supportive of structural differentiation. This means, first, that the component roles of these organizations are infused with value by being tied, through national ideology, to the achievement of community goals—thus formal role obligations are perceived by members of the community as involving public service;[34] and second, that Western culture sanctions the separation of roles into distinct spheres of social activity, so that the universalistic role obligations of the bureaucrat's official position need not actually conflict with the particularlistic obligations of his personal roles.[35]

The situation found in the "transitional" states of Africa is quite different. Here bureaucracies are not the product of a lengthy process of social change; they are the result of conscious emulation of organizational forms found in industrial societies. There is, as a consequence, a lack of congruity between the emulative institutions and their socio-cultural environment. The cultures and social systems of traditional Africa are organized around corporate descent groups, and although these societies are in the process of change, this traditional form of basic social organization, and the norms of interpersonal behavior that are appropriate to it, are an important aspect of the contemporary period. I have argued that this aspect of contemporary Africa prevents that separation of official roles from personal roles that is so necessary for the operation of public bureau-

[34] There is reason to believe that in the contemporary industrial societies this is no longer true for certain segments of their population. It would seem that in the post-World War II era the pure ideology or socially integrating myths of these societies have lost their power to generate affect and bring forth commitment, at least among a portion of their youthful members. The postwar years may indeed have brought an "end of ideology," but rather than providing the positive benefits predicted by its early observers, this may come to mean a deterioration of the moral cement binding the community, that is, a loss of legitimacy for its constituent roles.

[35] Much of the contemporary criticism of highly modern societies relates to the all-embracing pervasiveness of role separation in society and culture. Role compartmentalization is increasingly being alleged to rob men of their sense of "wholeness," to "separate them from their selves." Charles Reich, for example, argues that in contemporary America "as the individual is drawn into the meritocracy, his working life is split from his home life, and both suffer from a lack of wholeness." This, he alleges, is "the source of discontent and rage in the new generation" (*The Greening of America* (New York, 1970), p. 9). One need not agree with this particular formulation to recognize that while the integration between bureaucracy and culture in modern societies produces benefits from the point of view of organizational effectiveness, it can have negative consequences from other vantage points and in terms of other values.

cracy. Furthermore, because national political communities in Africa are so weak, the constituent roles of public bureaucratic organizations have been institutionalized more in their status than in their role or performance aspects. This means that the use of bureaucratic positions for personal and corporate-group status concerns will be socially sanctioned, even when such use violates the formal role obligations of the office. Thus the form in which "transplant" organizations have been institutionalized is congruent with, and in fact reinforces, the role expectations that are based in the corporate nature of traditional African social systems.

In the perspective adopted here, contemporary African social systems are malintegrated at the institutional but not at the individual level. At the formal institutional level organizational and extra-organizational role-sets are not reciprocally related, and consequently role performance within these organizations is unreliable and goal achievement suffers. However, this incompatibility between role-sets is not usually manifest in role conflict at the level of the individual actor. Since the dominant identification and commitment of most actors within African social systems is to role-sets external to the organization, there will be little social pressure placed on the individual to fulfill the universalistic obligations of his formal role, and a general consensus of role expectations in the direction of particularistic norms will exist. Thus, role conflict exists at the formal institutional level but not at the level of social interaction.

Obviously, there will be a certain number of actors with a personal commitment to their modern role and its universalistic criteria for behavior, who as a result will experience a great deal of role conflict. These are usually persons with a recent experience outside of their own social systems, such as attendance at a European university over a period of years. The commitment of these individuals to their official roles is unlikely to long survive their return to their own social systems, where they will find intense social pressure to honor personal obligations, together with a general absence of social support for their own commitment to organizational role behavior.[36]

From the perspective of the role model developed here, then, behavior in "modern" bureaucratic organizations within transitional

[36] Donald Levine found that in Ethiopia the university graduate who enters public bureaucracy and attempts to serve his country in terms of universalistic behavioral criteria "is likely to be criticized and even punished for maintaining [these] standards in the face of demands by superiors and relatives to do otherwise." According to Levine, most returnees from foreign universities, after a short period of resistance, make some form of adjustment to the demands of their home social environment. Donald N. Levine, *Wax and Gold* (Chicago, 1965), p. 205.

societies is viewed neither as a consequence of psychological malad-justment, nor as a result of the fact that bureaucratic rules violate immemorial tradition, nor as the outcome of marginality, cognitive confusion, and anomie, but rather as a consequence of the fact that the vector of social pressures placed on the individual by his significant others in most cases makes the violation of official norms and the absence of commitment to performance goals a rational pattern of behavior from the individual point of view. I am suggesting, not that the role pressures and resultant behaviors that I have attributed to transitional societies are totally absent in so-called modern social systems, but rather that in the latter case they are randomly distributed, and are considered to be deviant behavior, while in the former such behavior is systemic, *with deviancy represented by conformity to organizational norms.* It is the intensity, combination, and pervasiveness of dysfunctional role pressure and resultant behav-ior that is distinctive about bureaucratic organizations in transitional societies.

II

Setting, Method, and Sample

Setting

The empirical aspect of this study is focused on the role orientation of Ghanaian civil servants, and the role expectations and pressures directed at them by their "significant others" outside of the civil service organization. This discussion of role expectations and orientations can be usefully placed in context through a brief sketch of the history and structure of the Ghanaian Civil Service.[1]

As in other former colonial countries, the Ghanaian Civil Service as an organization was created by a European colonial power, in this instance Britain. It was created by the authority of the British colonial administration; the individuals who staffed the various boards and commissions charged with planning its formal aspects were appointed by the British, were in most cases themselves British, and explicitly utilized the civil service of Great Britain as the model on which to shape the public administration of an independent Gold Coast. And further, the Ghanaians who now hold the most senior positions in the civil service organization began their careers for the most part in what was still a British colonial civil service. It is not surprising, then, that in its formal aspects—its structure, organization, and governing norms—the civil service bequeathed to Ghana by

[1] Brief descriptions of the historical development of the civil service in Ghana can be found in Richard Symonds, *The British and Their Successors* (London, 1966), pp. 152-156; and D. K. Greenstreet, "The Development of the Ghanaian Public Service," *Journal of Management Studies*, II, 2 (September 1963), 23-29. For a detailed discussion of the formal structure and organization of the civil service in Ghana and Commonwealth Africa generally, see A. L. Adu, *The Civil Service in Commonwealth Africa*, passim. See also Lionel Tiger, "Bureaucracy in Ghana."

colonialism closely resembles the British variant of classical Weberian public bureaucracy. This remained so at the time of my study inasmuch as the Ghanaian governments that have ruled since independence was achieved on March 6, 1957, have not altered this legacy in any but marginal ways.[2]

The contemporary civil service organization and its staffing by Ghanaian personnel did not develop until very late in the colonial era. Only after World War II did the colonial administration give extensive thought to creating a civil service organization that would be appropriate to a self-governing entity. Only in the early 1950s were a number of governmental moves made to establish the structure and organization for the civil service of what was to become before the end of the decade the independent state of Ghana.[3] Steps were also taken to devise a means to "localize," "Africanize," or "Ghanaianize" the positions within the organization, that is, to replace the expatriate personnel of the erstwhile Colonial Service, and subsequent Gold Coast Civil Service, with Ghanaian citizens.[4]

"Ghanaianization" took somewhat longer than the creation of formal structure. Not until the middle 1960s was the Ghanaian Civil Service fully "Africanized." During the colonial era Africans were excluded by and large from administrative positions within the colonial bureaucracy. Posts in what was the Senior Service were known as "European appointments," while Africans were recruited into the Junior Service as clerks. In 1948 there were approximately 1,400 senior appointments (essentially positions above the clerical rank), and of these only 98 were held by Africans.[5] In the early 1950s, with the new civil service structure that abolished the formal distinction between Senior and Junior Service, and with the impending move of the Gold Coast toward self-government and independence, the situation changed rapidly. By 1952 there were 620 Ghanaians holding

[2] Under the Nkrumah regime the civil service and civil servants were constantly attacked by politicians for being a colonial vestige and for exhibiting a colonial "mentality," but these criticisms did not lead to any fundamental change in the formal aspects of the service's structure and organization.

[3] Most important of these was the "Lidbury Report" and its accompanying governmental White Paper. The official title of the report is *Report of the Commission on the Civil Service of the Gold Coast, 1950-51* (Accra, 1951).

[4] These steps included the creation of a Select Committee of the Legislature on Africanization in 1949; the appointment of A. L. Adu, a Ghanaian, as Commissioner for Africanization in 1951; the convening and report of the Lidbury Commission in 1951; the appointment of a Select Committee of the Legislature under K. A. Gbedemah to review the Lidbury Report in 1952; a review of the Africanization program by a working party of civil servants under A. L. Adu in 1953; and a major government statement on the program of Africanization in 1954.

[5] See Greenstreet, "Development of the Ghanaian Public Service," p. 24.

so-called European appointments, by 1954 the number had increased to approximately 1,000, and in 1957 it stood at slightly over 1,700. This increase in Ghanaian personnel did not necessarily mean a decline in the number of expatriate officers in the civil service, since the size of the organization was rapidly expanding as it took on the enlarged functions appropriate to a soon-to-be sovereign state. In fact, it was not until independence that the numbers of expatriate civil servants began to decline substantially, and even in 1960—some three years after independence—there were approximately 750 expatriates employed within the Ghanaian Civil Service.[6]

The higher reaches of the civil service were naturally the last to be fully Africanized. In 1954 none of the principal secretaries was Ghanaian; of twenty-two undersecretaries, only one, A. L. Adu, was African; there were only four Ghanaian principal assistant secretaries out of a total of thirty-four; and all but ten assistant secretaries were European. Even in 1960, some three years after independence, nearly one-half of the principal secretaries were expatriates, while Europeans occupied all of the undersecretary posts, and only twenty-two out of thirty-nine senior assistant secretaries were Ghanaian citizens.[7]

In short, the Ghanaian Civil Service is a very new structure in Ghanaian society, both in the sense of its existence as an organization, and in the sense of African participation in its roles and in roles of a similar nature in, say, the colonial bureaucracy. In this aspect Ghana, and African states generally, can be contrasted to other products of the British colonial empire such as India, where indigenous participation in the colonial civil service was already evident at the turn of the twentieth century, and became widespread by the 1930s.[8]

Method

The data on which the empirical aspect of this study is based were collected during 1968 and 1969 in three related attitude surveys. These are referred to as the Civil Servant Survey, the Clientele Survey,

[6] *Statistics on the Africanization of the Ghanaian Civil Service*

	1952	1953	1954	1955	1956	1957	1958	1959	1960
Africans	620	898	1,043	1,277	1,553	1,741	1,984	2,320	2,766
Expatriates	1,360	1,350	1,350	1,241	1,123	984	880	839	749

Source: D. K. Greenstreet, "The Development of the Ghanaian Public Service," p. 27.

[7] Official Government Civil Service Staff Lists, 1952 through 1962.

[8] See Richard P. Taub, *Bureaucrats Under Stress*, pp. 10-13.

and the Comparison/Clientele Survey.[9] These "dovetailing" surveys were designed, in line with a "role approach" to transitional bureaucracy, to assess the degree to which the environment provides or fails to provide social support for behaviors that are formally demanded of civil servants by virtue of their official membership in a bureaucratic organization. From the civil servants I sought to discover, among other things, the identity of their reference groups, or "significant others," their perceptions of the behavioral demands or role expectations held by these significant others, and the sanctions they believed were likely to be forthcoming if these expectations were violated. And from the public or potential clients of the public bureaucracy I sought the obverse of these—how they felt a civil servant should behave and actually would behave, and what their perception was of the consequences for the civil servant of one behavior as opposed to another. Standardized interview schedules and questionnaires were administered to a relatively large, randomly selected sample of the actual actors being analyzed (civil servants and clients). In the Civil Servant Survey, 434 Ghanaian civil servants were interviewed, and in the main Clientele Survey, 385 respondents filled out a rather lengthy questionnaire. Both the interviewer-administered and the self-administered questionnaires contained a combination of open- and closed-ended questions. Some of the questions were adaptations of those used with interesting results in other studies,[10] while others were created specifically for this study. The latter suggested themselves through events encountered and interviews held in Ghana prior to the final draft of the interview schedules.

In designing the survey items a concern with one problem was held uppermost—the danger of formalistic responses. The respondent, when faced with various behavioral alternatives, one of which is required by organizational rules, could be expected to give the formalistically appropriate response even if this differed from his actual beliefs and behavior. While the problem of formal as opposed to "truthful" responses is inherent in all survey research, it is magnified when one is asking about explicitly stated and legally defined norms of behavior. The solution to this dilemma was to avoid

[9] See Appendixes A, B, and C for complete interview schedules and questionnaires.

[10] Two sources especially influenced the construction of items for the survey instruments: the interview schedule developed by Morroe Berger in his study of Egyptian bureaucracy, and the questionnaire designed by Morris Janowitz and his associates in their stdy of public attitudes toward government bureaucracy in Detroit. See Morroe Berger, *Bureaucracy and Society in Modern Egypt*; and Morris Janowitz, Dale Wright, and William Delany, *Public Administration and the Public Perspective Toward Government in a Metropolitan Community*.

types of questions that were likely to be perceived by the respondents as demanding a potentially self-incriminating answer. Thus it seemed a fruitless enterprise to ask respondents about specific conditions under which they had in the past, or would in the future, violate the rules of the formal organization. I utilized instead a projective type of format, which presented a scenario in which hypothetical civil servants were depicted, and asked the respondent about the behavior of the civil servant in the imaginary situation, and about the actions of other actors in relation to the civil servant—for example, his friends, relatives, and the like. The assumption in this type of projective approach was that respondents will generalize from their personal experience when they comment on the imaginary situation, without having to feel threatened by their responses. In other words, the respondent can express things about himself and his significant others which if not projected onto an imaginary and thus neutral stimuli situation would be embarrassing, or in some other way threatening, and would thus probably be repressed.[11]

I have a great deal of confidence in the belief that the scenarios or imaginary situations that were presented to the respondents were good facsimiles of real-life situations in Ghanaian society. The manner in which the Ghanaian subjects responded to these items—a general ease of response that made additional interviewer probes unnecessary, the enthusiasm they showed in answering the open-ended questions, and the explicit comments they made about the ubiquitousness of the phenomenon being described—contributed to this conviction. In one such scenario the respondents were actually asked whether they thought the imaginary situation was realistic. Only 24 of the 434 civil servants interviewed responded that they thought the situation that was described was unlikely to actually occur.

Sample: Civil Servant Survey

In deciding on an appropriate sampling method for the Civil Servant Survey four considerations were taken into account. First, I desired a large enough sample of respondents to allow legitimate use of cross-tabulation in the analysis stage. Second, I sought a distribution

[11] There is evidence in the literature to support such assumptions. In a study by J. W. Gertzels it was found that when items were so phrased that the respondents were commenting on the actions of a third person rather than themselves they were more likely to reveal hostility to Negroes, and to express conflict with their parents. Furthermore, Gertzels' subjects reported that in responding to such items they usually thought of the imaginary person as "someone like myself." Gertzels' research is described in C. Selltiz et al., *Research Methods in Social Relations* (New York, 1959), p. 290.

of respondents at all levels of the civil service—in contrast to most empirical studies in the area of development administration, which have concerned themselves only with the topmost echelons of the administrative hierarchy. If senior officials cannot depend on middle- and low-level organization members to carry out routine tasks and make minor nonroutine decisions, then policy implementation will be seriously impaired, if not totally sabotaged. Thus any study of bureaucratic effectiveness should concern itself with the integration of lower members into organizational roles as well as with the commitment, ingenuity, and foresight of those in the top-level positions. A third consideration in making decisions about sampling method was the desire to take account of the heterogeneous social ecology of contemporary Ghana. Two dimensions of this heterogeneity stand out: its varied ethnic composition and the socio-economic and "life-style" gap between the relatively cosmopolitan capital city and the rest of the country. The fourth consideration that influenced the choice of sampling method relates to what might be termed organizational sensitivity. I felt that an effort to choose certain ministries or departments and then sample extensively within them would be perceived as a threat by supervisory personnel, who might conclude that if they were specific targets of investigation the results might be used to make invidious comparisons that would prove embarrassing. Therefore I decided to avoid concentration on any particular organizational unit and rather to seek a cross-section sample of the Ghanaian Civil Service. In that way a large sample could be obtained without interviewing a great proportion of persons in any particular office, and the impression that a single unit was being scrutinized could be avoided.[12]

The ideal sampling method would have been to draw a simple random probability sample of the entire Ghanaian Civil Service. But since such a sampling technique would have stretched my resources beyond their limit,[13] a method was sought which would fulfill the

[12] The problem of organizational sensitivity had at least one significant substantive as well as sampling consequence. Because of the sense that my ability to carry the research project through to fruition was precariously dependent on avoiding a perception of threat on the part of those in authority, I did not probe to the extent I felt optimally desirable into the internal social dynamics of the civil service organization, but concentrated more on the external social environment and the pressures it brought to bear on the civil servants. I believe this to have been a reasonable solution, under the circumstances.

[13] Utilization of a simple probability sample would have meant that individual civil servants would have had to be located and reached in all parts of Ghana, no small task for the lone researcher. Furthermore, since composition of the Ghana Civil Service is numerically dominated by the lower ranks, the sample, unless it was exceedingly large, would have been made up of too few respondents above the clerical rank to make analysis worthwhile.

four considerations just described and would, at the same time, be feasible. I decided to utilize a stratified random sample, with the civil servant population divided into strata according to geographic location and rank. Stratification by rank would provide an analyzable number of respondents from all positions within the bureaucratic hierarchy. Stratification by geographic locale, that is, the area to which the civil servant is posted, would build into the sample not only variation on the urban-rural dimension, but variation on the dimension of ethnic composition as well. Since in Ghana each administrative center is located in an area of different ethnic concentration, the drawing of the sample from regional administrative centers as well as the capital city provided variation in "ethnic ecology" as well as the degree of urbanization.

For reasons of geographic accessibility, civil servant respondents were chosen from four locations in Southern Ghana: the national administrative headquarters in the capital city of Accra, and the administrative centers of the three neighboring regions, the small cities of Cape Coast, Koforidua, and Ho. These four administrative centers differ in size, economic base, and ethnic composition. Accra is by far the largest, with a population of over 500,000 at the time of the official census in 1970, and Ho is the smallest, with a population of little more than 24,000.[14] Both Cape Coast and Koforidua are small towns compared with Accra, but they are larger than Ho, with approximately 51,000 and 46,000 inhabitants respectively. Accra is not only the administrative center of the country, it and its surrounding environs constitute Ghana's major commercial, manufacturing-industrial, and transportation node as well. Cape Coast, an important trading port in the precolonial days, is today chiefly noted as an educational center, with a number of important secondary schools and a university located there. Koforidua, lying astride the major rail and motor road routes between Accra and Kumasi, Ghana's main inland urban area, is primarily a nexus for domestic commerce and transportation. Ho's socio-economic ecology is primarily rural, with its small population and its location in the hinterland of a region whose economic basis is almost entirely small-scale farming or fishing. Within each of the four administrative centers the ethnic group that traditionally made its home in the area of the contemporary city predominates numerically, although the migration of job-seekers to the urban areas has tended to erode this traditionally dominant position. Thus the related Ga and Adangbe peoples make up a majority of the populace of Accra, while Fantis predominate in Cape

[14] Ghana, Central Bureau of statistics, *Statistical Year Book 1969-70*, (Accra, 1973), p. 8-10.

Coast; Ewes make up an overwhelming proportion of the inhabitants of Ho and its surrounding environs, and in Koforidua peoples from the Akim and Akwapim states are most numerous.

Staff lists of civil servants posted in the locality were obtained in each of the four administrative centers. The list for each locality was then divided into separate lists for the major ranks in the civil service hierarchy,[15] and respondents were drawn randomly from each list. In this way a geographic[16] and hierarchic cross-section sample of the Ghanaian Civil Service was obtained. The respondents worked in four different areas of Ghana and spanned the bureaucratic hierarchy. In addition, the chosen method of sampling drew respondents from a wide variety of ministries and departments. As a result, the civil servants interviewed came from thirty-one different organizational entities within the service. The sampling method also provided a good distribution of respondents on the dimensions of age and length of service (seniority).[17]

The Interviews

The respondents were first sent a personal letter, which described the research project in general terms, provided information on the researcher's academic affiliations, stated the source of the project's financial support, and solicited the potential respondent's participation. Within a few days of their receiving the letter each respondent was reached at his place of work, at which time the interview was conducted or an appointment was made for an interview at a later

[15] The ranks according to which I stratified the sample are the following: Clerical Officer, Executive Officer, Higher Executive Officer, Senior Executive Officer, Principal Executive Officer, Administrative Officer IV, Administrative Officer III, Administrative Officer II, Administrative Officer I. Within special departments of the civil service, such as the Department of Social Welfare and Community Development, grades or ranks are given different titles. Rank equivalency can be determined by equivalence in pay scale, and for the purpose of the sample the grades with special titles were placed in the appropriate grade in the hierarchy presented above. Excluded from the sampling universe were members of the professional class—for the most part doctors and lawyers in the medical and legal services. Since I was interested in those individuals whose main occupational role was as a civil servant, I eliminated that group whose members were likely to identify more strongly as medical and legal professionals than as civil servants.

[16] A complete geographic cross section would have included respondents from the five other regional administrative centers—Takoradi, Kumasi, Sunyani, Tamale, and Bolgatanga. Such an effort, however, was beyond the resource capacity of this particular project.

[17] Detailed statistical breakdowns on the structure of the civil servant sample in regard to location of posting, rank, seniority, and age can be found in Appendix D.

date. The bulk of the 434 interviews were conducted by six University of Ghana students who were hired, trained, and supervised by the author.[18] Interviews took about an hour to complete, and were conducted at the offices of the respondents. When the office was shared, an effort was made to ensure privacy. The response of Ghanaian civil servants to the interview situation was extremely cooperative. Only about 10 percent of the civil servants approached refused to be interviewed, a refusal rate which is considered quite respectable by the standards of survey research conducted in the United States.[19]

Sample: Clinetele Survey

The general purpose of the Clientele Survey was to provide data on the Ghanaian public's orientation to the client role in bureaucratic relationships, and to permit an assessment of the social support available to Ghanaian civil servants for various types of role behavior they are called upon to make in the course of their official duties. The label "clientele" is to be understood in a nonspecific, nontechnical way, in the sense that all members of the public are potential users of public bureaucracy, and therefore hypothetically its clientele.

The clientele sample was drawn from the student body of the University of Ghana. The choice of college students for the purposes of this study was subject to the same shortcomings as the great volume of social science research which has utilized this type of population group in the past—university students, especially in a country like Ghana, are atypical of the general population because of their high level of education. Be that as it may, a number of factors led to the choice of University of Ghana students as respondents in the Clientele Survey. First, and most obvious, was the factor of accessibility. Lacking the resources to obtain a probability sample of the Ghana population, I searched for a group that could economically provide a large number of respondents. University students, because they all lived in residence halls on the university campus, were such a group.

In addition to this economic rationale, there were four analytic

[18] Some interviews were conducted by an English woman, the wife of an expatriate lecturer at the university, and by the author. The responses in this group of interviews were compared with those obtained by the Ghanaian interviewers, but no systematic differences were revealed.

[19] Cf. Johan Galtung, *Theory and Methods of Social Research*, (New York, 1967), p. 147.

reasons for choosing university students for the clientele sample. First, university students, because of their atypical place in the Ghanaian social system, probably have had in the past and will likely have in the future more contact with the civil service than most other Ghanaians. Second, although university students represent a sample with a bias, it is a bias that runs counter to my major theoretical propositions, not one that would provide spurious confirmation of my hypotheses. It is my central thesis that the Ghanaian social system and culture are essentially hostile to the role behavior formally required by the civil service bureaucracy because the culture is dominated by role orientations and expectations that are not modern. Therefore, one would expect least evidence of this type of "hostile socio-cultural environment" among groups such as university students who occupy the so-called modern sector of their society. Any evidence of such a "hostile environment" which appears in the student sample can reasonably be expected to be amplified among less well educated, more "traditional" social groups. The comparison/clientele sample, discussed below, was designed to provide direct evidence for this proposition.

A third factor which made University of Ghana students an attractive sampling universe was the diversity in social background which characterizes the student body. In the last decade admission policies were so designed as to bring students to the university from all segments of Ghanaian society, not just the younger members of the highly Westernized Ghanaian social elite.[20] Because the University of Ghana student body is internally differentiated on dimensions such as parental literacy, paternal education and occupational background, size of community of origin, and the like, drawing a sample from this group permitted an assessment of the impact on role orientations of exposure to modernizing influences, one of the central aims of the study. Finally, since the Ghana Civil Service recruits for its high-level positions from those with university degrees, sampling the University of Ghana student body would permit an analysis of the orientations of Ghana's administrative manpower pool. I should be able to assess the attitudes of potential civil servants prior to their actual entry into the service, and to compare that group of students who are oriented toward careers in the higher civil service with those whose career orientations are in a different direction.

Thus, although a university sample for the Clientele Survey would

[20] Appendix E contains tables that provide a statistical breakdown of the structure of the university student sample on dimensions of paternal occupation, education, and literacy, and on size of home community.

create certain problems of bias, a number of considerations, in addition
to the obvious one of economic feasibility, suggested that University
of Ghana students would be an especially apt sampling universe for
my theoretical interests. The sampling technique was to select at
random equal numbers of students from each of the campus's five
residence halls.[21] Self-administering anonymous questionnaires were
distributed through the students' letter boxes, and the respondents
were instructed to return the completed questionnaires to a receptacle
located in the lobby of their residence halls. After two weeks a
follow-up letter was sent to those respondents who had not yet
returned their questionnaires. Of the 620 questionnaires distributed
in this manner, 385 completed questionnaires were returned, for a
response rate of 62.1 percent.

Sample: Comparison/Clientele Survey

In order to compare the role orientations of the university student
sample with role orientations of those less highly educated, a modified
version of the clientele questionnaire was administered to a small
sample of members of the Ghanaian public. The purpose was to obtain
interviews with people who could be classified as nonliterate or
semiliterate, whose educational background was minimal, and whose
occupations were those of low prestige in Ghana's urban areas. The
method of selecting respondents was akin to what Selltiz terms
"accidental sampling"[22]—individuals at lorry parks (depots for privately owned buses), taxi stands, and in various outdoor markets
were approached, and their participation in an interview was solicited.
Where sufficient motivation seemed lacking a small monetary gratuity
was offered as an added incentive. Interviews were conducted either
in English or, with the aid of an interpreter, in any of a number
of vernacular languages, depending on the facility of the respondent
in the English language. In this manner some eighty-one interviews
were carried out. Out of this total, some 57 percent of the respondents
had less than a secondary school education (high school in the United
States); 7.4 percent could not speak English at all, and another
66.7 percent could do so only haltingly;[23] less than one-half (48

---

[21] At the University of Ghana *every* registered student *must* live in one of these
residence halls.

[22] Selltiz et al., *Research Methods in Social Research*, p. 516.

[23] In Ghana, facility in English is a rough index of involvement in the "modern"
sector of society. It is the official language of contemporary Ghana; it is utilized in
all official government business and in all modern industrial and commercial enterprises.
As the language of the colonial power, it has been for more than a century, a prerequisiste
for mobility into and within the "modern" sector of the Ghanaian social system.

percent) could read English; and over three-fourths (78 percent) had occupations such as driver, trader, clerk, domestic (cook, steward, nurse-girl), and the like. Thus the Comparison/Clientele Survey makes possible a comparison of the responses of University of Ghana students with a sample that is more typical of the overall Ghanaian population.

Summary

The design for the research has a number of important strengths, I feel. The issues and questions dealt with are derived from a general theoretical perspective; the data that will be presented in an analysis of these were collected in a systematic manner; and the sampling universe utilized as a data base was varied and relatively large. At the same time it is important to acknowledge certain weaknesses. These are due partly to constraints in the research environment within which the field aspects of the study were conducted, partly to limited resources; and partly to limitations in the survey research method itself.

As a lone researcher operating with limited organizational and financial resources I could not utilize samples that were in the technical sense truly representative of the population universe under study. I attempted, however, to combine the need for respondents who were easily accessible with a conscious avoidance of the type of systematic sampling biases that would prejudice the findings in the direction of support for the arguments, and with an effort to build into the samples the type of diversity that would be "representative," even if not technically so, of the Ghanaian population aggregates that would be discussed. Also, because of resource limitations, I could hardly expect in the empirical portions of this study to cover all the lines of investigation and analytic propositions suggested by the theoretical framework adopted. I had to content myself with an attempt to provide some data on a number of the crucial foci within my theory of the social basis of administrative behavior in transitional polities; I could not deal with all of them.

Finally, we must recognize that there are limitations in the survey research method itself. It seems to me that the use of attitude surveys leads inevitably and correctly to questions about formalism and validation. How does one know whether the respondent's answer is a truthful reflection of his attitudes and perceptions? Is the interpretation one gives to the responses to survey items a truly valid one?

I feel that, although there can never be a fully satisfactory answer to these questions, the survey method is still a valuable research instrument for certain types of investigation, and in some contexts it is the best method available. I have commented already on how, in the context of this study, I attempted to handle the problem of respondent formalism. As for the second question, I would argue that the use of survey analysis involves a judgment about relative merits. In the last analysis, no matter what precautions are taken or validity tests devised, confidence in the validity of the data collected through survey techniques cannot be absolute, but rather is relative to what can be obtained through other methods. I feel that, when it comes to assessing role perceptions and orientations, survey methods are an improvement over impressionistic statements of observers and knowledgeable informants. At least in the former case the basis for making one's judgments—the survey items—is explicit, not subjective, and therefore the basis for accepting or rejecting validity is open to discussion.

Thus, faced with certain problems, I adopted a posture that, while not optimal, was best in the given situation. As such, the findings should be taken as tentative and partial. I make no claim to be presenting the definitive work on administrative behavior in "low income" countries, nor do the findings I shall present constitute a complete test of the theoretical framework developed in chapter 1. Rather, I view this study as a first and thus limited step toward linking "macro-level" social theory with the analysis of individual behavior, and toward the utilization of systematic data gathering and analysis in contemporary African studies. If it measures up to even that modest ideal, I will be satisfied that it makes a contribution to the scholarly literature on Ghana, on Africa, and more generally on the process of modernization.

III

Bureaucrat and Kinsman

Formal bureaucratic organizations are structures of specialized inter-dependent "social" positions, purposively created for the attainment of some goal. The superiority of such organization lies in its potential for large-scale teamwork, for the coordination of a great amount of human and material resources over an extensive geographic area. But whether potential will become reality, whether formal in-terdependence will be transformed into coordinated behavior, depends on the extent to which organizational members perform their constit-uent roles in required fashion. If they do not, interdependence will remain formal, and the teamwork and coordination that give bureau-cracy its superiority will not materialize. In short, organizational effectiveness depends in good part on personnel conforming to the requirements of their individual roles.[1]

When an actor conforms to the formal requirements of an organiza-tional role, he is responding to any one or a combination of three "forces": the institutional arrangements for sanctioning deviance, the internalization of organizational norms by the actor himself, and social pressure to conform from persons the actor cares about for reasons other than his immediate advancement within the organiza-tion. The two latter forces are primary because the institutional sanctions available—formal discipline, the withholding of promotion or salary increases, and the like—must be administered by individuals, and unless these persons are motivated either through the internali-zation of norms or through external social pressure to apply these sanctions in a manner that is related to the attainment of organiza-

[1] See Robert L. Kahn et al., *Organizational Stress*, p. 5.

tional goals, the mere existence of institutional sanctions will not necessarily be positively related to high levels of role performance. The extensive research by social psychologists into conforming behavior suggests, in addition, that social pressure is likely to be a more important element than is "internalization" in creating organizationally desirable role behavior. This literature provides powerful evidence that most individuals need social support for their beliefs and for their actions. When social pressure is homogeneous and in a direction opposed to his personal beliefs, it is a rare individual who can maintain his independent position.[2] Thus effective organizational performance, insofar as it is based on conformity to the requirements of organizational roles, is likely to depend on "human solidarity," that is, informal social pressures on organizational members that induce them to conform to the performance needs of the organization.[3]

Social pressure on organizational members can be generated either internally or externally. Internally generated social pressures are in principle subject to the control of leaders within the organization itself. At least leadership can communicate with members and, through the creation of ideology, the manipulation of symbols, and the operation of training or socialization programs, can attempt to foster the type of internal social solidarity that will be supportive of eufunctional role performance.[4] Externally generated social pressure is largely outside the control of the organizational leadership; it is generated by the nature of the social system in which the organization is embedded, its environment. The external social environment can affect the behavior of members within organizations in two basic ways. First, through the general process of socialization new members of society can be taught the requirements of centrally important organizational roles. Thus, for example, in the United

[2] See Solomon E. Asch, *Social Psychology*, 1952, passim; S. E. Asch, "Effects of Group Pressure upon the Modification and Distortion of Judgments," pp. 393-401; Kurt W. Back, "Influence through Social Communication"; R. S. Crutchfield, "Conformity and Character"; Muzafer Sherif, *The Psychology of Social Norms*, passim; M. Sherif and Carolyn Sherif, *Groups in Harmony and Groups in Tension*, passim; Stanley Schachter, "Deviation, Rejection, and Communication"; Edgar Schein, *Coercive Persuasion*, passim; Herbert McClosky and Giuseppe Di Palma, "Personality and Conformity: The Learning of Political Attitudes," pp. 1054-1059.

[3] For a discussion of "human solidarity" and its relationship to organizational performance, see Franz Schurmann, *Ideology and Organization in Communist China*, pp. 225-228; see also Amatai Etzioni's discussion of "social power" in his *A Comparative Analysis of Complex Organizations*, pp. 3-22.

[4] Philip Selznick, in his *Leadership in Administration*, argues that this is a central function of organizational leadership (pp. 90-133).

States an effort is made in the early school years to provide rudimentary knowledge of what kind of behavior can be expected of firemen, postmen, doctors, policemen, teachers, the president, and the like. If successful, such efforts are highly economical from the point of view of social organizations, since much of what new recruits or clients will need to know in order to perform their roles will have been learned prior to their contact with the organization and thus need not be taught by the organization itself.

The second way in which the social environment can affect behavior in organizations is related to the fact that organizational members will usually be members of multiple organizations and therefore will play many roles. Consequently, these organizations and roles will probably compete for the loyalty, time, and behavior of individuals who are mutual members. In other words from the vantage point of any given organization, there is the possibility of social pressure on members to violate role requirements in the name of commitment to some external informal group or formal organization. As was pointed out at length in the Introduction, social systems can and do ameliorate this problem of conflicting roles in one of two ways: social roles are either culturally defined in ways that are reinforcing rather than conflicting, or culturally compartmentalized into differentiated social spheres, within which different roles are given priority. It is generally accepted that the highly specialized and complex technology of societies commonly referred to as modern makes the first of these solutions largely irrelevant, and that such societies rely almost exclusively on the second method—structural differentiation and role compartmentalization.[5] In this way a limitation is placed on the generation of external social pressure that would undermine the requirements of role performance in any given organization.

The main thrust of the argument in chapter 1 was that administrative organizations in the new states of Africa are hampered by the fact that the social systems in which they are embedded do not operate so as to limit dysfunctional, externally generated social pressure on administrators. This, in turn, was viewed as a consequence of the fact that public bureaucracies in these countries are organizations whose role requirements assume role compartmentalization, but whose social environment makes little allowance for it. Put in terms of Talcott Parsons' pattern variables, we could say that while the formal organization demands universalistic behavior from its

[5] For one of the classic statements of this position, see Emile Durkheim's discussion of mechanical versus organic solidarity, in his *Division of Labor in Society*.

members, the actors in the social system whom the members care about are at the same time demanding particularistic behavior. The purpose of this chapter is to demonstrate this empirically, in the case of the Ghanaian Civil Service. I hope to show what sort of external social pressure is exerted on civil servants in Ghana, how they perceive it, and how they respond to it.

The Family in Ghanaian Society

There can be little doubt that in southern Ghana, where this study was conducted, the general portrait of traditional African society presented in chapter 1 holds true: descent groups—extended families and lineages—are corporate in nature and are the foundation of social organization. This quality was clearly noted by R. S. Rattray in his classic study of the Ashanti of central Ghana:

[The center of the social system] in Ashanti is not the King, or chief, or Clan, or Tribe, or even the individual; *it is the family*.[6] ... The society ... was regarded not as being composed of so many persons, but as consisting of an aggregation of units, each of which was a family group. ... The family was a corporation; action and even thought were corporate affairs.[7]

A similar assessment of the place of the family in the social system of the Ga, a tribal group in southern Ghana, was made by British anthropologist M. J. Field. In her pioneering work on the Ga people, she describes the family as corporate in nature, the lynchpin of social organization, and the chief mechanism for social control:

Responsibility for wrongdoing is a family affair. When a man is asked to appear before an elder's court it is not he himself who is called, but the head of his family—his father or elder brother—is requested to bring him. The head of his family is responsible for the payment of any costs he is ordered to pay. ... Always, until European influence was felt, responsibility was collective, not individual. ... The solidarity of the family, and the helplessness and destitution of an individual at variance with his family, was beyond all else what kept the individual law-abiding. An individual who offended his town offended his family and quarrelled almost with life itself.[8]

More recently, the central place of the extended family in the social organization of Ghanaian peoples was stressed by Justice N. A.

[6] R. S. Rattray, *Ashanti Law and Constitution*, p. 2. Emphasis added.
[7] Ibid., p. 62.
[8] M. J. Field, *Social Organization of the Ga People*, p. 109.

Ollennu of the Ghana Supreme Court. Writing in *A Study of Contemporary Ghana*, he noted:

> The basic unit of Ghanaian society is the family, not the individual. Almost everything affecting the individual is dealt with by his family. When the individual offends anyone, his conduct is reported to the head of his family who, with his elders, will go into the matter and take appropriate steps to make amends; if he achieves something good, his family gets the praise.[9]

Given the socio-cultural centrality of the extended family, and its corporate nature, it is not surprising that research has shown traditional standards of morality to involve primarily attention to family matters and adherence to its obligations. To quote from M. J. Field again, to the Ga, "life, health, and prosperity are the reward of goodness, and goodness is attention to family obligations and family ritual."[10] A similar orientation is found among the larger Akan-speaking group, which forms the majority of the population in southern and central Ghana. For example, Dr. J. B. Danquah, a leading Ghanaian intellectual and student of Akan custom and belief, has written that

> the Akan, above all else, held the family ... to be the supreme good, and that, to them, the worst vice was to bring dishonor or indignity or disgrace to the family name. Many Akan proverbs, scores of them, pointed to one truth, that the family, the neighbors, were those of the blood, the group held together by community of origin and obligation to a common ancestor. ... It was for this group that morality was of value and, for it, beneficence was truly beneficial and profitable in both senses, in worth and in increment.[11]

Although social changes over the last century—monetary income, new occupations, Western education, urban migration, and the like— have affected family structure and practice among the Ghanaian peoples, these alterations should not be exaggerated. Most observers of Ghanaian society would probably agree that the extended family is still a focal institution for Ghanaians of all social backgrounds, and that obligations to it are still strongly felt and generally honored. David Brokensha, in his study of an area in southern Ghana that had experienced profound economic changes and a great deal of missionary activity, and whose people have had a high level of exposure to Western education, found that "the family retains its

[9] N. A. Ollennu, "Aspects of Land Tenure," p. 254.
[10] Field, *Social Organization of the Ga People*, p. 216.
[11] J. B. Danquah, *The Akan Doctrine of God*, p. xxviii.

central place, Dr. Danquah's epigram applying equally in Larteh: 'What the Akan take to be the good is the family.' "[12]

On the basis of an analysis of Ghana's comprehensive 1960 population census, as well as his own independent surveys, the demographer J. C. Caldwell concluded that in Ghana the extended family continues to exist "as a network through which economic and other assistance, as well as obligation, run."[13] He notes that "the system may not be as secure as it has been," but he stresses that "the extent of ... change at the present time should not be exaggerated."[14] Data from the census shows that over one-third of rural households claimed to receive some money from relatives domiciled in the towns, and that nearly one-half of these said that money was received at least once a month. It was found that remittance was not a transitory phase of the migrants' lives, but continued even after they had been established in the town for many years—over four-fifths of the urban migrants claimed to send money to their "home" villages, with relatives receiving 99 percent of it.[15] A survey conducted at the University of Ghana similarly illuminated the continued strength of family obligations. The data showed that "the financial obligations of the extended family remained very strong." And, "on the whole, such obligations are not resented. ... Less than one-tenth of all students claimed that they resented it in any way. ... The majority approved, and one-third strongly approved."[16]

Surveys for this study also provide evidence of the considerable strength of the extended family in the area of financial obligations. Four-fifths of the civil servants in the sample claim to be providing financial assistance to at least one relative in addition to any wives or children they may have. Nearly one-third of them report supporting three or more such dependents; one-half say they provide assistance to one or two. As might be expected, the financial obligations deriving

[12] David Brokensha, *Social Change at Larteh, Ghana*, p. 266.

[13] J. C. Caldwell, "Population: General Characteristics," in W. Birmingham et al., eds., *A Study of Contemporary Ghana*, Vol. II: *Some Aspects of Social Structure*, pp. 17-74.

[14] Ibid. The following statement by anthropologist William Schwab about West African societies in general seems particularly to the point: "For many years anthropologists and sociologists asserted that Westernization undermined and destroyed extended kinship systems. More recently, this assertion has been questioned, and there is a growing realization that extended kinship systems may be very resilient even under unusual transitional stress. [While there is often a reduction in the scope of kinship rights and obligations, at the same time] kinship claims and loyalties persist and, although modified *the lineage system remains a primary* focus of cohesion and source of stability and control" ("Oshogbo—An Urban Community," p. 99). Emphasis added.

[15] Caldwell, "Population," p. 142.

[16] Ibid., p. 159.

from membership in an extended family increase with ability to pay and the position of the individual in his life-cycle. The "dependency ratio" thus increases with both rank and age.[17] The data from the main Clientele Survey also provides evidence on the extent of financial obligtion imposed by family membership within contemporary Ghana. Eighty percent of the university students who were the respondents in the survey report feeling under some form of financial obligation to their families which they will be expected to shoulder when they begin to earn salaries.[18] For male respondents only, this proportion increases to 85 percent. This obligation is perceived as taking the form of cash remittances or payment of school fees for younger members of the family. In many cases both forms of obligation are felt. The manner in which the question was asked makes it difficult to specify precisely where in the family the obligation lies, but one-fourth of those who felt some obligation did spontaneously mention that it included members of the extended family, that is, members beyond parents and immediate siblings.

If the family remains a primary source of individual identity, a unit in terms of which social morality is defined and measured, and a network of material assistance and obligation, then the questions for this study clearly become: What are the pressures, if any, placed by the family system on the civil servant in the performance of his role? How does he view these pressures—as legitimate or illegitimate? and, In what way does he respond to them?

However, before turning to the data relating to these questions, it is important to note that when Ghanaian civil servants are asked about the civil service role in the abstract an overwhelming number

---

[17] Of the respondents with low rank in the service (clerical officer), 30.6 percent say they have no dependents other than wives and children; only 9 percent of those with high rank (administrative officer) so report. On the other hand, 17.9 percent of the high-ranking officers report that they provide financial assistance to *five or more relatives*, while only 3.6 percent of the low-ranking group do so. Similarly, of the civil servants who are under thirty years of age nearly one-third (32.1 percent) report that they support only wives and children, in contrast to those over fifty, of whom only 18 percent report no dependents other than wives and children. Of the group who report that they support five or more "nonnuclear" dependents, we find that 25 percent of the "over fifties" are in this category, and only 5 percent of the "under thirties." Controlling for either rank or age shows that they have an independent influence on the dependency ratio. It should be noted that this type of financial obligation may incorporate reciprocal benefits. Often dependent kin are brought into the household and treated as full-time domestic servants. (I am grateful to Jon Kraus for pointing this out to me.)

[18] A survey carried out by J. C. Caldwell at the University of Ghana in the early 1960s obtained similar results. Two-thirds of the students expected to spend between 10 and 30 percent of their professional incomes on relatives other than their wives and children. See Caldwell, "Population: General Characteristics," p. 74.

view it in classic Weberian terms. Their abstract orientation, then, parallels the view set forth in the General Orders and the other official regulations that constitute the formal basis of the service. For example, when asked to agree or disagree with the statement "A civil servant should not allow his personal affairs to interfere with the carrying out of his duties," only 15 of 434 respondents disagreed, 43 percent agreed, and another 53 percent expressed strong agreement. Similarly, 96 percent of the civil servants agreed that a civil servant "should give equal treatment to all members of the public with whom he deals." But, as with research in other areas of attitude and opinion, the data show that consensus on a principle often quickly breaks down when it is placed within a social context.[19]

Familial Obligation and the Civil Servant Role

In order to tap the respondents' perception of familial role pressure, their orientation toward it, and their estimation of the likely response to it, I utilized a type of projective technique—an imaginary situation involving potential conflict between civil service and family roles was presented to the respondent and a series of questions were then asked about it.[20] In one such series the respondents were asked to "suppose a civil servant arrives at his office one morning and finds several people waiting to see him about routine business. One of these people is a relative of his." The civil servant respondent was then asked, "Would it be proper to keep this relative waiting because others have come before him?" Obviously, the purpose of this question was to determine which of his roles—civil service or family—the respondent believed should determine his behavior in this case. If he said that keeping the relative waiting was proper—that is, if he condoned universalistic behavior in the situation—the response was interpreted as ideally giving precedence to the civil service role; if he felt that universalistic role behavior in the situation was improper—that the relative should be seen first—his response was taken to be an indication that he ideally gave top priority to his role as family member. The

[19] See, for example, James W. Prothro and Charles M. Grigg, "Fundamental Principles of Democracy"; and also see Herbert McCloskey et al., "Issue Conflict and Consensus among Party Leaders and Followers."

[20] Three imaginary situations of this type were utilized: the "office scenario," the "transfer scenario," and the "scholarship scenario." The transfer and scholarship scenarios were lengthy and were presented to the respondent on a card by the interviewer. Questioning was begun after the respondent had time to read what appeared on the card. The office and transfer scenarios are modified versions of items utilized by Morroe Berger in his study *Bureaucracy and Society in Modern Egypt.*

next question was what the respondents thought "the average civil servant in Ghana would actually do in this situation." "Would he receive his relative before the others?" Here I was looking not for what the civil servants believed was the legitimate role orientation, but rather what they thought normal role behavior under the circumstances would be. The final question was about the relative in the imaginary situation: "Would he be likely to expect to be seen before the others, or would he expect to be seen only after those who came before him have taken care of their business?"

Table 1 clearly indicates that there is little correlation between what the respondents think is proper and what they expect will normally be done. Indeed, in the vast majority of cases what the

Table 1

Universalistic versus Particularistic Role Orientations in Response to the "Office Scenario"

	R Believes Legitimate Role Behavior to Be:	R's Estimate of Normal Role Behavior in Situation	R's Perception of the Relative's Role Expectation
Universalistic	75.3%	19.4%	5.1%
Particularistic	23.7	80.0	92.6
No Answer	.9	1.6	2.3
□ Total	99.9 (N=434)	101.0 (N=434)	100.0 (N=434)

civil servants thought would be normal procedure is the opposite of what they believed to be proper.[21] Of the sample as a whole, 75 percent said that universalistic role behavior would be legitimate under the circumstances, and only 19 percent expected that the average Ghanaian civil servant would actually act in such a fashion. Table 2 shows that, of the 327 respondents who considered a universalistic orientation to be proper, over three-fourths (76.7 percent) expect the average Ghanaian civil servant to behave in the opposite manner. The key to the situation, as can be seen in tables 1 and 3, is the role expectations of the relative. Nearly 93 percent said

[21] These findings closely parallel those obtained with a similar item by Berger in Egypt. Ibid., p. 139.

Table 2

*Respondent's Perception of Legitimate Role
Behavior and Estimate of Normal Role
Behavior: Office Scenario*

| | R Believes Legitimate Role Behavior to Be: | |
R's Estimate of Normal Role Behavior:	Particularistic (see relative first)	Universalistic (make relative wait)
Particularistic	87.3%	76.7%
Universalistic	12.7	21.7
No Answer	0.0	1.5
☐ Total	100.0 (N=102)	99.9 (N=327)

NOTE: Chi Square for table significant at .001 level.

Table 3

*Respondent's Perception of Relative's Role
Expectations and Estimate of Normal Role
Behavior: Office Scenario*

| | R Believes Relative's Role Expectations to Be: | |
R's Estimate of Normal Role Behavior	Particularistic	Universalistic
Particularistic	84.3%	18.2%
Universalistic	15.7	81.8
☐ Total	100.0(N=396)	100.0(N=22)

NOTE: Chi Square for table significant at .001 level.

that the relative would expect to be seen before the others—that is, that he would expect particularistic treatment from the civil servant. In other words, there was an almost complete consensus among the respondents that, in effect, the relative would expect the obligations of the family role-set to operate within the bureaucratic organization. As can be seen in table 3, there is a close fit between the respondent's perception of the relative's role expectations and his assessment of the way most civil servants would actually behave. The direction of the relative's perceived role expectations and the direction of expected role behavior correlates in 84.2 percent of the cases, a sharp contrast to the 37.3 percent of the cases in which a correlation exists between respondent's own sense of legitimate role behavior and his expectation of what will normally be done.[22] Clearly, then, for the Ghanaian civil servant the role expectations of relatives are seen to have a closer relationship to role performance than are the civil servant's own notions of what constitutes legitimate performance in the role. Such a finding suggests that violating the expectations of relatives is perceived as entailing costs for the civil servant. It suggests that the relatives can and do exert role pressure.

The other two imaginary situations that were utilized not only provide confirming evidence for the findings of the "office scenario," but also reveal the nature of the pressure exerted by the family role-set on the civil servant. First there is the "transfer scenario," in which the following imaginary situation was described:

A civil servant is officially informed that he is to be transferred from Accra to a new post in Tamale. The civil servant is from Accra, he speaks the local language, has all his friends and relatives there, and he is looking after his aged parents who are too old to move to the North with him. For all these reasons he does not want to be transferred to Tamale. He therefore goes to the head of his department, who happens to be his cousin, and asks to be kept in Accra.

This situation contains a potentially far more serious role conflict than the office scenario contained. In that situation particularistic behavior involved showing special courtesy to a family member and violating the "first come, first served" norm of bureaucratic universalism. In the transfer scenario the role demands of both organization and family are far more weighty. For the head of department, giving precedence to the family role-set would violate universalistic norms in regard to civil service personnel policy, and giving priority to the organizational role-set would cause hardship to his family. I sought first to determine whether in fact the Ghanaian civil servant was likely to experience role conflict in such a situation—that is, would his relatives expect him to violate bureaucratic norms and give precedence to family role obligations? The civil servant respondents were asked whether "in this situation," the head of department's relatives would "be likely to expect him to arrange to have his cousin

[22] These proportions were obtained from tables 2 and 3 by in each case summing the N of the congruent cells (universalistic/universalistic plus particularistic/particularistic) and dividing by the total number of respondents answering the question.

stay in the Accra post." There was an overwhelming consensus that the relatives' expectations would be in the direction of giving priority to the family role-set: 85 percent of the sample said that in such a situation the head of department would be expected by his relatives to overturn an official decision and arrange to nullify his cousin's transfer. At the same time, however, the respondents overwhelmingly considered these expectations illegitimate, as was the case in the office scenario. When the 365 respondents who said they thought the head of department's relatives would expect him to intercede for his cousin were asked whether they thought that the relatives "have a right to expect him to help his cousin in this situation," 81 percent of them responded that they did not have such a right. The fact that it was the overwhelming consensus among the civil servants that family role obligations were irrelevant (illegitimate) in the bureaucratic context again bears little relationship to their estimate of likely behavior. Only a minority think that the civil servant will be likely to refuse to help his cousin, that is, abide by the universalistic norm of his bureaucratic role. Of those who recognize the existence of cross-pressure in the situation—particularistic expectations on the part of relatives and belief in the legitimacy of universalistic behavior on the part of the respondent—65 percent think that actual behavior by the civil servant will be in line with the relatives' demands. The relative strength of these two independent variables in their impact on the respondents' estimates of actual role behavior can be observed by comparing tables 4 and 5.

Table 4

Respondent's Estimate of Role Conflict Resolution
and His Belief in the Legitimacy
of Familial Role Expectations

Method of Role Conflict Resolution	Legitimacy of Familial Role Expectations	
	Familial Expectations are Legitimate	Familial Expectations are Illegitimate
Particularistic (help his cousin)	77.1%	64.5%
Universalistic (refuse to help cousin)	22.9	35.5
☐ Total	100.0 (N=70)	100.0 (N=287)

NOTE: Question about legitimacy asked only of those respondents who thought that relative would expect particularistic behavior from the civil servant. Chi Square for table significant at .05 level. Gamma measure of association = .301.

Table 5

*Respondent's Estimate of Role Conflict Resolution
and His Perception of Relatives' Expectations*

Method of Role Conflict Resolution	Perception of Relatives' Role Expectations	
	Particularistic	Universalistic
Particularism	66.0%	14.0%
Universalism	34.0	86.0
☐ Total	100 (N=362)	100 (N=57)

NOTE: Chi Square for table significant at .001 level. Gamma measure of association = .845.

Although there is some relationship between how the respondents view the legitimacy of familial role expectations and what they expect the imaginary civil servant to do, it is clearly very weak compared with the relationship between perceived familial role expectations and expected role behavior. The former independent variable produces a difference in estimated role behavior of only 12.6 percent, the latter variable, a 52 percent difference.

The likelihood that a respondent will expect role behavior to be congruent with particularistic demands by the family role-set is not distributed equally throughout the service. Those with longer tenure and those with higher rank are more likely than their colleagues who have served a shorter period of time, or who occupy a lower rank, to expect civil servants to resist familial role expectations. (Tables 6 and 7 illustrate this relationship.) This is, of course, consistent with what is known generally about organizational and role commitment—it is usually directly related to rank and tenure of membership. However, what is striking about this aspect of our findings is the *limited* effect of rank and tenure on the weight that a civil servant is likely to give to his organizational role. The preponderant opinion in all categories is that in normal practice a civil servant yields to particularistic familial role expectations. Even within the high-rank category and among that small proportion of officers with more than twenty-two years of experience in the service, those who think it likely that in the transfer situation a civil servant would refuse to help his relative are in a minority; 44.1 percent of those with more than twenty-two years of service make such an estimate, and only 38.5 percent of those with ranks in the class of administrative or top executive officer.

Table 6

Respondent's Estimate of Role Conflict Resolution by Rank

Conflict Resolution	Respondent's Rank			
	Low[a]	Medium Low[b]	Medium High[c]	High[d]
Particularistic (help cousin)	67.0%	63.1%	64.0%	53.8%
Universalistic (refuse to help cousin)	31.9	35.1	31.0	38.5
Compromise or "It depends"	1.1	1.8	5.0	7.7
☐ Total	100 (N=94)	100 (N=111)	100 (N=100)	100 (N=52)

NOTE: Table includes only those respondents who perceived the existence of role conflict, i.e., who felt relatives would expect the department head to help his cousin stay in Accra.

[a] Clerical Officer.
[b] Executive Officer, Higher Executive Officer (or equivalent).
[c] Senior Executive Officer, Assistant Administrative Officer (or equivalent).
[d] Principal Executive Officer, Chief Executive Officer, Administrative Officer – Grades I through III (or equivalent).

The reason for the close link between respondents' predictions about behavior and their perceptions of familial expectations lies, I believe, not so much in the fact that they believe such expectations exist, but rather in their understanding of what consequences or sanctions would follow in the event such expectations are violated—that is, in their perception of the role pressures on public bureaucrats that are utilized by extended families within Ghana. In order to tap this type of consideration two questions were asked of the 371 respondents who thought that relatives in the transfer situation would have particularistic expectations. First: "What are the head of department's relatives likely to think of him if he refused to help his cousin stay in the Accra post?" The purpose was to discover the respondent's feeling about how a violation of role expectations would be understood by members of the family, and how he thought this understanding would affect the way the civil servant in the imaginary situation would be viewed by his relatives. I was seeking to discover what, if any, psychic costs were involved for a civil servant who ignored the obligations of his family role-set. In the second question, "Could the feelings of his relatives have any actual consequences for the

Table 7

Respondent's Estimate of Role Conflict Resolution and Seniority

Conflict Resolution	Length of Tenure (in Years)				
	5 or less	5-10	11-16	17-22	23 or over
Particularistic	70.0%	67.0%	63.8%	50.0%	44.1%
Universalistic	27.5	32.0	34.5	44.0	44.1
Compromise or "It depends"	2.5	1.0	1.7	6.0	11.7
☐ Total	100 (N=120)	100 (N=103)	100 (N=58)	100 (N=50)	99.9 (N=34)

NOTE: Table includes only those respondents who perceived the existence of role conflict.

head of department?" I sought to determine if the respondents were conscious of any social (including material) costs in giving priority to the bureaucratic role-set in a situation such as that described in the "transfer scenario."

The most striking aspect of the responses to the first question— What would the family think of a civil servant who refused to help his cousin?—is that the attitudes attributed to relatives show a complete failure to recognize the existence of conflicting role demands. That is, from the point of view of the civil servants interviewed, relatives in such a situation would fail to comprehend that the bureaucrat had organizational obligations that interfered with his ability to aid members of his family. The perceptions attributed to family members fall into three broad categories: The relatives will think that the civil servant's refusal to help his cousin is a manifestation of some general and negative personality characteristic; they will think it is a single example of a more generalized unfortunate social orientation such as selfishness; or they will think it is the result of an antifamily bias. The answers of some respondents attribute attitudes to family members that fall into all three categories. Of the 327 respondents who answered the item, 43 percent mentioned that the civil servant's general personality would be denigrated by his relatives. Specifically, they noted that the head of department in the transfer scenario would be thought of as a "wicked," "bad," "cruel," or "hard-hearted" man. Over a third (36 percent) of the respondents felt that the civil servant would be viewed by his relatives as a person who lacks a proper "social" orientation, one who is selfish, ungrateful, or inconsiderate. In the words of one respondent, a very high ranking administrative officer: "They [the family] would think that he is wicked and ungrateful because, no doubt, the head of department's relatives are sometimes of great help to him also in family matters."

Perhaps the most interesting group of responses (one-half of those answering) revealed a perception that the head of department's refusal to help his cousin would be taken as evidence of an antifamily bias on his part. Specifically, it was felt that the head of department's behavior would be interpreted as indicating he lacked an interest in helping his family, that he did not care for his relatives' well-being, that he had "abandoned" his family, and even that he had malevolent feelings about the family and was using this opportunity to "insult" it. As one higher executive officer with six years service put it, "They would think that he is not helpful to the family and that he is cruel ... that he does not want the aged dependents of his cousin to live comfortably."

Another respondent, this time a man with over fourteen years of experience, and at the time of the interview a higher executive officer in the Accountant-General's Department, offered a similarly typical answer: "They would think that the head of department who is their relative underrates the members of the family and that he does not [therefore] seek their interest." This respondent ended his answer by noting that the relatives would feel the head "lacks the typical Ghanaian family feeling." Typical of another type of response within the "antifamily" category are the following two statements that indicate family members may feel that the civil servant has abandoned his family as a consequence of his upward social mobility. Administrative officer, Organization and Methods Secretariat: "They would say because he has got somewhere he no longer wants to help his people"; higher executive officer, Ministry of Information: "He does not seek the family's welfare [since] he disrespects the family because he holds a high government post."

When it is recalled that in Ghana the family continues to be an important unit of personal identity and that moral worth is in good measure reckoned in terms of behavior toward it, then it is reasonable to assume that individuals would be strongly motivated not to be seen as cruel, hard-hearted, selfish, and inconsiderate toward their families, and that they would wish to avoid the impression that they did not have an interest in the family's well-being, or that they desired to purposely harm it. It is clear that the civil servants who were interviewed think that in Ghana the public bureaucrat who refuses to violate bureaucratic norms when the needs of his relatives demand it will have his motives misconstrued by the members of his family and consequently will be viewed in a highly negative light by them. Such a belief, in itself, represents severe subjective role pressure on the civil servant, but the consequences of ignoring family role expectations go beyond what the civil servant believes his relatives will think of him to how they will act toward him.

Two-thirds of the respondents agreed, in one form or another, with the civil servant who said, "The head of department would not feel easy to move among the relatives because of the strained relations that have been created." In many cases this strained relationship was linked to a loss in family position for the civil servant who had ignored the role expectations of his relatives. In the words of one respondent, he would "come to be regarded as an insignificant person in the family." And another felt that his relatives "would have little respect for him and treat him with contempt if he attends family functions." One-fifth of the respondents interpreted the notion of strained relations as involving actual ostracism from the extended family. Thus, in response to the question "Could the feelings of his relatives have any actual consequences for the head of department?" a senior executive officer gave what was a common response: "Definitely! A noticeable consequence among several others is that he would lose his rights as a member of the family. In fact in extreme cases he might be ostracized from the family affairs." Other respondents specified what ostracism would mean and the family rights that would be lost. "He would be isolated," went one such typical response. "Events like births, marriages, deaths, and so forth are of great family significance, and after this event I doubt if the head of department will be entertained at any of these functions." More than thirty respondents noted that failure to fulfill the relatives' particularistic role expectations would mean a loss of future family assistance should the civil servant find himself in need. And six respondents said that the head of department would be formally brought before the elders of his descent group to answer for his failure to meet family obligations—that is, they felt that institutionalized mechanisms of social control within the extended family would be brought to bear on the "deviant" member.

It is clear from the content of the responses to the open-ended questions that the Ghanaian civil servant, on the whole, believes that the members of his extended family will generally fail to recognize the validity of organizational role demands that conflict with obligations of the family role-set, that they would not be likely to engage in "role compartmentalization." Consequently, the civil servants interviewed believed that the violation of familial role expectations would most likely result in severe negative sanctions, both subjective and objective. It is thus a reasonable inference that they would violate these only with considerable trepidation, an inference supported by the fact that more than 60 percent of those who felt familial role expectations to be illegitimate in the transfer scenario nonetheless thought it likely that they would in fact be honored.

The findings and inferences generated by the transfer scenario are corroborated by the responses to a set of items that appeared at a later point in the interview schedule, and which relate to the "scholarship scenario." Again an imaginary situation was described.

"X" is a civil servant whose job it is to evaluate the records of secondary school graduates and recommend one hundred of them for scholarships to university. The final choice of some seventy-five awards will be made by a specially selected scholarship board, but before a name is presented to the board it must be approved by Mr. X. One of the students who has applied for a government scholarship is from X's hometown, and is the son of a man who helped X financially during the period of his own education.

While the boy is a very good student, he does not rank among the top one hundred applicants.

A number of people from X's village, including the applicant's father and X's own brother, have come to Accra to beg X to recommend the boy for a scholarship. X, however, ignores the pleas of his relatives and friends, and does not include the hometown boy in the one hundred names he submits to the scholarship board.

The primary purpose in presenting this situation was to eliminate the possibility that the role pressures perceived by the respondents in the transfer scenario were idiosyncratic to the particular types of role obligations built into that situation. Thus, when he had read the scholarship scenario, the respondent was asked to comment on how the behavior of X—giving priority to his bureaucratic role—would affect his relations with his relatives and other people in his home village. Table 8 presents a breakdown of the responses to this item.

Table 8

Consequences Perceived by Civil Servants of Giving Precedence to Organizational Role over Family Role: Scholarship Scenario

Consequence	No. of Respondents Mentioning Consequence
X would be thought of as ungrateful or selfish	188
Relations between X and village and family would be strained	103
Relatives and friends would be embittered toward X and/or X would be disliked	128
X would be thought of as a "wicked" or "bad" man	76
X would be ostracized	29
X would lose standing in the community	24
X would be spoken ill of	25
Relatives and friends would respect X more	4
X's actions would have no effect	10
Not answered	17

NOTE: Respondents were permitted to state more than a single consequence.

As in the transfer scenario, the coding categories in table 8 were generated by the responses themselves to an open-ended question—they were not preset. Although in the scholarship scenario the obligations to the family are less weighty than in the transfer situation—the implication of giving precedence to civil service norms will not have an immediate and direct impact on the physical and material well-being of family members, and the obligation is really quasi-familial[23]—the respondents view as remarkably similar the consequences for the civil servant of implementing policy according to civil service norms. All but 14 of 417 respondents who answered the question thought that giving priority to his civil service role would have negative consequences for X in terms of his relationship with his family. Only 10 respondents felt that X's action would have no effect on these relationships, and only 4 thought it would have any positive consequences. As with the transfer scenario, the verbatim responses to the scholarship situation are striking in the extent to which the respondents feel that the action of the civil servant will be perceived as stemming from his own volition rather than from constraints created by some binding obligation of his bureaucratic position. Thus, it is felt by the respondents that in the imaginary situation the act of the civil servant in refusing to violate regulations for the hometown boy will be seen as motivated by either personal enmity or some combination of selfishness and ingratitude. He will be seen to have disqualified the boy for a scholarship not because he had to but rather because he wanted to. The relatives and village people "would be annoyed with him," according to a senior executive officer in the Ministry of Education, "because they would feel that *he doesn't want to help* the people in his village." Another civil servant echoed a common theme when he noted that, to the people in the village, "X's action showed him to be wicked, and to have no interest in his relatives as well as the people in the village." Not uncommon was the notion that the failure to recommend the village boy for

[23] Ghanaian villages do not exhibit the quality of "amoral familism" which Banfield noted was characteristic of southern Italy. (Edward H. Banfield, *The Moral Basis of a Backward Society* [New York, 1958].) On the contrary, the hometown village is a strong unit of identification, and the common bond among village members tends to be strong even when more than one lineage resides there. The entire hometown is often thought of in kinship terms; for example, the category "brother" is used to refer to all of one's male peers within the village, rather than just to members related by blood or affinity. Thus the sense of mutual obligation characteristic of the traditional extended family is in many ways generalized to the entire village, a phenomenon that is reinforced by the fact that each constituent descent group will want to maintain a good position within the community and therefore will exert influence on its members to refrain from acts that will jeopardize harmonious relations with the other descent groups that make up the village.

a scholarship would be perceived as a conscious malicious act toward the village, family, or boy in question:

Clerk, Lands Department: "They [relations and friends] would think that because he is new he is *just trying to display his superiority*. They would feel ashamed."

Assistant accountant, Accountant-General's Department: "They would feel that X is a bad man and *does not like his people*. And, moreover, he is selfish. The boy's father would particularly think of X as ungrateful."

Senior administrative officer, Ministry of Health: "He is not very helpful, and is probably trying *to run the family down*."

Administrative officer, Organization and Methods Secretariat: "They [the relatives] would blame him [X] for snubbing his relatives. They would feel slighted."

The most commonly noted consequence is reflected in the comment of the assistant accountant in the above series—a large proportion of the respondents (50 percent) felt that X would be seen as ungrateful to the father of the hometown boy for the financial aid the man had previously given him; his action would be viewed as one of ingratitude. Some respondents went even further, noting that X's behavior would be seen as stemming from a certain haughtiness or a selfish desire to prevent the boy from attaining a social position equal to his own. For example, one respondent felt that the relatives "would think that X is wicked, proud, and pompous," and another noted that "they would think X would not like the boy to come to his rank in the future and is therefore selfish." Not surprisingly many respondents saw views of this kind directly and severely affecting social relations betweeen the civil servant in the scholarship scenario and his family and the other people in the village. In the words of one respondent, "They would dislike X and feel that he is ungrateful and not helpful. His village folks would deny him cooperation when the need arises—for example, funeral obsequies." Another respondent felt that "X might even be asked to refund all monies used on him when he was in school." Another group of respondents saw X's action as leading to his ostracism from the village community. Thus one respondent felt that the civil servant would be told that "he should no more come to the hometown," another felt that "he will be treated as an outcast," and a third felt that the antagonisms set up by his action were so great that "X is likely not to be able to go to the village because of fear of the safety of his life."

In summary, when presented with imaginary organizational situa-

tions involving conflict between bureaucratic and familial role obligations, there is a consensus among the civil servant respondents that
the family role-set will consider its obligations binding, expect them
to be fulfilled, and mobilize its considerable sanctional resources in
instances of their violation. The statements made by the respondents
to a number of open-ended questions revealed their belief that people
in Ghana generally fail to compartmentalize occupational and familial
roles, and instead see the obligations of the latter role-set penetrating
and taking precedence over the former. In consequence, most of the
civil servants that were interviewed felt that the average Ghanaian
civil servant would accept the expectations of his family role-set as
binding, even though the respondents themselves considered the
bureaucratic role-set to be the legitimate one under the circumstances. For reasons already discussed, the questions were asked in
such a manner that the respondent did not have to state explicitly
how he himself would act under the circumstances.[24]

Therefore, their statements about what the "average" civil servant
would do, and about what the imaginary civil servant is "likely"
to do, are taken to be reflections of what the respondents expect
and accept as the usual practice under the circumstances. For the
methodological reasons relating to projective-type items discussed
in chapter 2, because respondents sometimes answered the open-ended
questions in the first person, and because the respondents' predictions
of behavior were so closely linked to their perceptions of family
expectations, I feel that these statements probably also reflect what
the respondent himself would be likely to do under the circumstances
described to him. Further, I feel that the situations described were
meaningful to the civil servants interviewed, in that they were
reflections of "real," "normal," and "frequent" situations within the
Ghanaian social system. My confidence in this assessment was created
first by the ease of response to the open-ended questions. It was
not necessary for the interviewer to utilize numerous probes in order
to generate responses and explain the contents of the imaginary
situation, which indicates that our respondents had a general famil-
iarity with the type of situation being described. Second, my confidence in the "reality" of the imaginary situations was strengthened
by the responses to one of the questions that followed the scholarship
scenario. "Do you think that this imaginary situation is very realistic?
Do you think it likely that such a situation would occur? Would
a civil servant in X's position be likely to find himself under pressure

[24] See the discussion on pp. 46-47.

from relatives and friends?" Only 24 of 434 civil servants interviewed said that the imaginary situation was unrealistic, and of the 94 percent who said that it was indeed realistic many were emphatic in their responses, adding such remarks as "definitely," "most certainly," and "it is happening all the time" to the simple "yes" or "no" that was asked for by the interviewer.

There is one further reason to feel that role pressures and role behaviors described by the civil servant respondents are an accurate reflection of Ghanaian social reality—their perceptions are corroborated by the observations of the student sample. Built into the clientele questionnaire was the possibility of comparing the civil servants' expectations and perceptions regarding familial role pressures with those of Ghanaians who were not members of the service. The transfer scenario was appropriately modified, and a set of questions similar to the ones asked of the civil servants were posed. Here the person being transferred was described as the father of the respondent, and the head of department was described as the respondent's uncle by marriage.[25] The respondents were asked to comment on how they thought their families were likely to act under the circumstances described. The pattern of responses by the student sample was strikingly similar to those offered by the civil servants. When asked whether a member of their family would ask the head of department to have the transfer nullified, 80 percent of the sample thought such behavior was likely. It will be recalled that 85 percent of the civil servant sample thought that relatives would have particularistic expectations in the transfer situation. The descriptions offered by the university students of the consequences for their uncle if he should refuse to nullify the transfer strongly confirm the perceptions of the civil servants.[26] Three-fourths of the respondents thought that if their uncle behaved in such a manner his relationship with the family would be seriously damaged. It is perfectly clear from their open-ended responses that this large proportion of respondents believed that their families would consider the head of department's commitment to the universalistic norms of his offical role to involve a breach of a most serious family obligation, which would be received

[25] The content of the imaginary situation was as follows: "Your father is a civil servant who is posted in Accra, and he has just got notice that he will be transferred to a new post in Tamale. Your entire family lives in Accra, and if your father must move your family life will be seriously disrupted. Now, your mother's sister is married to a man who is the head of your father's department, and therefore he has the power to arrange to have your father keep his Accra post."

[26] The student sample was asked, "What would be the reaction of your family if your relative refused to fix things for your father? Would his refusal affect his relations with them? If so, how?"

by much ill will within the family, and would lead to sanctions such as refusal of aid in the future and complete ostracism.

"My family," went one typical response, "would feel it had been let down by somebody whose duty it was to help it. ... The relative would be looked upon as somebody who ignored a most essential duty to his kinsmen. ... He would be regarded as a bad man and members of the family might refuse to have anything to do with him again." A number of respondents noted explicitly that their families would react negatively because they would see in the head of department's behavior a violation of traditional norms. For example, a twenty-five-year-old male member of the coastal Fanti tribal group stated, "Yes, relations between the head and my family will be greatly affected. In Akan custom the services of any member of the family should be placed at the disposal of other members of the family. His refusal is a flagrant violation of what obtains in our traditional custom."

Another respondent made the same point in a different and illuminating fashion: "They will brand him as not being interested in the welfare of the larger family and say that *he is a Black-European*." Like the civil servants, a large group of student respondents felt that their families would view the head of department's refusal to help his relative as a malicious act motivated by malevolent designs toward the family. The following responses are typical:

My family would be annoyed with the relative. *They might even consider him a saboteur*. Though this reaction might seem unreasonable, that's the most probable thing to expect. It doesn't mean I endorse it.

If my relative refused to fix things for my father, *we must think he hates us privately*.

Relations would be strained for we would have nothing to do with the gentleman again as *he does not want us to prosper*.

Many of the respondents mentioned that by slighting the family through his refusal to nullify their father's transfer the civil servant opened himself up to retaliation in kind. As one person put it, "As you make your bed so must you lie. ... I will only wait a chance when his need arises." Often complete ostracism from the family was seen as the likely price the head of department would have to pay for his behavior.

They [my family] might even go to the extent of slandering him and maybe completely refusing to accept him in the family.

The family will regard the relative as a very wicked person and almost every member of the family will keep away from such a person.

The relationship would be strained. My father would not have anything to do with the relative as long as they live.

A few respondents felt the break in family relations would be so complete that their aunt would be likely to divorce the head of department. Table 9 presents a numerical breakdown of all the open-ended responses grouped into general categories.

Table 9

*Consequences Perceived by Student Sample of Giving Precedence
to Organizational Role over Family Role: Transfer Scenario*

Consequence	No. of Respondents Mentioning Consequence
Relative will be ostracized	56
Relations will be strained	112
Relative will be considered to have abandoned family	70
Relative will be disliked	50
Relative will be considered a "wicked," "bad," or "hard-hearted" man	30
Family will retaliate by refusing aid to relative when he is in need	15
Family will feel snubbed, insulted, or slighted	19
Relative will be considered an enemy of the family (his behavior will be interpreted as a malicious act)	28
Other, Don't Know, or Not Answered	13
No consequences	77

NOTE: Respondents were permitted to mention more than one consequence.

One last observation about the perceptions of the clientele sample as they were revealed in responses to the open-ended question: It is quite clear that the "offense" committed and the resultant hostility generated by the head of department's action involved not merely the two individuals directly involved—the head and the respondent's father—but rather the two family groups of which each was a member. A number of responses made this quite explicit. For example, one respondent thought that the head's refusal to aid his father would "also bring about a chain of hatred between my family and my relative's children." Another felt that "my family will have nothing to do with the other family until the case is settled by elders." It was suggested earlier that this would occur in a cultural environment in which obligation and responsibility are defined in corporate terms.[27] It has significance for the role pressure placed on a person in a bureaucratic position such as the department head in the imaginary transfer situation, because by his action he jeopardizes not only himself but many other members of his descent group, and offends not only the person seeking help but also the members of his branch of the extended family.

Given their belief in the intensity of negative affect that the head of department's behavior was likely to arouse, and the severity of the sanctions they thought the family was likely to mobilize against him, it is not surprising that an overwhelming number of the respondents in the Clientele Survey thought that in such a situation their relative would come to the aid of their father. Such a belief was expressed by 83 percent of the 385 respondents. This is a higher proportion than those who thought that the head would be approached for a favor, and thus indicates that some respondents felt that members of their family would not ask their uncle to prevent the transfer, because they assumed he would honor the obligations of family membership without being asked to do so.

In sum, then, the Clientele Survey produced evidence that lends strong support to the conclusions thus far drawn from the responses of the civil servant sample: (1) that in the contemporary Ghanaian social system people generally perceive the family role-set as "penetrating" the social sphere of the formal bureaucratic organization, and as having priority over obligations of the organizational role-set; (2) that the social pressure supporting the familial role-set is highly uniform and severe; and (3) that as a consequence the obligations of the family role-set are usually binding on the Ghanaian civil servant, even when he is acting within the context of the bureaucratic organization.[28]

[27] See the discussion on page 32.

[28] There is some evidence that this pattern of dominance by the familial role-set over the personal preferences of individuals exists in other areas of social activity also. In particular, research into the changing nature of courtship and marriage patterns has revealed the continued strength and effectiveness of traditionally based role pressures, within the general context of change. Peter Omari, in a study of orientations

Conclusion

Public bureaucracy, like all other formal organizations, depends for its effective operation on the individual role performance of each of its constituent members. The ability of members to so perform requires the social compartmentalization of official roles from all other roles, so that only the requirements of the organizational role-set need be attended to, and conflict with the member's other social roles can be avoided. The data presented in this chapter indicate that in the Ghanaian social environment such role compartmentalization is generally not permitted by a basic unit within that social system, the kinship group. The respondents indicated that a civil servant who ignored a family obligation because it conflicted with requirements of his organizational role would be the likely recipient of rather severe negative sanctions from his descent group, whose members would be prone to define the family role obligations as primary. Indeed, since role compartmentalization in the situational context was not believed to be widely practiced, many respondents felt that the honoring of organizational norms would be commonly misconstrued as a malevolent act, intentionally directed at the family by the civil servant relative. It was not surprising, therefore, that a large proportion of the respondents felt that under the circumstances Ghanaian civil servants would conform to the expectations of their kinship group.

---

to selecting marriage partners among Ghanaian young adults, found that while a large majority personally favored individual choice and "romantic love" as the primary bases of marriage choice, only one-fourth said they would defy parents who insisted on the traditional practice of arranged marriage. The sociologist Gustov Jahoda, also studying contemporary attitudes toward love and marriage in Ghana, comments on the reasons for the continued strength of traditional practice in terms that have equal significance for this study: "Youths or girls may have their own ideas about the kind of marriage partner they want, yet at the same time they are frequently not able or willing to ignore the pressures or objections of their elders who remain attached to traditional standards. Severing of the ties which bind them to the kin group is not only difficult because it runs counter to deeply entrenched sentiments, but would also be risky in practice in a society where as yet no safety net is provided by the welfare state. Even educated Africans derive comfort and security from their kin if they should happen to fall upon evil days; it requires a very independent cast of mind to be able to cut oneself loose under such circumstances."

Clearly the responses of the subjects in this study to the open-ended questions asked of them provide ample support for Jahoda's assessment about the consequences for the individual of breaking with his descent group. See T. Peter Omari, "Changing Attitudes of Students in West African Society Toward Marriage and Family Relationships," p. 204; and Gustov Jahoda, "Love, Marriage, and Social Change."

IV

Stability and Change
in Familial Obligations

The relationship between bureaucratic and familial roles was described in chapter 3 from a static point of view; in this chapter the question of change is addressed. Since the study concerns the general problem of the effectiveness of public bureaucracy in contemporary nonindustrial societies, the focus here is on those changes that indicate the development of congruence between the role requirements of formal "modern" organizations in such societies and the role behavior of persons who staff them. Let us examine, first, the extent to which the socio-cultural changes taking place in Ghana are creating a social environment that permits role compartmentalization, where it becomes accepted practice for occupational roles, under certain circumstances, to be separated from and take precedence over personal roles; and second, the changing "size" of the family unit, and the relationship of that to the ability of bureaucrats who are family members to perform in their official roles.

Social Mobilization and Role Orientation

In the contemporary literature concerned with "development," attempts to analyze and explain the widespread adoption of modern role orientations in previously traditional social systems have focused on the concept of social mobilization as it has been developed by Karl Deutsch.[1] This literature generally contends that in societies

[1] See, especially, Deutsch, "Social Mobilization and Political Development"; see also, Deutsch, *Nationalism and Social Communication.*

that are "late-comers" to industrialization, modernizing social change is produced as individuals increasingly come into contact with new social forms that introduce them to, and sometimes force them into, modern forms of role orientation and behavior. It is contended that exposure to these so-called modernizing influences—the market economy, Western education, urban life, nontraditional occupations, mass communications media, and the like—generates a process "in which major clusters of old social, economic, and psychological commitments are eroded or broken down and people become available for new patterns of socialization and behavior."[2] The empirical work relating to social mobilization theory has tended to support its central proposition—that the above "mobilization variables" or "forces of modernization" are related to the acquisition of modern role orientations.[3] Much of this research, however, has focused on individual orientations rather than behavior, while tacitly making the inference that the latter will follow from the former.[4] Such an inferential leap is unjustified, since there are powerful theoretical and empirical reasons for suspecting that the two need not be closely correlated. Since there are material and social costs to the individual for his behavior, his own orientation toward action is only one of a number of factors determining the final "behavior-event." At least as important as the individual's own orientation are the orientations of those he considers his "significant others." Thus, even if an individual has been extensively and intensively exposed to "modernizing influences," he is not likely to behave in ways congruent with these influences unless those he interacts with, both socially and psychologically, have been similarly influenced. Usually the consequence of this phenomenon is to slow down the process of behavioral change. It is possible, of course, for a socially mobilized population to coalesce into a "deviant" subcultural solidary. In such situations social change, that is, behavioral change, is not inhibited by interaction between socially mobilized individuals and "unmobilized" significant others; instead, the members of the deviant solidary provide social support for each other in new forms of action. The Calvinists in Western European modernization, and Leninist political parties in the twentieth century, may be historical cases in point.

[2] Deutsch, "Social Mobilization and Political Development," p. 494.

[3] See, for example, Daniel Lerner, *The Passing of Traditional Society* (Glencoe, 1958); James Coleman, *The Politics of Developing Areas* (Princeton, 1960), pp. 532-576; and Alex Inkeles, "Participant Citizenship in Six Developing Countries," *American Political Science Review*, 63:4 (December 1969), pp. 1131-1141.

[4] See Lerner, *Passing of Traditional Society*, and Inkeles, "Participant Citizenship," passim.

In Africa generally, and in Ghana particularly, such a deviant subculture does not seem to be in evidence. Rather, most observers have characterized the Ghanaian social system as open in its informal interaction across lines of differential social mobilization and status.[5] The strength of kinship has meant that socially mobilized individuals are tied into large networks of interaction and identification, the majority of whose members are at present relatively low on the dimensions of social mobilization, and likely to remain so for some time to come. As Gustov Jahoda has noted of the Ghanaian social system, "The sense of loyalty to both tribe and kin, as well as the feelings of dependence on these, remain sufficiently strong to ensure the persistence of frequent personal contacts (e.g., visits, joint participation in rituals) among people of widely disparate status levels."[6]

Furthermore, since educational opportunities have not been as open to women as to men, the man who has had a great deal of exposure to such social mobilization variables as a university education, a modern occupation, and foreign travel is likely to marry a woman who has been far less exposed to such influences. This has inhibited, for the time being, socially mobilized elements of the society from developing into a cohesive social group through the practice of endogamy in regard to social ties and interaction.[7]

The clear implication of the above discussion is that we should expect social mobilization variables to have only a limited impact on actual social behavior, even if they do have a dramatic impact when individual orientations are measured. Although the survey instruments in this study obviously do not provide information on actual behavior, they do provide some data that permit inferences that are relevant to this discussion. The data already presented strongly support the claim that it is a fallacy to posit a strong link between individual behavior and exposure to so-called modernizing influences. A large majority of both samples expressed personal role orientations that were in line with the thrust of social mobilization theory: over 80 percent of both groups indicated universalistic, or modern, role orientations when presented with imaginary organiza-

[5] In contemporary Ghana high social status is based in part on attributes whose attainment involves exposure to modernizing influences—university education, professional occupations, travel abroad, and the like. Consequently, there is likely to be a strong relationship between a person's social status and his position on the various dimensions of social mobilization. (Of course, in the transitional nature of African societies, high status is also attributed to those who can make traditional claims to it.)

[6] Gustov Jahoda, "Social Aspirations, Magic and Witchcraft in Ghana: A Social Psychological Interpretation," p. 202.

[7] Ibid.

tional situations. Since as civil servants or as university students these respondents can be considered to have extensive contact with modernizing influences, these results are what one would expect on the basis of mobilization theory. Of greater significance is the fact that a majority of these same individuals believed that actual behavior would most likely be quite different and would conform instead to the traditional role expectations and pressures coming from members of the civil servant's extended family. From the point of view of role behavior, then, the impact of mobilization variables on the actor's own role orientations may not be as important as the degree to which the influence of these variables on the individual is generalized to his significant others. Data relevant to this question are available through the Clientele Survey.

It will be recalled that the university students in the clientele sample were presented with the transfer scenario and were asked what their families would expect of a head of department who was their uncle by marriage. The survey also elicited a variety of demographic information—father's occupation, father's and mother's educational background, parents' literacy level, and the like—which provides a rough index of the degree to which a respondent's family can be considered to have been exposed to the social mobilization variables.[8] By relating these social background factors to the respondents' estimate of what their families' role expectations would be in the transfer scenario, we can essay the impact of social mobilization variables on an important determinant of role behavior. That is, we can determine if those respondents whose immediate family background indicates a high level of exposure to these variables are more likely to feel that their extended family would compartmentalize its role expectations and not demand particularistic behavior in a bureaucratic situation than are those whose family background lacks such influences.

The analysis of the data from the Clientele Survey reveals a clear and statistically significant relationship between the degree to which a respondent's family has been exposed to modernizing influences and the likelihood that its role expectations will appear to the respondent as universalistic. Tables 10 through 16 illustrate the relationship for six social background factors. Table 16 presents a summary of the findings by showing the percentage differences in

---

[8] For a discussion of these demographic variables as modernizing influences, see Deutsch, "Social Mobilization," and Inkeles, "Participant Citizenship"; see also Daniel Lerner, "Communication Systems and Social Systems. A Statistical Exploration in History and Policy."

perceived particularism between the "highs" and "lows" on each of the background indices.

Table 10

Familial Role Expectations and Place of Family Residence

Familial Role Expectation	Place of Residence		
	Village[a]	Town[b]	City[c]
Particularistic	81.1%	85.8%	69.0%
Universalistic	18.9	14.2	31.0
□ Total	100 (N=90)	100 (N=176)	100 (N=71)

NOTE: Table reports respondents' perceptions of their own family's expectations. Chi Square for table significant at .01 level.
[a]   Less than 2,000 inhabitants.
[b]   Between 2,000 and 30,000 inhabitants.
[c]   Over 30,000 inhabitants (over half of this category reside in Accra, the largest city in Ghana, with a population of over 500,000 at the time of the interviews).

Table 11

Familial Role Expectations and Parents' Literacy Level (in English)

Familial Role Expectation	Literacy Level		
	Low[a]	Medium[b]	High[c]
Particularistic	88.5%	79.3%	74.2%
Universalistic	11.5	20.7	25.8
□ Total	100 (N=130)	100 (N=150)	100 (N=93)

NOTE: Table reports respondents' perceptions of their own family's expectations. Chi Square for table significant at .01 level.
[a]   Both parents are nonliterate in English.
[b]   One of the parents is semiliterate in English; or one is literate and one is nonliterate.
[c]   Both parents are literate in English.

Table 12

Familial Role Expectations and
Occupation of Respondent's Father

Familial Role Expectation	Occupation		
	Traditional[a]	Marginal[b]	Modern[c]
Particularistic	87.0%	78.9%	75.5%
Universalistic	13.0	21.1	24.5
□ Total	100 (N=154)	100 (N=95)	100 (N=102)

NOTE: Table reports respondents' perceptions of their own family's expectations. Chi Square for table significant .05 level.
   [a] Traditional occupations are farmer, fisherman, and traditional authority (chief).
   [b] Marginal occupations are those that do not demand a great deal of "modern" skill in their performance — petty trader, clerk, non-officer policeman.
   [c] Modern occupations include senior civil servant, professional or managerial positions, businessman, and clergyman.

Table 13

Familial Role Expectations and Annual Income
of Respondent's Father

Familial Role Expectation	Income		
	Below $600	$600 — 2,000	$2,000 — 6,000
Particularistic	89.4%	83.6%	72.9%
Universalistic	10.6	16.4	27.1
□ Total	100 (N=113)	100 (N=128)	100 (N=59)

NOTE: Table reports respondents' perceptions of their own family's expectations. Income as reported by respondent. Chi Square for table significant at .02 level.

Table 14

*Familial Role Expectations and Educational Background
of Respondent's Father*

Familial Role Expectation	Educational Background		
	Low[a]	Medium[b]	High[c]
Particularistic	87.9%	83.0%	64.2%
Universalistic	12.1	17.0	35.8
☐ Total	100 (N=165)	100 (N=141)	100 (N=67)

NOTE: Table reports respondents' perceptions of their own family's expectations. Chi Square for table significant at .001 level.
[a] No formal schooling, attended primary school.
[b] Attended middle school, middle school + special training, teacher training college.
[c] Attended secondary school, secondary school + training course, university, postgraduate.

Table 15

*Familial Role Expectations and Educational Background
of Respondent's Mother*

Familial Role Expectation	Educational Background		
	Low[a]	Medium[b]	High[c]
Particularistic	84.8%	80.0%	56.5%
Universalistic	15.2	20.0	43.5
☐ Total	100 (N=230)	100 (N=125)	100 (N=23)

NOTE: Table reports respondents' perceptions of their own family's expectations. Chi Square for table significant at .01 level.
[a] No formal school.
[b] Primary or middle school, or middle school + special training course.
[c] Teacher training college, or secondary school.

Table 16

*Percentage Differences in Particularism Produced
by Six Social Background Variables*

Variable	Percentage Difference
Father's Occupation	-11.5
Place of Residence	-12.1
Parents' Literacy	-14.3
Father's Income	-16.5
Father's Education	-23.7
Mother's Education	-28.3

NOTE: Figure arrived at by subtracting the proportion of respondents reporting particularistic role expectations from their families in the "high" mobilization category from the proportion in the "low" category.

The tables show that all six social background factors are related to a decrease in particularistic familial role expectations as reported by the respondents. Urban residence, literacy in English, high income, modern occupational experience, and secondary and higher education would seem, according to the reports of the respondents, to increase the likelihood that families will compartmentalize their role expectations and allow the bureaucratic role-set top priority within the organizational context. Table 16 clearly indicates that the educational background of the respondent's parents has the strongest influence on the direction of family role expectations.

There are at least two reasons for this. First, research has shown that formal education is generally the most powerful demographic variable affecting orientations and beliefs. Alex Inkeles, in studying the relationship between some forty-five social factors and participant citizen orientations in six "transitional" societies, notes that "formal education is clearly the most consistently powerful influence."[9] Similarly, Almond and Verba wrote in the *Civic Culture* that "among the demographic variables usually investigated—sex, place of residence, occupation, income, age, and so on—none compares with the educational variable in the extent to which it seems to determine

[9] Alex Inkeles, "Participant Citizenship," p. 1132.

political attitudes."[10] The second reason that parents' education is the most powerful social background variable in this study is that it correlates highly with other modernizing influences.[11] A person whose father ranks high on educational experience (secondary school or university) is likely to be a person whose parents both are literate and whose father holds an elite occupation in the urban sector. Therefore, a high score on Father's Education indicates that the respondent's family has been exposed to "modern" influences in more than this one important respect. That is probably why the dimension of Mother's Education has the most influence. Within the Ghanaian social structure it is almost certain that a woman who has a secondary education will marry a man of similar or more advanced educational training, one who is employed in a modern occupation as well. Thus the influence that a high score on Mother's Education has on family role expectations is really a composite that includes high scores on Father's Education and Father's Occupation also. The dimensions of place of residence and income, which are more or less independent of the other four measures,[12] show a weaker but still positive relationship with universalistic familial role expectations that is statistically significant at the .02 level for income and the .01 level for urban residence.

Although there is a clear and statistically significant relationship between social mobilization variables and perceptions of universalistic role expectations, equally striking, and just as important theoretically, is the fact that this relationship is extremely weak. Shifts toward universalism are clear and in the expected direction, but they are extremely small. None of the variables has the effect of reducing the proportion of respondents who estimate their family's role expectations as particularistic to less than a majority, as can be seen in tables 10 through 15. Thus, for example, 64 percent of the families that rank high on Father's Education, and 57 percent of the families that rank high on Mother's Education, have particularistic role expectations, according to the members of these families that were interviewed.

[10] Gabriel Almond and Sidney Verba, *The Civic Culture*, p. 379.

[11] The Tau-B measures of association for Father's Education (FAED) and Father's Occupation (FAOC), Mother's Education (MOED), and Parents' Literacy (PARLIT) are .650, .619, and .739 respectively. The Tau-B statistics for Mother's Education and FAED, FAOC, and PARLIT are .619, .542, and .679.

[12] The level of association between Place of Residence and Father's Occupation, Father's Education, Parental Literacy, and Mother Education measured in Tau-B terms is .349, .340, .298, and .231 respectively. For the relationship between income and the above four social background factors the Tau-B statistics are .355, .389, .334, and .333. The level of association between income and place of residence is Tau-B .266.

The explanation for the limited effect of social mobilization variables on perceived role expectations relates back to the discussion
of the open or fluid nature of Ghanaian social structure. Although
the social background characteristics that were measured relate
exclusively to the nuclear family, it is clear from the responses to
the open-ended questions that respondents, when commenting on
familial role expectations, had in mind the much larger extended
family. Thus, in order for "modernizing influences" to greatly affect
familial role expectations and role pressures within the Ghanaian
social system, a much larger group than the immediate nuclear family
must be exposed to them. The spread of such exposure is still
somewhat limited within contemporary Ghana. Thus, in 1960, 78.8
percent of the adult male population had no formal schooling, only
1.4 percent had been to secondary school, and a mere 0.3 percent
had been to university.[13] The percentages for women who have
attended secondary school and university are a small fraction of the
proportions for adult males. Even the randomly selected sample of
university students in this study reveals the narrow penetration of
mobilization variables in Ghana. Only 18.4 percent of the nuclear
families of these students have an urban residence; in only 24 percent
of the families were both parents literate in English and in 27 percent
did the father have an occupation that could be classified as modern;
and fathers had secondary school or university educations in only
17.4 percent and mothers in a mere 0.4 percent of the cases.[14] The
inference to be drawn from these statistics is that the individuals
who have experienced a great deal of exposure to the kinds of
modernizing influences discussed so widely in the literature are in
most cases rather special in this respect within their extended families,
and thus role expectations and consequent role pressures coming from
the extended family tend to be predominantly particularistic. The
aggregate of socially mobilizing forces in Ghana may be relatively
large, by contemporary African standards, and if it were concentrated
in a single status group it would probably have considerable influence
on the behavior of its members. But most observers have noted, and
my data on the social backgrounds of civil servants and University
of Ghana students indicate, that this is not the case, that these forces
are dispersed.[15] Consequently, as the responses to the survey questions

---

[13] Philip Foster, *Education and Social Change in Ghana*, p. 243.

[14] Ghana is correctly thought of as one of the tropical African countries that have
experienced the greatest exposure to modernizing influences. This, however, is more
a reflection of the lack of such influences elsewhere than of their extensiveness within
Ghana.

[15] Only 20 percent of the sample of civil servants come from families in which both
parents are literate in English, and 29 percent have parents neither of whom is literate;

have suggested, social mobilization variables do not have a great deal of impact on familial role expectations and pressures. And to the degree that such role pressures determine the actions of individuals, these variables will have limited effect on behavior as well. Thus, 83 percent of the university student sample felt that in the transfer situation their uncle would resolve the conflict between bureaucratic and family role-sets in the particularistic direction, fulfilling obligations to the family and violating bureaucratic norms.

This is not to suggest that no change is occurring. On the contrary, these data clearly show that the introduction of modernizing influence into a society does have an effect on role expectations, and consequently, it could be inferred, on role behavior as well.[16] But the results indicate that this effect is far less dramatic—that overall social change is far less rapid—than is usually imagined. If social mobilization means a break with past social ties and psychological orientations, such that the individual becomes available for reintegration into a new system of interaction, identification, and belief—as it was originally defined by Deutsch—then, based on the data obtained here, it cannot be said that exposure to modernizing influences will produce social mobilization on any substantial scale. Most of the people who have been exposed to modernizing influences, such as the students and

---

43 percent come from villages or towns of fewer than 10,000 inhabitants; 35 percent have educational backgrounds extending only to middle school, and only 20 percent have attended university; only one-third (29 percent) have fathers whose occupations are clearly "modern" in character. There is a clear relationship between rank and the kind of social backgrounds that indicate exposure to modernizing influence. Position in the civil service hierarchy is positively related to such variables as paternal occupation, parental literacy, and respondent's own educational attainment. However, a significant subset of even the highest ranking officers have social backgrounds that indicate a very limited exposure to "mobilization" influences. Thus among the respondents who ranked from Senior Executive Officer on up in the bureaucratic hierarchy (including equivalent ranks outside the Administrative Class) only one-half (52 percent) had attended university, and 15 percent had gone only as far as middle school; approximately 30 percent had fathers with a traditional occupation (farmer or fisherman), 20 percent had fathers with semitraditional occupations (petty trader, driver, unskilled worker), and only 43 percent had fathers whose occupations could clearly be classified as modern (civil servant, lawyer, engineer, manager, technician).

[16] Since the survey data indicate that education is the most potent variable in changing role expectations, it is important to note that there has been a vast increase in the availability of educational opportunities since Ghana became independent in 1957. However, it should also be observed that, while the results of the survey show that education at the secondary school level produces the most dramatic change, the availability of educational opportunity in Ghana has increased most at the presecondary level. Thus, while some form of presecondary school education is presently available to a large majority of Ghanaian children, those attending secondary schools are still a small minority and are likely to remain so for some time. In 1966-1967 there were some 42,276 pupils enrolled in secondary schools, 280,866 in middle schools, and 1,116,843 in primary schools. See *Report of the Commission on the Structure and Remuneration of the Public Services in Ghana* (Accra, 1967), p. 45.

civil servants in these two samples, continue to be socially and psychologically tied to groups, most of whose members have far less exposure than they to such influences. Consequently, the social support necessary for a change in behavior is generally not available.

Such social support can become available in one of two ways— through the growth of new social solidarities that are homogenous in terms of exposure to modernizing influences and endogamous as regards social interaction, or through the gradual aggregation of modernizing influences throughout a social system, so that old social solidarities such as kin groups become relatively homogeneous in terms of extensive exposure to these influences.

It is my guess that those respondents who reported the role expectations of their families as universalistic come from extended families in which formal education, literacy, urbanism, and the like have spread more broadly than in the families of those who felt that their families would expect particularistic consideration. It would take further research, in which the spread of modernizing influence is sociometrically mapped within extended families, to test this hypothesis. However, some measure of support is provided by the strength of the effect that father's and mother's secondary school education has on reported familial role expectations. In all likelihood, most of the adults with secondary school education who are old enough to have children at university had received that education during the 1940s, if not earlier. Since in 1940 there were in all Ghana (the Gold Coast) two government, three government-assisted, and twelve nonassisted secondary schools with a total student population of 2,635,[17] it can be assumed that university students with parents who have secondary school educational backgrounds come from kin groups whose access to modernizing influences was very early and practically unique, relative to that of the rest of the Ghanaian population. This would be even more true with mothers who had secondary education, since families who sent their daughters to secondary school before 1945 represented the most acculturated group in colonial society. Thus it is likely that those respondents who had parents who ranked high on the educational background indices come from extended families that have been broadly exposed to the modernizing influences that were a part of Western penetration under colonialism. It is perhaps for this reason that father's and mother's education show twice as much influence on reported familial role expectations than do the other social background factors.

In sum, the data show that role orientations and expectations tend

[17] Foster, *Education and Social Change*, p. 115.

to be altered under the influence of social forces that were originally exogenous to the Ghanaian society. The data suggest, however, that changes in actual behavior are far less dramatic than changes in stated personal orientations. One possible explanation for this is that in countries like Ghana exposure to modernizing influences is not equally distributed throughout society. Consequently, highly exposed individuals, whose personal role orientations have become nontraditional, interact within a network of socially significant others, most of whose members have not undergone a similar change in role orientation. The result is that the social pressure directed at the changed individual will continue to demand traditional forms of role behavior, and he is likely to yield to this pressure, despite his own personal orientation, because of the high cost of nonconformity.

The Parameters of Familial Obligation

The data that have been thus far analyzed relate to changes in the extent to which role compartmentalization is socially permitted by Ghanaian families so as to allow the separation of familial and bureaucratic obligations. A second dimension of familial change is of potential significance from the vantage point of bureaucratic organization, that of familial size. The question is whether exposure to social mobilization variables alters the specific kin relationships that would arouse expectations of particularistic behavior on the part of civil servants. The data generated by the two clientele surveys permit a tentative and admittedly partial step toward an answer.

The traditional Ghanaian family can be described as "large" in two senses: in the weight of obligation that membership in a corporate unit imposes, and in the size and extent of the family unit—the traditional extended family as a functional unit including several generations and numerous collateral relatives. For the student of contemporary bureaucratic organizations, the first aspect of family "largeness" should be viewed as primary. It is the definition of obligation that membership entails that poses problems for effective role performance from the organizational point of view. The size of the family unit would mean little if membership did not involve obligations that conflicted with the requirements of formal organizational roles for any of its number who are public bureaucrats—that is, if role compartmentalization was socially sanctioned. But once such organizationally dysfunctional role expectations and pressures are found to exist, it is important to take cognizance of the size aspect of the family unit. Size will define the extent of the "circle" within which particularistic expectations are likely to predominate, and it will determine in part the number of situations in which the public bureaucrat will find himself under familial role pressure to violate organizational norms.[18] Thus a society in which the kinship system was characterized by nuclear families that defined membership in corporate terms would be a more hospitable environment for bureaucratic organizations than would a society in which family membership was similarly defined corporately, but in which family structure was of the extended form. Consequently, social change that altered family structure from extended to nuclear forms, even if it did not alter the corporate nature of membership, would be significant for the operation of bureaucracy.

Contemporary research into kinship and marriage patterns in Africa, and in Ghana, has revealed that among urban dwellers the nuclear family based on conjugal ties is a far more important social institution than it is for residents of the rural hinterland.[19] This difference is apparently most pronounced among the more highly educated and the professionally employed.[20] The movement away from extended kinship and to some form of a nuclear family arrangement appears to be produced by a combination of factors. In urban forms of employment the extended family loses much of its functional value as a unit of production and income; urban architecture, particularly in middle- and upper-class neighborhoods, is not congenial to the maintenance of households much larger than the nuclear family; and where urban residence involves migration from natal villages, it places the individual at a distance from his kinship group and thus to a degree frees him from its mechanisms of social control. Although research has shown that in urban Ghana the nuclear family has increasing significance and that the ties of extended kinship are reduced by virtue of urban migration, the same research does not permit the conclusion that the extended family kinship system is presently in a state of general collapse, or that even among the high-income professionally employed the extended family is an unimportant social institution. To the contrary, this research indicates that all segments of the urban population continue to interact with

[18] See Lloyd Fallers, *Bantu Bureaucracy*, p. 231.

[19] For Africa in general see A. Phillips, *Survey of African Marriage and Family Life*; and D. Forde, ed., *Social Implications of Industrialization and Urbanization in Africa South of the Sahara*. For Ghana, see, Margaret Peil, *The Ghanaian Factory Worker*, pp. 190-217; J. C. Caldwell, *Population Growth and Family Change in Africa*, pp. 52-95; and Christine Oppong, *Marriage Among a Matrilineal Elite* (Cambridge, England, 1974), passim.

[20] See Caldwell, *Population Growth*, passim; and Oppong, *Marriage Among a Matrilineal Elite*, passim.

their extended families, participate in its ceremonies and rituals, honor its financial obligations, and depend on it for economic security and social status.[21] Moreover, although research has been quite clear and consistent in the finding that urban occupational modes and residence patterns have tended to make the conjugal unit functionally independent of the larger kinship group and have thus introduced a good deal of tension in the fulfilling of extended kinship obligation, it has been far less precise about the extent to which tension has been translated into a willingness to avoid obligations, or into a redefinition of which obligations are appropriate.

The concern here is not with the parameters of kinship obligation in general, but rather with those parameters that affect the relationship between bureaucrats and their kinsmen. A series of items was designed for the Clientele Survey that would permit an assessment of the relationship between kinship distance from the respondent and the respondent's belief in the existence of familial obligation, in an effort to discover the extent to which close kin relationships were more likely than more distant ones to generate particularistic expectations, and to illuminate whether differences in expectation toward close and distant kin were related to exposure to modernizing influences.

Each respondent was asked to imagine that he was dealing with a civil servant in a government office, and was then presented a series of items that described the civil servant in question as having various kin relations to the respondent. The respondent was asked whether he would expect better treatment, worse treatment, or the same treatment as other people using the services of the government office.[22] Six different kinship relations were presented in this manner:[23] father's brother (FaBr); brother-in-law's brother (Br-in-law's Br); mother's cousin—mother's mother's sister's son (MoMoSiSo); grandmother's sister's husband (MoMoSiHu); brother of father's brother's wife (FaBrWiBr); husband of father's brother's wife's sister (FaBrWiSi-Hu).

Figure 1 is a kinship map that designates the relationships appearing in the survey items (Ego represents the respondent). These six kinship

[21] See the discussion in chapter 3, p. 60-61. Christine Oppong, utilizing a sample of eighty-three Ghanaian senior civil servants, found that *all* respondents reported making regular financial remittances to rural members of their extended kinship group, in addition to intermittent monetary contributions on visits home, at funerals, and on festive occasions. She also reports that about half of her urban "elite" sample owns shares in family property located in rural villages. See Oppong, *Marriage*, pp. 53-55.

[22] For the exact form in which the series of items was introduced see Appendix B., item 23.

[23] The six items in the kinship series were presented in random order.

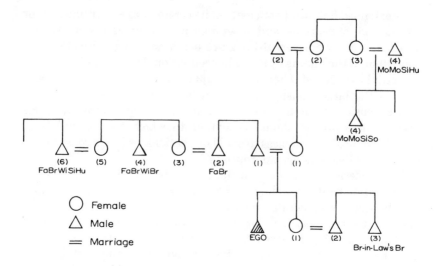

Figure 1. Kinship map of "Extended Family." Relationships Are Those Appearing in Survey Items.

relations are not intended to comprehensively cover the relationships found within the contemporary or traditional Ghanaian notion of the extended family, nor were they chosen because they traditionally connoted differences in degree of closeness and therefore obligation. The anthropological literature apparently does not contain the type of information that would permit such judgments for the major Ghanaian tribal groups, nor, of course, would such literature provide insight into the way traditional kinship relationships translate into obligation in the bureaucratic setting. Instead, these kinship relations were chosen because they logically appeared to represent variation in "distance" on the dimensions of consanguinity (biological ties), affinity (marriage ties), and generation (age ties). Thus we have one item that represents what would appear to be a very close collateral biological relative, the respondent's uncle, or father's brother, and others that represent seemingly more distant biological relatives, mother's cousin, and still others that combine distance in terms of both biology and marriage, the rather remote husband of father's brother's wife's sister, for example.

Table 17 presents the results of these items for the main clientele sample, that is, the sample of University of Ghana students. This table suggests (1) that a substantial portion of the sample recognizes extended family ties as relevant within the bureaucratic context

Table 17

Percentage of Respondents Who Expect Better Treatment from Civil
Servants Who Are Related to Them in Designated Manner

Civil Servant Is	Percentage of Sample Expecting Better Treatment
	(N=385)
FaBr	69.4
Br-in-law's Br	57.3
MoMoSiSo	52.5
MoMoSiHu	39.6
FaBrWiBr	36.7
FaBrWiSiHu	36.7

described in the survey item, and (2) that not all relationships of extended kinship are equally likely to be so recognized. It is particularly striking, and significant from the point of view of this study, that over one-third (36.7 percent) of the university students would expect special consideration from a civil servant who is as remote a relative as their father's brother's wife's sister's husband. For the moment, let us ignore generational differences and distinctions between blood and marriage ties, and measure distance in the number of kinship "steps" by which Alter is removed from Ego (see the numbers below the kinship positions in fig. 1). In this manner, FaBr (2) would be the closest relative, Br-in-law's Br (3) the next closest, and FaBrWiSiHu (6) the most distant. The findings on particularistic expectations parallel this rank ordering of kinship distance, with the likelihood of such expectations decreasing as we move from FaBr to FaBrWiSiHu. But if we observe the three relationships that are four steps removed from Ego, it would seem that more is involved than distance measured by this crude "step method." The relations of MoMoSiHu and FaBrWiBr generate about the same likelihood of particularlistic expectations—that is, in 40 and 37 percent of the cases—while the relationship of MoMoSiSo, also four steps removed from Ego, generates particularistic expectations in 53 percent of the cases. One factor that may account for this difference is that the latter relationship is one of consanguinity—it is a biological tie—while in the former two relationships the ties with Ego are of the marriage or affinal variety. This suggests that biological ties are more likely to carry obligations that are those of marriage.[24]

Discussion of the variation in the likelihood of particularistic expectations should not obscure a second interesting finding. It is striking and significant, from the point of view of this study, that as many as a third of the university students sampled would expect special consideration from a civil servant who is as remote a relative as their father's brother's wife's sister's husband. Indeed, a rather large proportion, 31 percent, maintain particularistic expectations across the entire spectrum of kin relationships with which they were presented. Of the 257 respondents that expect favored treatment from a civil servant who is their father's brother, nearly one-half, a full 47 percent, also expect such treatment from the distant husband of their father's brother's wife's sister.[25]

Although table 17 suggests the continued importance of the extended family, even for those highly exposed to Western forms of education, it also reveals that, for most of the respondents, relationships of extended kinship are not undifferentiated. Rather, the likelihood that particularistic expectations will be held by the respondent in his capacity as a client of public bureaucracy varies with his kin relationship to the civil servant with whom he is dealing. The apparent dimension of this differentiation is kinship distance.

[24] It is possible, of course, that the variation observed in table 17 is a function, not of kinship distance, but rather of the representation of groups in the sample that reckon kin membership differently. Since the sample does contain individuals from both matrilineal and patrilineal ethnic groups, it might be thought that the variation in expectations toward specified civil servant relatives is a consequence of the distribution of matrilineal and patrilineal groups within the sample. On this line of reasoning particularistic expectations would vary according to which side of the family the relationship was on, with those from matrilineal tribes being more likely to have particularistic expectations in the case of relatives on the mother's side, and those from patrilineal groups on the father's side. The survey data, however, reveal that for the type of expectations being considered here this distinction in terms of lineage reckoning is irrelevant. Controlling for tribal background turned up no differences in the likelihood of particularistic expectations for any of the six kin relationships tested. It appears that differences in the way lineage membership is determined may bear little relation to expectations in this type of context, although it is important in other contexts, such as in determining inheritance.

[25] In pretests of the series of extended-family items it was observed that Ghanaians had no difficulty in locating and identifying even the most distant relative mentioned. Thus, for example, when the item specifying "the husband of your father's brother's wife's sister" was read to the respondents they could almost instantaneously place a real person who was known to them in the category. When Americans have been tested informally on these items, they have had great difficulty in locating the more distant relatives in even a theoretical sense, and rarely have any personal knowledge of the actual identity of these distant "relatives."

Within the context of this discussion, the primary question raised by table 17 is whether the variation in particularistic expectations according to kinship distance is a function of the traditional social system or a product of social change consequent upon the exposure of individuals to modernizing influences. Does the variation indicate a shrinkage in the parameters of familial obligation, a movement toward a more nuclear family arrangement?

In an attempt to answer this question, table 18 presents two subsets of the student sample which are high and low on indices of exposure to modernization and compares their role expectations for the six relationships within the extended family.

Note first that for each of the kin relationships presented, exposure to "modernizing influences" reduces the likelihood that client role expectations will be particularistic. Those whose families live in urban areas, whose fathers have modern occupations, whose mothers have at least middle-school-level educational backgrounds, and those whose fathers have been to secondary school or university are, with one minor exception, less likely to expect better treatment from a civil servant who occupies any of the kin relationships mentioned than are respondents who have families that reside in rural areas, or have fathers in traditional occupations, or have parents with little or no formal education. Second, of the four variables, the educational background of the respondent's father appears to have the greatest influence. For each of the six kin relationships, the proportional difference in particularistic expectations between high and low subsets that is produced by father's educational background is practically twice as big as the differences produced by the three other independent variables.[26] The greater effect of father's education can be seen even more clearly if we compare the means of the percentage differences created by the independent variables across the six kin relationships: father's educational background creates a mean percentage difference of 13.7, compared with 8.2 for father's occupation, 6.6 for mother's education, and 5.1 for place of residence.

These findings are clearly in line with the results obtained from the analysis of the "transfer scenario": exposure to modernizing influences increases the likelihood that respondents will exhibit universalism in their personal role orientations, and a high level of formal education is the most potent social background variable in creating such orientations. Less clear than this, however, is support

[26] There is an exception in the case of the father's brother relationship, where father's occupation reduces particularism to a greater extent than does the educational background of the respondent's father.

Table 18

Effect of Exposure to Modernizing Influences on Expectations of Better Treatment from Civil Servant Relative
(University Student Sample)

			Percentage Expecting Better Treatment from			
	FaBr	Br-in-law's Br	MoMoSiSo	MoMoSiHu	FaBrWiBr	FaBrWiSuHu
Residence						
Urban	69.6	58.0	49.3	33.3	30.4	29.4
Rural	67.1	58.3	52.9	42.4	41.2	34.1
% Difference	+ 2.5	- 0.3	- 3.6	- 9.1	-10.8	- 4.7
Paternal Occupation						
Modern	62.7	56.4	53.5	36.6	33.3	31.7
Traditional	77.0	59.6	58.3	46.1	42.8	40.1
% Difference	-14.3	- 3.2	- 4.8	- 9.5	- 9.5	- 8.4
Maternal Education						
High	66.7	52.4	42.9	33.3	37.9	28.6
Low	71.9	56.8	51.8	43.2	42.9	35.0
% Difference	- 5.2	- 4.4	- 8.9	- 9.9	- 5.0	- 6.4
Paternal Education						
High	65.2	53.8	43.1	29.2	30.3	22.7
Low	77.5	62.5	55.3	47.5	43.7	40.0
% Difference	-12.3	- 8.7	-12.2	-18.3	-13.4	-17.3

for the hypothesis that a differentiated set of expectations within the extended family is also a consequence of exposure to modernizing influences. For this hypothesis to be confirmed, we should find that for those with low levels of such exposure there should be little decline in the likelihood of particularistic expectations as we move across the kinship spectrum from close to distant relatives, or at least there should be less of a percentage falloff in particularism than among the subset of respondents with a great deal of exposure to modernization. But the data in table 18 indicate that even for the low-exposure subset there is a considerable falloff in the proportion of particularistic expectations as one moves outward from close to distant relatives. For three of the social background variables the contours of the falloff, that is, the percentage decline from one relative to the next, for both high and low groups is quite similar. However, in the case of father's education there does appear to occur a slightly less dramatic decline in particularism among those scoring low than among those scoring high. By comparing the slopes of the two lines in figure 2, we can see that the decline in particularism is greater for those whose fathers

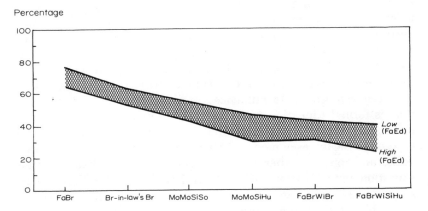

Figure 2. Father's Education (FaEd) and Expectation of Better Treatment from Relatives.

have had secondary or university education. But quite clearly the relative difference that is revealed is not dramatic and can be taken only as a hint of evidence in support of the hypothesis.

The hypothesis need not, however, be abandoned. It is possible that lack of confirmation obtained from the data presented in table 18 is a function of the sample being utilized. Because these respondents are university students, and therefore have all been extensively exposed to "modernizing influences," it is possible that their own experience has flattened out differences that would otherwise be produced by variation in social background. Since the Comparison/Clientele Survey has a sample of respondents who have experienced less in the way of formal education, it provides us with the means to further test the hypothesis. Table 19 and figure 3 offer presentations of the data obtained by the Comparison/Clientele Survey and permit a comparison with the responses of the university student sample. The respondents in the Comparison/Clientele Survey are varied with respect to the exposure to modernizing influences, but none has had as extensive a formal education as have the university students in the main clientele sample. Forty-one percent of them have attended secondary school but one-fourth (24.6 percent) have had no schooling at all or have only completed their primary level education. Column 2 of table 19 presents the proportion of this sample who expected better treatment from a civil servant relative in each of the six kin relationships. Column 3 presents the percentage breakdown within a subset of this sample—those respondents who cannot read English at all or who do so only slightly.[27] In Ghana, literacy in English is an excellent barometer of the extent of an individual's exposure to modernizing influences. Since as a consequence of colonial imposition the "modern sector" (government, business, schools) conducts its written business almost entirely in English, a facility in reading the language is a good indication of the extent to which an individual is involved in the sector and thus has been exposed to its influences. It is a better indicator of this than is formal education, since on the one hand a person who has had no such educational background, but who is actively and intensely exposed to the forces of modernization, can informally obtain literacy skills, and, on the other hand, a person who has had a formal education, but who afterward is relatively uninvolved in the "modern sector," may lose these skills as a consequence of disuse. Column 3 in table 19, therefore, represents a group of respondents who are fairly closely tied to the traditional institutional network. Most of them speak little or no English, and are employed as drivers, domestic servants (stewards, nurse-girls, watchmen), or petty traders.

Two things can be observed in the comparison of the two clientele samples. First, in line with what was found to be true on the basis of the university sample alone, the less the exposure to modernizing influences of a population group taken as a whole, the greater is

[27] Ability to read English was easily determined by the interviewer, since in a number of items the respondent was handed a card on which was printed, in English, an imaginary situation which he was asked to read. If the respondent indicated difficulty in reading the material, the interviewer described the imaginary situation verbally.

the likelihood that role expectations will be particularistic. For each of the kin relationships tested there occurs a dramatic increase in the proportion of respondents manifesting particularism as we move from the university sample to the nonuniversity-educated sample to

Table 19

Percentage of Respondents with Particularistic
Expectations for Specified Family Relationships,
by Exposure to Modernizing Influences

Relationships	(1) University Student Sample	(2) Total Non-University Sample	(3) Nonliterate or Semiliterate Subset
FaBr	69.4	79.5	83.8
Br-in-law's Br . . .	57.3	70.4	80.6
MoMoSiSo	52.5	72.6	87.9
MoMoSiHu	39.6	65.8	70.6
FaBrWiBr	36.7	53.5	71.0
FaBrWiSiHu	36.7	58.3	74.2
	(N=385)	(N=81)	(N=37)

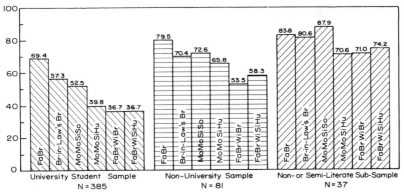

Figure 3. Percentage of Respondents Who Expect Better Treatment from Civil Servant Relatives. By Relationship and Exposure to Modernization.

the traditional subset. Second, the phenomenon of differentiated responses—in which closer kin relationships are more potent than more distant ones in producing particularistic role expectations—tends to disappear in the more traditional group. Among the nonliterate and semiliterate subset a majority of more than 70 percent expects better treatment from a civil servant relative who fits any of the specified relationships. This not only represents a larger proportion of particularistic expectations than even the closest relative produced in the university sample, but also reveals that the more traditional respondents were most likely to have particularistic expectations across the entire spectrum of kin relationships that we specified. The graph in figure 2 visually represents this latter point. If we observe the differences in the likelihood of particularism from one relationship to another, we can see that the decline from the relationship with the greatest likelihood to that with the least likelihood is less drastic in the nonuniversity sample taken as a whole than it is in the university sample, while in the semiliterate subset the differences tend to "flatten out" even further.

The conclusion that follows from this analysis is that exposure to "modernizing influences" not only reduces the overall likelihood of familial role expectations in a bureaucratic context, but does so at different rates within the varied relationships of the extended family. The more distant the relative the more drastic is the reduction in the likelihood of particularistic role expectations based on family connection. Obversely, the more traditionally involved the individual, that is, the less his exposure to modernizing influences, the less likely he is to differentiate between relatives in his expectations—all relatives alike are expected to recognize family connections and behave accordingly. The survey data suggest, then, that one aspect of modernization in Ghana is the shrinking of the "circle" within which family ties are expected to affect behavior in nonfamilial institutional contexts. However, the data also suggest that this process is as yet far from complete within the total Ghanaian population. Of the three population aggregates presented in table 19 and figure 3, it is the semiliterate group which comes closest to approximating the social characteristics of what is probably the numerical majority of Ghanaians.[28] And it is this group which manifests very high levels of particularistic role expectations for all the kin relationships represented in the survey items, with nearly three-fourths of the group expecting better treatment from a civil servant who is as remotely

[28] Since most of these respondents are residents of Ghana's capital city or its environs, they should in that respect probably be seen as more highly exposed to modernizing influences than the majority of Ghanaians.

related to them as the husband of their father's brother's wife's sister. Therefore, the data indicate that at present familial role expectations and pressures that can influence organizational performance can and will be mobilized in a wide array of relationships and by a large number of persons. From the point of view of the civil servant, the Ghanaian family would appear to still be very large, although there are forces at work within the social system that are beginning to shrink the family in terms of the relationships that impinge on him in the performance of his role.

In the decade of the 1960s scholars viewed the process of social and political change in Africa as one of upheaval and rapid transformation, an orientation captured in the phrase social mobilization. "Every well-informed person knows," wrote a Ghanaian sociologist in a statement typical of the period, "that there is 'ferment' in Africa and that political, social, and economic changes are going on at a 'jet-propelled' rate."[29] The findings presented in this chapter strongly suggest that more conservative assumptions about the extent and rapidity of social change should be brought to the study of contemporary Ghana. It would seem that change tends to be syncretic rather than wholesale, and that the "winds of change" are so scattered that systemic forces can operate to dampen their effect.

[29] T. Peter Omari, "Changing Attitudes of Students in West African Society Toward Marriage and Family Relationships," p. 197.

V

The Bureaucrat-Client Relationship: Client Role Orientations

Thus far this study has concerned those role expectations and consequent role pressures on Ghanaian civil servants which have been generated by "significant others" who have had some personal relationship to the civil servant in question. Hypothetically, role pressure can also be exerted by those the civil servant interacts with even when they have no personal tie to him. The reason for this can be found in what might be termed the mutuality principle in interpersonal behavior. As Talcott Parsons has noted:

It is a fundamental property of action ... that the actor develops a *system* of "expectations." ... [And] in the case of interaction with social objects, [part of] ... ego's expectation, in many cases the most important part, consists in the probable reaction of alter to ego's possible action, a reaction which comes to be anticipated in advance and thus to affect ego's own choices.[1]

The social psychologists Krech, Crutchfield, and Ballachey make the same point in a somewhat different manner:

We would emphasize that action in the standard interpersonal behavior event is determined jointly by the individual's own predispositions ... and by the expectations and sanctions, as apprehended by the individual, of other persons in the behavior event who are enacting complementary roles. Both the characteristics of the individual and the way in which other persons

[1] Talcott Parsons, *The Social System*, p. 5.

108

respond to him as a taker of a given role must be taken into account in seeking to understand his behavior.[2]

These theoretical statements encompass both the condition in which Alter has a personal relationship to Ego and the condition in which he does not. Obviously, in the former case Alter's influence over Ego's behavior is likely to be greater since he is capable, in ways already discussed, of mobilizing important sanctions against an Ego that does not conform to his expectations. But the mere fact that Alter has expectations of behavior on Ego's part, even in the absence of clear sanction, can affect, albeit to a lesser degree, the behavior of Ego. This is perhaps most clearly true in the context of formal organization, because here the norms governing role behavior are reciprocally defined. "What characterizes the organizational role, or office," writes Theodore Caplow, "is its rigorous polar relation to other offices, without which it cannot be activated. The role of husband depends on the reciprocal role of wife. The role of foreman depends on the role of workman. The role of physician depends on the role of patient. Neither can function at all without the other."[3] Caplow could easily have added that the role of bureaucrat depends for its effective functioning on the role of client. If a bureaucratic organization is to work effectively, the client as well as the bureaucrat must have role expectations that are congruent with formally defined and coordinated roles. That is, if those members of society who interact from time to time within bureaucratic organizations do not understand or act on the norms which supposedly govern their behavior vis-à-vis the bureaucrat, then the bureaucrat will have difficulty in applying the formal rules of his office to them. The reverse, of course, is also true. The client cannot easily follow the rules associated with his organizational role unless the bureaucrat adheres to his. Katz and Eisenstadt have commented succinctly on this phenomenon in the context of their observations on the workings of the Israeli public service:

It is expected by the bureaucrat and the bureaucracy that the client will bring with him to the bureaucratic context certain knowledge of expected roles from "outside," even though he may have had no previous contact with this particular bureaucracy. In Western society, for example, one is prepared for one's first encounter with a customs inspector by virtue of

[2] David Kretch et al., *Individual and Society* (New York, 1962), p. 348.
[3] Theodore Caplow, "The Criteria of Organizational Success." pp. 1-9.

one's single-purpose relationship with other officials, tradesmen, and the like. [In Israel] when this preparation is lacking, the bureaucrat himself ... added a dimension—teaching—to his relationship with the client. ... The bureaucrat teaches the client how to be a client so that he (the bureaucrat) can go on being a bureaucrat.[4]

In Israel, as described by Katz and Eisenstadt, civil servants added a teaching dimension to their roles and instructed "unsocialized" individuals in proper role behavior for bureaucratic clients. It is clear from the examples cited by the authors that the teaching role was added because the bureaucrats cared about organizational goals and viewed proper client role behavior as a necessary condition for their effective attainment.[5] However, where bureaucrats do not care strongly about organizational goals they are not likely to be motivated to take on extra teaching functions; rather, they are likely to mesh their behavior with the expectations of clients regardless of the consequences for organizational goal attainment. This would especially be true where the dominant values of the society are supportive of the nonbureaucratic orientations of the clients and where there exists little social support for the bureaucrat who seeks to adhere to organizational norms by teaching reciprocal norms to the citizens with whom he must deal.

From the theoretical point of view adopted in this study we would expect the social environment of a transitional society such as Ghana to produce clients of bureaucracy whose own notion of their client role and whose related beliefs about the behavior they can expect from bureaucrats is such as to undermine role performance on the part of the bureaucracy. First, individuals who have been socialized in traditional culture and society, to which formal bureaucratic organization is a foreign institution, are not likely to possess the requisite role expectations regarding the client role. Second, and more significant, the traditional socialization process is likely to create *general* expectations about the basis of interpersonal behavior that are directly opposed to the universalistic principle on which the role of the bureaucratic client, as well as all other roles in bureaucracy, is based.

As was noted in chapter 1, social interaction in systems based on the corporate family are generally of the type that the nineteenth-century social theorist Ferdinand Toennies called gemeins-

---

[4] Elihu Katz and S. N. Eisenstadt, "Response of Israeli Organizations to New Immigrants," p. 124.

[5] See S. N. Eisenstadt, *Essays on Comparative Institutions*, pp. 259-263.

chaften.[6] Interaction takes place on a foundation of personal, often face-to-face, relationships that bind the interacting individuals together in a manner that transcends any given interaction "event." Modern bureaucracy, however, defines its role interactions in the opposite manner, the relations between interacting individuals being ideally based on gesellschaft considerations. The relationships between clients and bureaucrats are supposed to be functionally specific and impersonal, with individuals bound to each other only by the limited purpose for which they are interacting. What, then, is the orientation of an individual, socialized to have stable expectations about interaction only when personal ties are present, when he must deal with government bureaucracy? It is my hypothesis that such a client, believing he cannot expect service from one who is essentially a "stranger," will seek out some way of establishing a personal tie between himself and the bureaucrat with whom he must deal, even if he has a formal right to such service as a consequence of official public policy. Only in this way can such a client feel confident that the service he seeks will in fact be granted.

Civil servants, consequently, not only will have to deal with particularistic role expectations when their own kinsmen or village neighbors are directly involved, but will constantly be approached by individuals who attempt to establish a particularistic relationship with them, either directly or indirectly. Of course, civil servants may have similar beliefs that personal relationships create the necessary basis for fruitful social interaction, hence such perceptions on the part of clients could be not only a product of socialization in a corporate-based social system but also an accurate assessment of what is required of one doing business with public bureaucracy. Indeed, since civil servants have been socialized in essentially the same social system as their clients, they are likely to have similar expectations about the proper basis of interaction, although given their special experience they are more likely than the average member of their society to have learned new expectations. When civil servants share with clients the notion that productive social interaction does not occur between "strangers," there will occur a complimentarity of personalistic role expectations, and particularistic role behavior in public bureaucracy can be considered systemic.

The survey data do not provide empirical evidence for all aspects of the above argument, but they do allow observation of what the

[6] See Ferdinand Toennies, "Gemeinschaft and Gesellschaft," in Talcott Parsons et al., eds., *Theories of Society*, vol.1, pp. 191-201.

Ghanaian public views as necessary behavior for a person who is doing business with the civil service. Each of the samples was presented with an item that listed alternative methods of getting things done at a government administrative office, only one of which involved a universalistic approach: "You go directly to the government office and state your business." The respondents were asked which they thought was the most effective method in terms of getting things done. Thus, to the civil servant sample, the following item was presented:

Suppose that an ordinary citizen finds it necessary to go to a government official concerning ordinary official business. Which of the methods listed on this card would be the *most effective* for him to use in order to accomplish his purpose? (a) He should see a relative of his who is also a government official. (b) He should go directly to the official's office and state his problem. (c) He should see a friend who knows the government official.

In addition, the civil servant respondents were asked what they thought would be the second most effective method, and which of the methods they thought the average Ghanaian would actually be likely to use first.

A majority of the civil servants interviewed believed that the universalistic approach was the most effective one to use when doing ordinary business with a government office, 63.6 percent stating that the client should "go directly to the official's office and state his problem." At the same time, however, nearly a fourth of the sample (22.8 percent) thought that this was the least effective of the three methods, which indicates that a sizable portion of the Ghanaian civil servants believe that establishing even an indirect particularistic relationship with a public official is more efficacious than relying on the impersonal universalistic application of official policy.[7] To the question about what the average Ghanaian would be likely to do when dealing with public officials, only 14.7 percent of the civil servants interviewed believed that the average citizen would in fact go directly to the official's office and state his problem; fully 85.3 percent believed that Ghanaians would first attempt one of the two particularistic approaches. Although we cannot directly test the accuracy of this assessment of the social environment in which the Ghanaian public bureaucracy must operate, it must be acknowledged

[7] The belief that a universalistic approach is *least* effective does not vary with seniority. When the sample is broken down by rank there appears a slight tendency for higher-ranking civil servants to be more likely than lower-ranking ones to judge the universalistic approach as least effective, but this relationship is not statistically significant.

that the respondents are in a unique position to make such an assessment, since they are speaking from personal experience.

From our clientele samples, however, there is data that allow an independent assessment of what non-civil-servant Ghanaians believe is the type of behavior that will get things done at government offices. A modified version of the item presented to the civil servants was presented to the sample of University of Ghana students:

We are interested in the most effective ways of getting things done at government offices in Ghana. Let us say you had some *routine* business with a government bureau or agency. Below are listed five alternative ways of getting your business done. Which of these would be the most effective, i.e., would get the business completed successfully in the shortest time?
1. You see a friend who knows the official with whom you must deal.
2. You go straight to the government office and state your business.
3. You visit the official in charge at his house prior to going to his office, and offer to "do something."
4. You find someone to "fix things" with the responsible official.
5. You go to the office and "dash" the official with whom you must deal.

Note that in this version of the item a time dimension has been explicitly added and made part of the definition of the problem, efficacy here is getting the business accomplished " in the shortest time." This wording favors alternative (2)—the universalistic approach—over alternatives (1), (3), and (4), since the latter involve activities—finding an intermediary, and visiting the official at his home—that require a greater expenditure of time than simply going to the government office. Nevertheless, a majority of the student sample felt that a particularistic approach would be more effective— would get their routine business completed in the shortest time. Only 46 percent of the sample believe going straight to the government office would be most effective. Among Ghanaians with less formal Western-type education, an even smaller proportion believes that going directly to government offices is an effective way to get things done. Of the comparison/clientele sample, 42 percent thought the universalistic approach to doing business with the civil service would be most efficacious, and of the nonliterate or semiliterate subset of that sample, only 28.2 percent felt that such an approach would be more effective than one of the particularistic methods.

The nature of the samples and of the survey instruments does not permit a determination of whether semiliterates show less faith in a universalistic approach than university students show because they have lower social status or because they are more traditionally oriented. On the one hand, it might be that university students feel they can get service at government offices because their educational attainment gives them a type of social status that will carry weight with civil servants, and that semiliterates, lacking such social status, feel they do not count at government offices. On the other hand, semiliterates might be more likely than university students to favor a particularistic approach because, lacking the exposure to modernizing influences of the latter, they maintain traditional role orientations and modes of role behavior. It is feasible, of course, for both factors to operate simultaneously, and indeed I strongly suspect that they do. However, there is some slight evidence that the acculturation factor operates independent of any status concerns. The length of time a student has spent in the university environment influences the likelihood that he will regard the universalistic approach as most efficacious. There is a mild increase in the proportion of students assessing the universalistic alternative as most effective with each successive year spent at the university—41 percent of the first-year students favor going directly to government offices, 45 percent of those in the second year, and 50 percent of the students in their third year. Since third-year university students are unlikely to have appreciably more social status than those in the first year, it is a reasonable interpretation that the extended period of time spent within the Western-influenced environment of the University of Ghana is responsible for these differences.

The foregoing findings concern a situation in which the business being transacted at the government office has been defined as routine. If the situation is altered so that the respondents perceive the business that must be attended to as urgent rather than routine, they are even less likely to put their trust in the impersonal operation of government bureaucracy. When the question focused on urgent business, the proportion of the sample believing in the universalistic approach dropped considerably.[8] Only 32 percent of the students responding to the item thought that, in such a situation, going directly to the government office would be the most effective method of getting things done, almost seven out of every ten preferring one of the particularistic alternatives. A large proportion of the respondents felt that *any* of the particularistic alternatives would be more effective

---

[8] The wording of the item in the urgent condition was as follows: "Now let us suppose that the business you had to transact was urgent and demanded rapid attention. In this case would the most effective alternative be the same as in the previous question or would it be different? If you answered 'different,' could you write down the number of the alternative which you believe is most effective in this case." This form of the question was asked of the university student sample only.

than the universalistic one. Thus, approximately 45 percent of those student respondents who answered felt that going directly to the government office would be the *least* effective means of getting either routine or urgent business accomplished at government offices in Ghana.[9] Tables 20 and 21 summarize these findings, presenting the percentage breakdowns for each of the five alternative approaches to both the routine and urgent situations, and providing a comparison of university and nonuniversity samples.

Table 20

Respondents' Evaluations of Alternative Methods
of Doing Business at Government Offices:
University Student Sample

Method	Routine Business		Urgent Business	
	(1)	(2)	(3)	(4)
	Most Effective	Least Effective	Most Effective	Least Effective
1. See a friend who knows the official with whom you must deal	27.9%	12.1%	27.0%	11.6%
2. You go straight to the government office and state your business	46.1	43.8	32.2	45.8
3. You visit the official in charge at his house prior to going to his office, and offer to do something	13.7	10.9	19.4	8.6
4. You find someone to fix things	10.3	16.9	14.8	19.3
5. You go to the office and dash the official	2.1	16.3	6.6	14.6
☐ Total	100.1	100.0	100.0	99.9
	(N=380)	(N=313)	(N=366)	(N=301)
Not answered	5	72	19	80

[9] A large number of respondents failed to answer the item concerning the least effective alternative, and the percentages reported are for those answering, not the total sample.

Table 21

Alternative Methods of Doing Business at Government
Offices: Comparison of Clientele Samples

	Most Effective Method		
Alternative Methods	University Student Sample	Comparison/ Clientele Sample	Non- and Semi-literate Subset
1. See a friend who knows the official with whom you must deal	27.9%	24.7%	28.2%
2. You go straight to the government office and state your business	46.1	42.0	28.2
3. You visit the official in charge at his house prior to going to his office and offer to do something	13.7	24.7	33.3
4. You find someone to fix things	10.3	6.1	7.7
5. You go to the office and dash the official	2.1	2.5	2.6
☐ Total	100.1	100.0	100.0
	(N=380)	(N=81)	(N=39)

Personal Relationships and the Dash System

The findings presented in tables 20 and 21 are interesting not only for the patterns they reveal in regard to universalistic versus particularistic role orientations but also for the pattern revealed among the four particularistic alternatives. Each of these alternatives concerns a somewhat different type of particularistic relationship, and some discussion of them is in order before an analysis of the findings is presented. Alternatives (3) and (5) explicitly involve the transfer of a material gratuity—in Ghana called dash—between client and civil servant.[10] The practice of dashing public servants is generally recog-

[10] Alternative (4) may or may not involve such a transfer. "To fix things" is an idiom in common use in contemporary Ghana, generally meaning to expedite some

nized as widespread in Ghana and in Commonwealth West Africa.[11] The type of corruption represented by dash should be distinguished from other forms of malfeasance, such as extortion, graft, or payoffs.

Unlike these other forms, which are usually employed to obtain some legally nonlegitimate service, or to have some existing regulation ignored, dash is demanded and offered for the provision of services that are the legal right of the client. It can be found to be present in even the most routine matters. A client seeking a copy of his birth certificate, a passport, an application form for a driver's license, admission to a government secondary school, clearance of goods from customs, and the like will often provide a material gratuity to the relevant official even in those situations in which he has a legitimate right to such services.[12] Observation indicates that the size of the gratuity varies with the wealth of the client and the routine nature of the service.[13] Dash is somewhat like the tip that is so common in the United States, but it differs significantly in that it occurs prior to the transaction and is a prerequisite for it, rather than following it as an appreciation of services rendered. Although there is considerable evidence from the Ghanaian press and from government documents that corrupt practices such as graft, extortion, embezzlement, and the like are widespread in Ghana's public agencies,[14] the dash system is worth special attention. The system of dash is more pervasive than these other practices because it potentially

transaction involving bureaucratic organizations. The particular means by which business is expedited is not specified by the phrase, and can involve some personal intervention as well as the offering of monetary consideration. In contrast, the idiom "to do something" which appears in alternative (3) is quite specific, meaning to offer some material consideration to the bureaucrat in question.

[11] In Nigeria before the coup of 1966, a prominent cabinet minister in the federal government was somewhat affectionately referred to as King of Dash.

[12] The author has personal knowledge of dash being both demanded and offered in each of the types of instances noted.

[13] Thus a very simple routine matter, such as the issuance of a copy of a birth certificate, may involve a small dash of less than a dollar, while something like clearing goods at customs may involve a considerably larger sum. During 1968, when the author was in Ghana, it was a common practice for shipping agents to include in their fee a miscellaneous charge that was explained as necessary for the purpose of dashing the customs officials.

[14] See the numerous reports of Commissions of Enquiry published by the Ghana government between 1966 and 1970. See also annual reports of the Auditor-General issued by the Auditor-General's Department, Accra. A recent edition of these reports was summarized this way by the *Legon Observer*, Ghana's leading intellectual and political periodical: "Serious financial irregularities, frauds, and losses in Ghana involving the majority of city, municipal, and local councils were reported in the accounts of Ghana by the Auditor-General. . . . The irregularities included . . . overexpenditure and improper payments; . . . embezzlement . . . direct misappropriation of cash by treasurers; fraudulent purchases which invariably involved collusion between council and official suppliers." *Legon Observer*, April 23, 1971, p. 26.

affects every citizen in his relations with government bureaucracy, and it has, I believe, a special basis in the socio-cultural system.

The term *dash* is usually translated, both inside and outside West Africa, as the English word *bribe*. I believe that this translation gives an inaccurate image of what is involved, for the word *bribe* does not encompass aspects of what is involved in dash and it does include moral connotations that are not necessarily accurate. It is my belief that dash performs two very important functions simultaneously. First, it is an institutionalized mechanism for establishing a personal tie between client and bureaucrat in a situation in which the two are "strangers." In a socio-cultural system in which personal relations are the dominant basis for stable expectations in social interaction, dash provides social cement for institutions whose scope extends far beyond the realistic reach of any single gemeinschaft community. Second, the giving of dash is a symbolic act that verifies and gives testament to the unequal status of the two interacting individuals. The act of dashing an official makes a statement about the superiority of the civil servant in relation to the client; it is a concrete form of deference.

The contemporary system of dash has strong roots in traditional social practice. In Western thought, both lay and sociological, the transfer of material objects is almost always thought of in instrumental terms: as related to utilitarian calculations about interpersonal behavior, and as distinct from, indeed mutually exclusive of, ties based on interpersonal affect. In fact, Western sociology since the nineteenth century has viewed such material transfers as the distinctive feature of social relations in modern society.[15] However, material transfers are a prominent feature of traditional society generally, and of West African traditional societies particularly. Anthropologist Robert T. LeVine notes that "[personal] relationships are frequently characterized by Africans primarily in terms of the type of material transaction involved: who gives what to whom and under what condition." When they describe relationships of equality and inequality, "Africans emphasize ... obligations to give material goods—food, gifts, financial help, property, and babies."[16] The difference, of course, between the contemporary Western orientation toward material

[15] Thus, Ferdinand Toennies, for example, identifies gesellschaft relationships as the foundation of "bourgeois society" and goes on to define gesellschaft in this manner: "In Gesellschaft every person strives for that which is to his own advantage.... Buyer and seller in their manifold types stand in relation one to the other in such a manner that each one, for as little of his own wealth as possible, desires and attempts to obtain as much of the wealth of others as possible." In T. Parsons et al., eds., *Theories of Society*, vol. 1, pp. 200- 201.

[16] Robert A. LeVine, "Personality and Change," p. 288.

transactions and that of traditional African societies is that the former stresses the calculative, utilitarian, or payoff aspect of such transactions, while the African orientation emphasizes its sharing aspects. The sharing of material resources in a subsistence economy, in which they are naturally very scarce, is a fundamental demonstration and validation of the strength of the ties that bind individuals. As such, in the traditional societies of southern Ghana, as well as elsewhere in Africa, the transfer of material objects and especially food and drink, is an essential part of almost all important social events, and formally marks the occurrence of many important role transactions. Central features of all traditional festivals and religious rituals are the pouring of libations and the offering of food and drink to the gods, ancestors, and other members of the community. As a concrete expression of the ties that bind the individual members, the sharing of food in this manner testifies to the personal links between community members—both living and dead—and symbolizes the unity of the group.[17] The transfer of food and drink is also granted a significant place in the traditional approach to secular events. Hospitiality and trust between visitors and their hosts are expressed in this way; traditional economic transactions such as the selling of land to "strangers,"[18] and the establishment of an apprenticeship relationship

[17] An excellent illustration of this can be found in the following description of an important Akan traditional ceremony, the Adae Butu. "The drums summoned the chief and elder to the stool-house (nkongua-fi), where the stool-custodian (nkongua-hene) opened the door.... The chief presented a bottle of schnapps, part of which was poured as a libation by the stool-custodian for the stool, the gods, and the previous chiefs. Some schnapps was poured on the stool and [a prayer was] recited.... After the rest of the schnapps had been passed around among the elders, the chief asked the stool-custodian for permission to withdraw.... [On the second day] the chief offered a sheep and schnapps, and again the stool-custodian poured libation for the living and the dead. The ankobeahene offered rum, the balance of the drinks being consumed in each case....

"As the libation was being poured, the executioner slaughtered a ram ... the meat being cut up and cooked.... At 11:30 all assembled ... to receive their share of the cooked meat, ... the chief receiving his first, then the leader of the four egyitase on behalf of their people. The meal, eaten communally, signified the unity of all who partook, and anyone who betrayed the chief after sharing the meal was, according to the elders, punished by the ancestors. Throughout the ceremony the unity of the town and Kubease was stressed." David Brokensha, *Social Change at Larteh, Ghana*, pp. 162-163.

[18] In southern Ghana when land is sold the *guaha* ceremony is performed. Polly Hill reports that in this ceremony, after the intended purchaser applies to the one who owns the land, the "customary presentation of rum is generally made to the vendor." See Polly Hill, *Migrant Cocoa-Farmers of Southern Ghana*, p. 141. David Brokensha, in a discussion of land sales among the southern Akan, also mentions the significance of customary drink in the transaction: "As in other ceremonies the acceptance of rum before witnesses seals the contract." Brokensha goes on to note that "rum is used in the generic sense, and may refer to any type of spiritous liquor, though specific types—and even brands—may be preferred for particular ceremonies." See Brokensha, *Social Change at Larteh*, pp. 36-37.

are sealed in this manner.[19] To quote Professor LeVine once again:

> In contrast with the Western attitude (genuine or hypocritical) that the emotional component in interpersonal relations is more important than any transfer of material goods involved ... Africans are frankly and directly concerned with the material transfer itself *as indicative of the quality of the relationship.* This is best illustrated with respect to food and feeding. Volumes could be written on the social and cultural meanings of food and feeding in African societies. Family relationships are often described in terms of feeding or providing food. Visitors are accepted, honored, or rejected in terms of the food and drink provided for them, and they in turn show their friendliness and trust by accepting food and drink.[20]

The emphasis placed on the exchange of food in traditional social relations is a particularly significant key to the meaning of the contemporary institution of dash. A commonly used synonym for dash is the term *drink*. A person will often say, "I bought him drink," when referring to having paid dash. Here of course the word *drink* is being used in a symbolic sense; it does not necessarily refer to consumable liquid. Thus language commonly in use in contemporary Ghana shows that dash is perceived as being related to the traditional practice of underscoring important role transactions and social interactions through the transfer of liquor from one actor to another. Indeed, there is further linguistic evidence for this point of view. In present-day Ghana, as elsewhere in English-speaking West Africa, a government official who takes money as a prerequisite for carrying out his official duties is often said to be engaged in "chopping money." "To chop" is a pidgen English idiom meaning, among other things, "to eat." Thus, in this way too, the connection between the system of dash and the traditional practice of food exchange is established. Just as a chief under certain circumstances must offer food and drink to the ancestors, members of his retinue, and his elders, or a junior member of an extended family must offer it to a more senior one, so within government bureaucracy a client must offer "drink" to a civil servant. By such an act a personal link is established between the two role incumbents, a traditional seal is placed on the role transaction, and the client demonstrates his acknowledgment of the superior status of the bureaucrat in the given context. In short, a

[19] Brokensha reports that when a father arranges for his son to become an apprentice to a goldsmith "the agreement is sealed by the presentation to the master of money and schnapps." And when the apprentice has completed his course his father "presents the master with sheep ... and drinks.... The presentation is made before all the assembled craftsmen, who share the drinks, advise the apprentice on expected standards of behavior, and welcome him formally to their ranks." See ibid., p. 259.

[20] LeVine, "Personality and Change," p. 288. Emphasis added.

traditional basis for stable role expectations is substituted for the impersonal and universalistic norms on which expectations in bureaucratic roles are supposed to be formally based. This phenomenon was clearly revealed in the statements of one of the respondents, an elderly Ga market woman. She was emphatic in her preference for a civil servant who expected and accepted dash, because, she said, "He gives me peace of mind—I know he will finish my business." On the other hand, the civil servant who refuses dash is "a very wicked man—he worries me, I don't know what he will do."

The institution of dash—the transfer of "drink" in a nontraditional context—is not something new to the Ghana scene. On the contrary, it can be traced back to the period of earliest commercial contacts between Europeans and Africans on the Guinea Coast. When the European sea captains, merchants, and factors made their way to the coast of what is now Ghana, they could engage in commerce only after they had first given customary gifts to the African traders and the chiefs of the towns and villages at which they moored their boats and endeavored to do business. As early as 1602 the Dutch navigator and trader Pieter de Marees published a work that described life and commerce along the Gold Coast and clearly revealed the existence of the institution of dash, or "dache" as he called it.[21] Descriptions of the institution can be found in later accounts also. For example, an American, J. A. Carnes, who traveled to West Africa on a merchant ship in the mid-1800s, gave this description of a typical commercial transaction:

The usual palaver had hardly commenced between our krumen and the latter [African "head man"] . . . before it was obvious enough that it would be no easy matter to deceive either the king or his men. . . . The first article offered was a quantity of ostrich feathers, that were really beautiful. For these an offer was made, by our captain, of such . . . things as he thought would insure a purchase. . . . His majesty, glancing his eyes upon these, shook his head in the negative, and informed our tradesmen that "dash" was wanting. *So we were compelled, as it were, in order to succeed in our trade, to present his highness with "a bottle of rum," and his men with a "dash" or glass each.*[22]

If, as I have argued, dash is an adaptation of a traditional mode of social behavior, then one would expect exposure to modernizing influences to affect the likelihood that an individual will engage in such behavior. From the findings recorded in table 21, it is apparent

[21] See Freda Wolfson, *Pageant of Ghana*, (London, 1958), p. 4.
[22] J. A. Carnes, *Journal of a Voyage from Boston to the West Coast of Africa*, excerpts reprinted in Wolfson, pp. 129-130. Emphasis added.

that this is indeed the case. Alternative (3)—"you visit the official in charge at his house ... and offer to 'do something' "—shows that approximately one-seventh of the university students believe that offering dash in the stated manner is the most effective method, and that the proportion increases to nearly a fourth of the nonuniversity sample and a third of the semiliterate and nonliterate respondents. In other words, those who have had less exposure to forces of "modern" acculturation are more likely to believe that the use of dash is the most effective method of getting things done at Ghana government offices.[23] Indeed, for the least acculturated group, the semiliterate and nonliterate subset, alternative (3) is the most popular of the five methods offered.

The effectiveness attributed to the method of going to the official's home and dashing him is not shared by method (5)—"You go to the office and dash the official." A smaller proportion of respondents in each of the categories in table 21 believe this method to be the most effective than is true for any of the other four alternatives. Only 2 percent of the university students and only slightly more than 2 percent of both the comparison/clientele sample and the semiliterate and nonliterate subset believe that simply going to the government office and dashing the official will be the most effective way to get things done. The fact that so few respondents view alternative (5) as effective compared with the alternative of going to the official's house and dashing him, provides support for the argument that the function of dash is the creation of a personal tie between client and official rather than the creation of a "contract" based on utilitarian considerations. When entreaties for help are made at the *home* of the official, the dash performs the customary functions of demonstrating respect or deference, verifying a personal tie (established through the visit), and sealing an agreement. When, however, dash is presented at the official's office, it has the appearance of a "contract"; it is impersonal, and it thus falls outside the framework of customary behavior. And, to judge by the responses to the questionnaire, it is generally perceived as having less potency. The belief in the need to visit the public servant at his home is a dramatic

[23] A breakdown of the student sample on the basis of various social background factors turns up few differences in the methods the respondents believe to be most effective. However, the time a student has spent at the university does appear to have an effect. A student who has been at the university for over two years is less than half as likely as one who has been there only a year to believe that visiting the official at his home will be the most effective way to get things done. Twenty percent of the first-year students, and only 9 percent of the third-year students, believe visiting the official to be the best method.

illustration of the existence of a traditional socio-cultural role orientation.[24] Such a practice obviously runs counter to what Max Weber considered a social prerequisite for effective bureaucratic organization—the separation of office and home.[25] In Ghana it may in fact be an extension into a new social realm of the traditional practice whereby the business of the community and of the family is conducted at the compounds of the chief and the family head. If this were so, it would fit nicely with the theory that dash is an extension of a customary practice.

A number of other interesting things are revealed in tables 20 and 21. Note that alternative (1), which involves finding an intermediary with a personal tie to both client and civil servant, but which does not involve dash, is more favorably viewed by the more highly educated respondents. In table 21 we can see that the university students are twice as likely to believe in seeing a friend who knows the official than they are to think that visiting the official at his home will be effective; in contrast, the respondents in the nonuniversity comparison/clientele sample are just as likely to believe in visiting the official as in seeing a friend, and those respondents who are nonliterate or semiliterate are more likely to evalute visiting the official as the most effective method. This is not surprising, since the latter group of respondents are less likely than the university students to have friends in the civil service. The university student respondents can thus more realistically expect to find an intermediary with some personal tie to them, while the nonliterates and semiliterates must establish their own personal relationship with the civil servant in question, visiting him at his home and offering to "do something."

The respondents also believed that switching from a situation in which the business to be transacted is routine to one in which it is urgent increases the value of visiting the official and offering him

[24] Although I know of no other "hard" data that permit an estimate of how widespread the practice of visiting officials at their homes is, the literature does contain some impressionistic evidence of the practice. For example, a Ghanaian civil servant involved in a major population resettlement project reported the following about his experience: "The people believed it was a good thing to see the 'big man' in his own house, and they were never turned away whenever they called to see him, but quietly encouraged to call later at the office. On certain occasions upon waking up early in the moring, the Welfare Officer would find five or six people waiting to talk to him" (G. W. Amarteifio, *Tema Manhean*, p. 19).

[25] "In principle, the modern organization of the civil service separates the bureau from the private domicile of the official, and, in general, bureaucracy segregates official activity as something distinct from the sphere of private life." In C. W. Mills and Hans Gerth, *From Max Weber*, p. 197.

dash.[26] Compare columns 1 and 3 in table 20. It is apparent not only that moving from a routine to an urgent condition increases the general belief in the efficacy of a particularistic approach to the civil service, but that alternative (3)—visiting the official at his home and dashing him—receives the greatest increase among the four particularistic alternatives. Table 20 also reveals that of all the alternatives listed, alternative (3) has the smallest proportion of respondents who believe it is the *least* effective method; this holds true in both the routine and urgent situations. This indicates that many respondents who may consider some other method the *most* efficacious believe at the same time that going to the official's home and dashing him is a viable method of doing business with government bureaucracy.

The findings presented thus far tend to underestimate the degree to which the institution of dash is a part of the role orientation of bureaucratic clients in Ghana. This is so because the survey items whose findings we have been discussing provided the respondent with the alternative of approaching the bureaucracy through a personal friend, thus making other forms of establishing a personal connection, such as through the proper utilization of dash, unnecessary. But in most situations citizens are unlikely to have a personal friend who happens to know the official with whom they must deal, and therefore such an alternative is not open to them. Therefore respondents were presented with an item that attempted to tap the extent to which Ghanaians thought that dash influenced the behavior of civil servants with whom they might have to deal. The following situation was described to the clientele samples:

Now, suppose you were attempting to carry out some routine business at a government office. You have visited the office *three* separate times, but each time the civil servant in charge says your forms are not ready and that you should "go and come." What would you conclude is the trouble?[27]

The respondents were asked to choose an explanation for the difficulty from a list of five possible reasons, or, if none appeared satisfactory, to specify something else. Table 22 presents the list of explanations and the percentage breakdown on the item for the university student sample. Apparently a substantial majority of the

---

[26] This finding is for the university student sample. Only the routine condition was presented to the comparison/clientele sample.

[27] "Go and come" is an idiom widely used in Ghana by "service" personnel to inform clients that they will not be served at the present time.

Table 22

Respondents' Perceptions of Reasons for Delays
at Government Offices: University Student Sample

Alternative Reasons for Delay	Percentage of Respondents Offering Given Reason
1. The staff is overworked	3.8%
2. The staff is lazy	12.4
3. The official is looking for a dash	63.7
4. The staff is incompetent	11.3
5. The official is trying to show his importance	8.0
6. Other	.8
☐ Total	100 (N=372)
Not answered	13

student respondents think that slowness and delays in the Ghana Civil Service are the result of the fact that civil servants demand dash before performing services. Sixty-four percent of the sample felt that the civil servant in the imaginary situation was looking for a dash—that they had been told to "go and come" as an indication that dash was necessary if the desired service was to be obtained.[28] The comparison/clientele sample responded to the item in a similar nature: 64 percent of the total sample believed that the civil servant was looking for dash, and 69 percent of the semiliterate and nonliterate respondents felt so.

If the expectation that dash is required for service from government bureaucracy is, at least in part, a function of an orientation toward traditional modes of social behavior and not simply a reflection of empirical reality, one would expect estimates of the importance of

[28] A number of informants had told the author that the expression "go and come" was often used as a signal that dash was necessary to get work done in an expeditious fashion. For that reason, and because the idiom appeared to be so commonly utilized, the item presently being discussed was constructed and included in the survey instruments. It is interesting to note that the expression "go and come" provides no reason for delay, nor does it specify a time for the client to return, indicating that its use is not directly related to the effective dispensing of organizational services, and thus lending credence to its interpretation as a signal for dash.

dash to be related to exposure to "modernizing influences." And, indeed, this turns out to be the case. As such exposure increases, the reliance on dash as an explanation for delays is reduced. For example, table 23 presents a breakdown of the student respondents'

Table 23

*Parental Literacy Level and Explanation
for Delays at Government Offices*

	Parental Literacy Level		
Alternative Explanations	Low[a]	Medium[b]	High[c]
1. Staff overworked	3.1%	5.4%	2.2%
2. Staff lazy	10.2	10.7	18.0
3. Official expects dash	71.1	65.8	49.4
4. Staff incompetent	8.6	9.4	19.1
5. Official showing importance	6.3	7.4	11.2
6. Other	.8	1.3	0
☐ Total	100.1 (N=128)	100.0 (N=149)	99.9 (N=89)

[a] Both parents nonliterate.
[b] At least one parent semiliterate.
[c] Both parents literate.

answers according to the level of their parents' literacy. Explanation (3)—that the official expects or is looking for dash—is clearly more prevalent among students with nonliterate parents than among those students whose parents both are literate in English. The table also reveals that respondents whose parental background includes high levels of literacy are twice as likely as those with a background of low literacy levels to blame delays on staff incompetence or "status demonstration" by the civil servant. We should not lose sight of the fact, however, that even among those respondents whose parents are both fully literate nearly 50 percent believe that delays are produced by the failure to offer dash. Findings of a similar magnitude and in a similar direction are obtained when we test for the influence of other social background variables—maternal and paternal education, urban or rural place of family residence, and paternal occupation. In addition, the personal experience of the respondent appears to be related to the centrality of the institution of dash to his client role orientation. The more cosmopolitan an individual, as indicated by his travel experience, the less likely he or she is to view the delays described in the imaginary situation as the results of a civil servant's looking for dash. Sixty-nine percent of the respondents who have never traveled outside of Ghana believe that failure to dash is responsible for delays, compared with 60 percent of those who have traveled only to other African countries, and 46 percent of those who have spent time in the highly industrialized societies of Western Europe, North America, and the Soviet Union. This relationship is presented in table 24.

Table 24

*Respondent's Travel Experience and His Explanation
for Delays at Government Offices*

	Travel Experience		
Alternative Explanations	None	Africa outside Ghana	Europe N. America U.S.S.R.
1. Staff overworked	2.1%	8.0%	2.7%
2. Staff lazy	10.9	11.0	24.2
3. Official expects dash	68.7	60.0	45.9
4. Staff incompetent	10.4	12.0	13.5
5. Official showing importance	7.0	9.0	13.5
6. Other	0.9	0	0
☐ Total	100 (N=230)	100 (N=100)	99.8 (N=37)

The length of time the respondents have been part of the university community also appears to be related to the likelihood that they will perceive the working of government bureaucracy to be related to the use of dash. Nearly three-fourths of the first-year students and about half of the third-year students think that delays at government offices are caused by officials "looking for dash," which indicates once again that exposure to modernizing influences tends to reduce the prevalence of the institution of dash in the client role orientation. Table 25 summarizes these data on the relationship between year at university and the respondent's explanation for delays at government offices.

Table 25

Respondent's Year at University and His Explanation for Delays at Government Offices in Ghana

Alternative Explanations	Year at University of Ghana		
	First	Second	Third
1. Staff overworked	5.6%	2.0%	3.2%
2. Staff lazy	7.9	15.8	11.6
3. Official expects dash	73.0	63.4	55.8
4. Staff incompetent	6.3	11.9	15.8
5. Official showing importance	5.6	6.9	12.6
6. Other	1.6	0	1.0
☐ Total	100 (N=126)	100 (N=101)	100 (N=95)

In summary, we can draw three basic conclusions from the findings already discussed. (1) Particularism is a prevalent aspect of the general orientation toward client roles in Ghana. Civil servants believe that Ghanaians will seek to establish a personal tie to officials with whom they must deal if no such direct relationship exists, and such an assessment appears to be confirmed by the data from the clientele surveys. (2) The use of dash is a prevalent part of client role orientations. It is in fact a social institution with deep roots in customary social practice and with a long history in its nontraditional form. (3) The likelihood of generalized particularism in client role orientations, and the prevalence of dash within such orientations, are inversely related to the extent to which an individual has been exposed to forces of social change usually associated with "moderni-zation." Thus students at the University of Ghana are almost twice as likely as semiliterate and nonliterate Ghanaians to believe in the effectiveness of a universalistic approach in the client role. The latter group is almost three times more likely than the university students are to believe that utilizing dash is the most effective method of getting things done at government offices in Ghana. Similarly, the students are less likely than those who have not been exposed to the acculturative aspects of the University of Ghana to believe that delays at government offices are a signal that dash is required if services are to be forthcoming, and the longer a student is in the university environment the less likely he or she is to have such a view. Once this relationship is recognized, the effect of modernizing influences should not be exaggerated. Even among the most highly exposed respondents, generalized particularism in client role orienta-tions, and the reliance on the institution of dash, can be found in a majority of cases: 54 percent of the University of Ghana students believe that a particularistic approach to civil servants is the most effective and efficient way to get business accomplished, and 64 percent believe that delays at government offices are a function of expectations of dash on the part of civil servants. A possible explana-tion for the limited effect of so-called forces of modernization has been discussed at length in chapter 4.[29]

The Client Role and Service Orientation: An Overview

The titles "civil service" and "civil servant" imply that the orienta-tion that ideally underlies the purposes of public bureaucracy is public service. And by extension, truly effective role performance by public bureaucrats, especially those who deal directly with clients, is depen-dent on officials approaching their roles with a service orientation. That is, such bureaucrats should have a sense of obligation to dispense government services to all citizens who qualify under the rules governing their offices. The Ghana Civil Service itself takes official cognizance of the importance of a service orientation for effective public administration. In the service's *Handbook for New Entrants*, the following passage appears:

The civil servant is first and foremost the servant of the people. Your service to members of the public is, therefore, one of the most fundamental things you have to remember. You must therefore be absolutely fair to all persons,

[29] See pp. 83-95.

polite and courteous and possessed of tact in your dealings with them. Also, you must ... as far as the rules and practices of your department permit, show sympathy and offer as much help as possible to those who come in official contact with you.[30]

Like so much else in bureaucracy, a prerequisite for a service orientation is the notion of the separation of office and person. If bureaucratic positions are conceived of as personal possessions, then they are likely to be used as a resource to be exploited for personal benefits, rather than as a means to further the service ends of public policy. But whether or not a particular socio-cultural environment allows for the compartmentalization of personal and official roles, there are aspects inherent in the bureaucrat-client relationship that make the creation and maintenance of a service orientation on the part of public servants a universal problem for civil service bureaucracy. The very real power over citizens that bureaucratic positions provide—in terms of information and services that could be withheld—creates a situation conducive to the use of such positions for the personal enhancement of the bureaucrat, if not in material then in ego terms, to the detriment of fair and impartial dispensation of government services.[31] If such temptations are to be counteracted, there must exist positive incentives for bureaucrats to adopt a service role orientation. Incentives of this kind can be provided in a number of ways and can exist in a number of contexts. They may be internal to the organization—for example, in a reward structure that is tied to some objective and rational measure of performance, in an internal organizational or professional ideology that stresses the value of service to the public, or in the existence of informal social pressure from superiors and peers within the organization that is supportive of a service role orientation. Incentives can also lie outside the organizational structure per se. Here an important aspect of the relationship between bureaucrat and client is manifested. The service orientation of public agencies can be enhanced if clients themselves come to the organization with a service expectation—that is, with a belief that as citizens they have a right to government services and that it is the duty of the civil servant to serve them. Clients of this type are likely to demand attention from civil servants who manifest a lack of commitment to service norms and thus provide an exterior counterweight to the potential failure of internal incentive

[30] Ghana, The Civil Service, *A Handbook for New Entrants*, p. 6.

[31] Thus in a study of a social welfare agency in Chicago, Peter Blau and Richard Scott report widespread dissatisfaction on the part of clients about the manner of treatment they receive from agency personnel: 74 percent said they were treated as inferiors by the bureaucrats. See Blau and Scott, *Formal Organizations*, p. 77.

mechanisms. However, when clients generally lack this expectation of service, any antiservice orientations that may exist in public bureaucracy will be reinforced.

I would hypothesize that one aspect of the social environment of public bureaucracy in transitional societies such as Ghana is a general lack of clients with service expectations. I am not suggesting that in highly modern societies service expectations are a universal characteristic of clients, or that they are randomly distributed throughout the population. On the contrary, the poor in such societies, because of a limited knowledge of bureaucratic organization and because of the "class" difference that exists between themselves and public servants, are much less likely than middle-class and upper-class persons to have such expectations. But in transitional societies the lack of service orientations on the part of clients are likely to be more generalized throughout society and are produced by at least two basic factors in addition to the extensiveness of a low-income condition within those societies.

The first factor is a part of the general problem of national and political integration that faces such societies. Since the states of Africa are new, in the sense that as entities they are products of a colonial era that has only recently ended, and since they are not yet truly nations, in the sense of being made up of a single people, it is not likely that the socialization mechanisms in these societies will prepare individuals to be "citizens" of the new political units. The institutions of primary socialization in the states of Africa are part of, and are therefore oriented toward, different political communities and regimes, ones that existed prior to the establishment of the postcolonial state. Consequently, those perceptions, orientations, rights, and duties that constitute the "citizen role-set" have probably not been transmitted to most people in the new state. This has a bearing on the role orientations of the clients with whom government bureaucracy deals. In the postcolonial state, public bureaucracy is part of the new "apparatus" of what David Easton refers to as the "political regime," but the client role that should exist along with the formal organization, like the more general citizen role-set of which it is a part, is not likely to be included in the role learning that individuals undergo during their socialization. The rights and expectations that are a prerequisite for a service orientation in the client role are not likely therefore to be part of the role orientation of most people when they come to deal with government bureaucracy.[32]

---

[32] Public bureaucracy in its colonial form has existed in most of Africa and in Ghana since the beginning of the twentieth century. But it could hardly be contended that the colonial bureaucracy constituted a public service organization vis-à-vis the African

The second factor that is basic to an understanding of the limited number of clients with service expectations involves the dependence of such expectations on a prior perception that roles exist in a socially compartmentalized fashion. When, as in transitional societies, members of a social system do not readily engage in role differentiation, then citizens will tend to view civil servants as *personally possessing* the power and services attached to their offices. With such an orientation clients come to the civil service, not with expectation that services are due them as a right of citizenship, but rather with the belief that these are the property of the civil servant to dispense according to his whim and fancy. Jose V. Abueva, describing bureaucrat-client relations in the Philippines, provides an excellent illustration of this phenomenon:

It appears that many officials tend to feel they are providing services or benefits not so much out of a sense of duty but as personal favors that accrue to their official status. In turn many citizens who approach officials for assistance do so feeling more that they are asking personal favors than seeking what is theirs by right. The ... well known concepts expressed in the democratic saying, "Public office is a public trust," and in the terms "sovereign people" and "civil servant," *collide with customary expectations in interpersonal relations.*[33]

When government services are viewed as privileges at the personal disposal of public officials, then it becomes incumbent on the client to behave so as to deserve such favored treatment. In the discussions of familial particularism and of the institution of dash, note was taken of two methods of activating public bureaucrats when a service ethic or orientation does not exist. That is, personal connections established throught kin relations or some other mechanism such as dash can be used by the citizen to obtain what are supposedly public services. Another mechanism that can, or indeed must, be utilized, either independently or simultaneously with the other two, is status deference. With a public display of deferential behavior toward the civil servant, a client makes a "status payoff," demon-

---

population. Until the last years of the colonial era the colonial administration in most colonies performed "law and order" functions as an instrument of colonial domination, with only a minor social service aspect. Furthermore, any services that were provided through the colonial apparatus were dispensed as a paternalistic favor from the colonial "master," not as a response to any citizen rights possessed by Africans. Thus it can be said that from the African vantage point no *public* bureaucracy existed until the era of self-government and independence. In Ghana this means until the 1950s.

[33] Jose V. Abueva, "Administrative Doctrines Diffused in Emerging States: The Filipino Response," p. 585. Emphasis added.

strating the superior status of the official, and at the same time acknowledging the civil servant's personal right and power to decide who will receive the values under his official jurisdiction. A display of deference is essentially a public declaration that the right to service resides in the personal discretionary power of the public official rather than in the quality of citizenship.[34]

Service Orientations and the Client Role in Ghana

Turning to the situation in Ghana, it is this writer's impressionistic observation that deference is a prevalent aspect of bureaucrat-client relationships. The frequency with which deference is displayed, and the degree of obsequiousness that it involves, appear to vary with the social status of the client. Thus individuals with high social status—persons who are mature in years, persons of wealth, education, and professional occupation—do not appear to be expected, nor themselves to expect, to show deference to civil servants. Indeed, if their social or political status is high enough—if they are considered "big men"—it is the civil servant who may display deference toward them. On the other hand, individuals of low status can commonly be observed engaging in lavish displays of deferential behavior. It is not uncommon, for example, for such a client to approach the desk of a civil servant, bent at the waist and clasping his hands in the traditional posture of deference, while muttering the phrase, "I beg you, master."[35]

These impressionistic observations on the importance of status and on the operation of deference at government offices in Ghana led to the inclusion within the Clientele Survey of two items whose purpose was to tap this dimension of the bureaucrat-client relationship more systematically. The first item sought to discover the respondents' perceptions about the general nature of the relationship

[34] This type of bureaucrat-client relationship is characteristic of traditional patrimonial administration. As Max Weber has noted, in patrimonialism there exists "the regulation of all relationships through individual privileges and bestowals of favor, ... at least in so far as such relationships are not fixed by sacred tradition." Quoted in C. W. Mills and H. Gerth, *From Max Weber*, p. 198.

[35] Brokensha notes that such "begging" is a widespread traditional practice among the Akan of Ghana. He notes that "once a person begs it is difficult to refuse his request. ... For by begging one usually obliges the person asked to accede to the request by placing the full moral responsibility on him" (*Social Change at Larteh*, p. 133). The use of this institution in the context of bureaucrat-client relations is an indication that the client perceives the valued objects he seeks from government to be under the personal discretionary control of the bureaucrat, rather than as rights that are his and that the civil servant is obligated to provide.

between bureaucrats and clients—who is the servant of whom? "Now suppose," the respondents were asked, "that you were teaching a child how to deal with the government civil service. Which of these three ways would you tell him to use when approaching civil servants for help?"

1. As a government employee he is your servant, and it is his job to give you prompt help. You should simply state what you want from him.
2. He is in a position of authority and therefore you must show proper respect if you expect help from him.
3. Although civil servants are employed to serve people like you, it is best to show respect if one wants some help from them.

I interpret method (1), in the above, as a straight service orientation—service is seen as a right inherent in citizenship. Method (2) is the opposite—the civil servant, being in a position of authority, is seen as having privileges which he can bestow to those he deems deserving. The orientation of a client in this case can be referred to as "dispensatory." In the third instance the client's orientation is neither truly one of service nor one of dispensation. He recognizes his formal right to service, but doubts it will be recognized by the civil servant, and since the bureaucrat has power over objects he values, he adopts a posture of instrumental deference. It should be noted that, in terms of acting as a pressure or check on bureaucrats to help maintain a service orientation, both method (2) and method (3) have no utility. In both cases, if a civil servant lacks a commitment to service norms, the client's behavior will be reinforcing; indeed, his action will serve to acknowledge the legitimacy of this lack of commitment. Only if method (1) is a fairly common client role orientation will civil servants who lack a service commitment be placed in the type of awkward position that might pressure them to adopt a service posture.

Table 26 shows the percentage breakdown for the three types of client role orientation in the university student sample, the comparison/clientele sample, and the semiliterate and nonliterate subset. The findings revealed in the table offer only partial support for the position I have been arguing. It is true that only a small minority of all three groupings of respondents manifest a service orientation, but the largest proportion of respondents fall into category three, in which deference is used instrumentally in response to a belief about the civil servant's power. It was expected that the largest cells in the matrix would be those corresponding to a complete absence of service

Table 26

Respondents' Beliefs about Proper Orientation
in the Client Role

	University Sample	Comparison/ Clientele Sample	Semi- and Nonliterate Subset
1. Service orientation	14.7%	23.8%	20.5%
2. Dispensatory orientation	11.9	20.0	30.7
3. Instrumental orientation	74.2	56.3	48.7
☐ Total	100.8	100.1	99.9
	(N=385)	(N=81)	(N=39)

orientation, that is, the "dispensatory" orientation. Only a minority of even those most closely tied to traditional social relations—the semiliterates and nonliterates—believe that deference should be displayed because it is the legitimate right of those in authority. At the same time it should be noted that respondents in this group are three times more likely to express such an opinion than are the more acculturated university students. This finding is clearly in line with the position I have been arguing. However, highly incongruous from this perspective is the finding that the proportion of persons having a service orientation is smaller among the university sample than among the sample of respondents less highly exposed to institutions of Western education.[36] This may be explained in part by the fact that the wording of method (1) presented to the comparison/clientele sample differed somewhat from that presented to the university student sample.[37]

The second item used to test the proposition about the general lack of service expectations among bureaucratic clients in Ghana

[36] The social background of the student respondents—maternal and paternal education, place of family residence, paternal occupation, and parental literacy—made no difference in the responses to this item.

[37] In the survey administered to university students, method (1) was described in this manner: "As a government employee he is your servant, and it is his job to give you prompt help. You should simply state what you want from him." In the survey administered to the comparison group, method (1) was described in this manner: "As a government employee the civil servant is there to serve people like you, and it is his job to give prompt help. Therefore, when going to see a civil servant you should simply state what you want from him."

provided stronger support for my position than did the first. An item was designed that would allow one to infer the type of client orientation characteristic of the respondent from his statements about how he would act in a particular situation. The following situation was described:

Suppose you go to a government office to take care of some routine business. The business should take only a few minutes to transact, but you find yourself waiting three hours. Then the government official calls you over and simply says "go and come." What would be your likely reaction to this situation?

Which of the following statements comes closest to your probable reaction?

1. I would realize that "this is the way things are," that it is to be expected, and I would come back the next day.
2. I would become angry and demand an explanation from the civil servant.
3. Becoming angry, I would demand that the civil servant serve me, and if he did not I would go and see his superior, or supervisor.
4. I would offer to "do something" if he would finish the business straight away.

It was reasoned that statements (2) and (3) are based on the existence of a service orientation on the part of the client. Anger at having to wait and not being served in a simple and routine matter is a relevant emotion only when the actor makes certain assumptions about his right to service in the given situation. When however, the client's orientation is dispensatory—when he believes that the civil servant's relationship to himself is one of an authority with the power to bestow privileges to those he deems deserving—then he is likely to explain delays and refusals as "the way things are." Such a client is also likely, I reasoned, to offer to "do something," that is, give dash, because he views the bureaucratic position as the personal property of the civil servant. Table 27 presents the proportions of the samples opting for each of the statements as reflecting the respondents' probable behavior under the circumstances described. It can be seen that 65 percent of the university student sample attribute reactions to themselves that indicate a service orientation, but that the opposite is true when we are dealing with the comparison/clientele sample, a group of respondents who are much more typical of the Ghanaian population in terms of their exposure to modernizing influences. In the latter case, 68 percent of the respondents opt for the two statements that reveal the lack of a service expectation. Among the subset of this sample with the least exposure

Table 27

*Respondents' Estimates of Their Probable Reaction
to Bureaucratic Delays*

Reactions to Delays and Refusals	University Sample	Comparison/ Clientele Sample	Semi- and Nonliterate Subset
1. Belief that "this is the way things are"	29.1%	55.1%	64.1%
2. Become angry, demand explanation	44.1	22.9	5.1
3. Become angry, see supervisor	20.8	8.9	7.7
4. Offer to "do something"	6.1	12.7	23.1
□ Total	100.1	99.6	100.0
	(N=385)	(N=81)	(N=39)

to these modernizing influences this proportion is increased to a full 87.2 percent. Notice that the semiliterate and nonliterate respondents are more than twice as likely to express fatalism—"this is the way things are"—than the university students, and almost four times more likely to offer a dash. Finally, note that even among the highly acculturated university students more than a third of the respondents opt for one of the two statements that reveal a dispensatory orientation in the client role. In summary, when confronted with an imaginary situation that described extensive bureaucratic delays, the respondents predicted behavior about themselves which revealed client role orientations that in a large proportion of cases lacked a service expectation. An expectation of service, and consequently a feeling and expression of anger when this expectation is violated, appears to be widespread only among those persons with extensive Western-oriented formal education.[38] This seems to indicate that in

[38] Columns 2 and 3 differ not only in that the proportion of semiliterates and nonliterates in the former is smaller than in the latter, but also in the proportion that have little or no formal education. In the total comparison/clientele sample 27 percent of the respondents have gone only as far as primary school; in the semiliterate subset these respondents constitute 47 percent of the total.

Ghana a service orientation in the client role is a product of exposure to certain types of modernizing influences.[39]

Such an indication cannot, however, be transformed into a conclusion, because there is an alternative plausible explanation for the responses shown in table 27. It is likely that in any bureaucratic context a display of anger toward a bureaucrat or a complaint to a supervisor may be irrational from an instrumental point of view, unless the individual so behaving has the resources to protect himself from negative reactions on the part of the bureaucrat. And it is plausible that high social status brings with it such resources, or at least the perception of their existence on the part of the offending bureaucrat. Persons of low social status, therefore, may avoid displays of anger, or fail to complain to supervisors, because of an accurate perception that such action would not bring them any benefits and might well do them harm. Since the respondents in the comparison/clientele sample are predominately low-status individuals, their tendency to opt for statement (1) in table 27 could represent response to a "fear of reprisal" at the hands of civil servants who are more powerful than they, rather than lack of service orientation. The university students in the main clientele sample may view themselves as part of a social elite, and therefore as secure enough to make their demands and displeasure known to civil servants. Unfortunately, the survey instrument did not include an item sensitive enough to separate an acquiescent posture based on fear from an acquiescent posture based on a dispensatory orientation.

Whatever the explanation of the distribution of the responses in table 27 may be, whether it is seen as a product of modifications in personal role orientations in the process of social change or as a product of differential concern for reprisals among individuals of different social status (and the two may well be operating simultaneously), the responses do indicate that service oriented *behavior*, as distinct from personal role orientations, is likely to occur to only a limited extent in Ghana. In the sample that most closely approximates the characteristics of the majority of Ghanaians, the comparison/clientele sample, a large majority reported that in the situation

---

[39] Note that the responses of the university students are not affected by social background characteristics such as father's education and occupation, parental literacy, and the like. The potency of the respondent's own formal education experience in producing service expectations is, however, explicable in terms of my argument. Since the traditional mechanisms of socialization do not include learning the role of bureaucratic client, and do not support the phenomenon of role compartmentalization, Western-influenced formal education is one of the few institutional contexts in which role definitions that include a service expectation in the client role are at least formally presented to the individual.

of bureaucratic delays described to them they would behave in an acquiescent rather than in a service-oriented manner.[40] Since it is the manifestation of service orientations in client behavior that can act as a check on civil servants, the absence of such manifestations is of importance for the operation of public bureaucracy.

Conclusion

It has been the supposition here that the general lack of service-oriented behavior on the part of clients will have negative consequences for the performance of the Ghana Civil Service. Although the empirical data do not allow a test of this proposition, it would seem tentatively supportable on the basis of logical plausibility. The organizational performance of major elements of civil service bureaucracy, particularly those that deal directly with the public, will be greatly enhanced if civil servants maintain a commitment to service. But, at the very least, the asymmetric nature of power and authority in the bureaucrat-client relationship will tend to favor an orientation of domination on the part of civil servants rather than one of service. When clients acquiesce in this posture of domination, they will legitimize and thus reinforce this tendency. On the other hand, when clients come to the public bureaucracy expecting service, and when they feel it is safe to manifest this expectation, they will encourage the civil servant, who is their alter in this interpersonal behavior event, to adopt a service posture. For the civil servant to do otherwise will violate the client's role expectations, and will produce interpersonal friction, risk official complaints, and in other ways create a situation that, from the civil servant's point of view, is better to be avoided.

[40] In a personal communication to the author, Jon Kraus suggests that the responses of the comparison/clientele sample are less relevant in this context than those of the university students, since the social position of the former indicates that they and people like them are likely to have little contact with government bureaucracy. Although I know of no data on "use rates" that could settle the issue, my own sense of the situation is quite different. My impression is that the average Ghanaian, especially in the urban areas, has considerable contact with public bureaucracy—health clinics, post office, police, license bureau, labor department, schools, and the like. And because of the widespread existence of petty trade, and of travel between Ghana and her neighbors, even agencies such as the Passport Office, the Bank of Ghana, and the Ministry of Trade have substantial contact with individuals of relatively low socio-economic status. Although individuals with status similar to university students might have far more contact with the higher echelons of the public bureaucracy, the same would not seem to hold for the "service" agencies whose functioning entails dealing with the public.

VI

The Social Basis of
Administrative Corruption

No single issue in Ghanaian political life in recent years has received as much attention on occasions of public oratory as has the issue of corruption in government, in both its political and its administrative aspects. The heads of Ghana's successive governments have made strong and extensive statements about the phenomenon, and a plethora of government-sponsored "commissions of inquiry" have been constituted to look into institutions it is believed to affect.[1] Articles on the topic frequently appear in Ghana's leading and influential political-intellectual periodical, the *Legon Observer*. There appears to be a consensus at least among Ghana's politically articulate stratum that corruption in the public sector of Ghanaian society is pervasive, highly detrimental to developmental goals, and seemingly resistant to any short-run remedy.[2] The two statements that follow,

[1] There has been no inquiry into the civil service. However, shortly after the military coup of 1966 a commission was established to inquire into the Cocoa Marketing Board and the civil service. But the commission was mysteriously disbanded after it had completed its work on the Marketing Board and was about to begin its investigation of the civil service.

[2] The surveys in this study turned up evidence of a common belief that corruption was widespread in the Ghana government at that time. The client sample was asked the following question: "About how many of the high government officials would you say are probably dishonest or corrupt? Many of them, some of them, just a few of them, or none of them at all?" Of the 378 University of Ghana students who answered this question, only 28 thought that just a few officials were corrupt; 348, or 92 percent, answered that some or many were probably corrupt. The same question asked of the comparison/clientele sample obtained results of a similar direction and magnitude. Whether similar perceptions exist today, during the second military regime, is of course not indicated by our data.

the first by a lawyer and the second by a political scientist, are from the pages of the *Legon Observer*, and can be taken as typical of the views of the Ghanaian intelligentsia, at least until the military regime that came to power in 1972:

Corruption pervades life in Ghana. It is to be found in high and low places; it is practised by public and judicial officers, professional men, labourers and even by children. So prevalent is it that many consider it a natural way of getting a job or promotion or making money. ... Corruption exists in spite of all the laws that have been passed to deal with it.[3]

The general impression one gets after reading the two reports [of Commissions of Inquiry] is the appalling and disheartening high level of the corruptibility of all sections of Ghanaian society. Intellectuals, politicians, farmers, messengers, civil servants, businessmen, women, men, etc., etc. are all easily susceptible to corruption. One only has to glance through the list of names mentioned in the two reports in order to satisfy oneself of the validity of this point.[4]

Much attention to the issue of corruption has also been paid by Western scholars who are concerned with comparative politics and comparative administration in "low income" regions of the world. In this group there is a general perception that, although political and bureaucratic corruption are present to some extent in all polities, it is most pervasive in societies and polities undergoing those changes that are characteristic of the process of modernization. Samuel P. Huntington has summed up this view in his *Political Order in Changing Societies*:

Corruption obviously exists in all societies, but it is also obviously more common in some societies than in others and more common at some times in the evolution of a society than at other times. Impressionistic evidence suggests that its extent correlates reasonably well with rapid social and economic modernization.[5]

[3] Kwame Oduro, "The Law and Corruption," p. 18.
[4] J. A. Peasah, "Institutionalised Corruption," p. 12.
[5] Samuel P. Huntington, *Political Order in Changing Societies*, p. 59. Huntington goes on to state: "Political life in eighteenth-century America and in twentieth-century America, it would appear, was less corrupt than in nineteenth-century America. So also political life in seventeenth-century Britain and in late nineteenth-century Britain was, it would appear, less corrupt than it was in eighteenth-century Britain. Is it merely coincidence that this high point of corruption in English and American public life coincided with the impact of the industrial revolution?"

When we move beyond the question of what type of society and polity experiences the greatest amount of corruption, agreement quickly breaks down. For example, although scholars once agreed that corruption was a phenomenon with negative consequences, this agreement no longer exists. In recent years a "revisionist" view of the phenomenon has come to dominate the literature on the subject. Based on a type of functionalist analysis pioneered by Robert Merton in his classic treatment of the urban political machine in the United States,[6] this new school of thought has attempted to show that corruption is functional for economic development and modernization, and therefore should be seen to benefit low-income countries.[7] It is impossible to definitively settle the debate about the consequences of corruption because of the difficulty of empirically verifying the relationships asserted between the independent variable (corruption) and the dependent variable that is of concern—organizational effectiveness, economic development, modernization, or whatever. Indeed, the arguments on both sides of the issue are almost invariably "data free," and rely exclusively for their validity on logical plausibility. On this basis, it is my view that the conclusions of the functionalists about the beneficial consequences of corruption have little reality for Ghana and for low-income countries like it. This is so because the functionalist arguments are marred, I believe, by one or a combination of two analytic weaknesses—what I shall term "empirical irrelevance" and "myopic selectivity."[8]

Empirical irrelevance occurs when the logical connection between an independent variable (corruption) and a dependent variable (say, economic development) depends on intervening conditions that are highly unlikely to exist in empirical reality. Myopic selectivity involves making a claim of functionality based on logic, without taking into account (1) possible concommitant costs, and (2) alternative

[6]:Cf. Robert Merton, *Social Theory and Social Structure*, pp. 72-82.

[7] Although functionalists explicitly claim only that corruption *can* be beneficial, I have the distinct impression that they are really arguing that it *is* beneficial. For the strongest statements of the functionalist point of view see Nathaniel H. Leff, "Economic Development through Bureaucratic Corruption"; and David H. Bayley, "The Effects of Corruption in a Developing Nation"; see also Jose V. Abueva, "The Contribution of Nepotism, Spoils, and Graft to Political Development." A less forceful advocate of the revisionist position on corruption is J. David Greenstone, in "Corruption and Self-Interest in Kampala and Nairobi."

[8] This discussion will be confined to arguments about *administrative or bureaucratic corruption*. Functionalists also claim beneficial consequences for "political" corruption—corrupt behavior by ministers, members of parliament, mayors, and so forth, usually involving the building of political support—but these phenomena are beyond the scope of this study.

and less costly means.[9] An excellent illustration of empirical irrelevance and myopic selectivity is the common functionalist argument that corruption contributes to capital formation, and thus to economic development, because it is a form of taxation that diverts resources from consumption to investment.[10] This argument assumes, of course, that the corrupt public bureaucrat's marginal propensity to invest is greater than that of the person he has "taxed." Unfortunately, there seems to be little empirical basis for such an assumption, at least in African countries. There, most observers report, resources obtained by corruption are usually either consumed or hoarded, or if invested, are used in relatively unproductive real estate speculation.[11] Furthermore, the functionalist argument neglects the fact that

[9] With the use of myopic selectivity there is little that cannot be shown to have beneficial consequences. Take, for instance, this somewhat humorous treatise on the social and economic benefits of crime: "A philosopher produces ideas, a poet verses, a parson sermons, a professor text-books, etc. A criminal produces crime. But if the relationship between this latter branch of production and the whole productive activity of society is examined a little more closely one is forced to abandon a number of prejudices. The criminal produces not only crime but also the criminal law; he produces the professor who delivers the lectures on this criminal law, and even the inevitable text-book in which the professor presents his lectures as a commodity for sale in the market.... Further, the criminal produces the whole apparatus of police and criminal justice, detectives, judges, executioners, juries, etc., and all these different professions, which ... develop diverse abilities of the human spirit, create new needs and new ways of satisfying them. Torture itself has provided occasions for the most ingenious mechanical inventions, employing a host of honest workers in the production of these instruments.

"The criminal produces an impression now moral, now tragic, and renders a 'service' by arousing the moral and aesthetic sentiments of the public.... The criminal interrupts the monotony and security of bourgeois life. Thus he protects it from stagnation and brings forth that restless tension, that mobility of spirit without which the stimulus of competition would itself become blunted. He therefore gives a new impulse to the productive forces." Karl Marx, *Theorien uber den Mehrwert*, (translated in T. B. Bottomore, ed., *Karl Marx* (New York, 1964), pp. 158-160.

[10] "Corruption, whether in the form of kickbacks or of payments originating with the briber, may result in increased allocations of resources away from consumption and into investment. Contrary to common expectations, it may be a supplemental allocative mechanism compatible with the goals of economic development" (Bayley, "The Effects of Corruption," p. 728).

[11] In 1967 a Ghanaian political scientist had this to say about the use to which corruptly obtained resources were put in his country: "The saddening thing is that, in a country where skills are in such short supply, the beneficiaries of such a corrupt system are not generally the persons who would make good use of their booty. Their first reaction is to consume and not to engage themselves in any profitable enterprise.... [He] who gets a 'windfall' of N₵10,000 [ten thousand dollars] immediately imports a Benz and that is the end of it because he knows no better use of his money; at best, he imports iron sheets, rods, and cement for a mansion" (J. A. Peasah, "Institutionalised Corruption," p. 12). Also see Rene Dumont, *False Start in Africa* pp. 78-87; and Franz Fanon, *The Wretched of the Earth*, p. 122. Although there are many impressionistic observations that African civil servants have high marginal propensities to consume, there is little or no real data on the subject.

corruption can and often does occur in government agencies whose goal is capital formation, with the consequence that the ability of the government to extract resources for investment is reduced. The argument regarding capital accumulation maintains its logical "validity" only by assumptions that are improbable and by a type of abstraction that neglects empirical context so that the costs accompanying alleged benefits are not visible.

A similar conclusion can be made about the often repeated argument that corruption frees alien entrepreneurial minorities from the effects of stifling government discrimination and interference and permits them to continue to carry on productive economic activity.[12] This argument ignores, first, the reality that such minorities are most commonly involved in types of commercial enterprise with little potential for economic development and whose benefits are at best short term. Second, it ignores that fact that, since these minorities are alien nationals who often dominate key sectors of the host countries' economy, the purpose of discriminatory government policy may be to dislodge the group and to open the sector to indigenous participation and control.[13] Corruption, then, whatever its alleged benefits in terms of the economy, would be thwarting policies directed at other goals, and would thus have political and social costs that the functionalists do not recognize in their logical equation. Another example of this sort of myopic selectivity is the claim that corruption contributes to economic development by cutting bureaucratic red tape, preventing delays, and providing the "direct incentive necessary to mobilize the bureaucracy for more energetic action on behalf of the entrepreneurs."[14] This is a possible outcome of corruption, but other outcomes are just as likely—for example, the undermining of economically rational regulations and the mobilization of bureaucracy to serve the interests of entrepreneurs whose self-interest may not coincide with that of the society. Thus, in a country that issues import licenses so as to cut down the outflow of scarce foreign reserve on luxury manufactures, corruption may help a factory manager who has an urgent need for spare parts, and who is facing bureaucratic delays, but it may also permit the importer of luxury consumer goods to continue his activity fraudulently, thus undermining a rational economic policy.[15] Rather than corruption, a saner solution to the

[12] See Nathaniel H. Leff, "Economic Development through Bureaucratic Corruption," p. 10.

[13] This is the position in which the Lebanese and Syrian communities in Ghana find themselves. In East Africa the Asian community is in a similar position.

[14] Leff, "Economic Development," p. 10.

[15] This was precisely the situation during the later years of the Nkrumah regime.

problem of bureaucratic red tape would be the elimination of needless regulation and the establishment of controls to improve bureaucratic role performance. This solution would seem to have all the benefits alleged for corruption without its costs.

Taken as a whole, most functionalist arguments about bureaucratic corruption in low-income countries demonstrate an underlying and tacit belief in and preference for the laissez-faire market mechanism in the process of economic development. With such a preference, political development—the increasing capacity of a political system to control its environment—must be viewed as a major threat to economic growth because it contains the potential for government interference in the economic sphere. Corruption, then, is ultimately beneficial, because for a time it undermines political development and allows entrepreneurs to purchase freedom to pursue their economic self-interest unimpeded. The available evidence, however, suggests to me that in Ghana as well as in most other low-income countries the opposite perspective is justified. This perspective holds that in such societies only the government has the organizational, entrepreneurial, and resource *potential* to deal effectively with the obstacles to economic development and social modernization. Political development, which involves turning potential into actual capacity, is, then, a prerequisite for the achievement of economic and social goals. Corruption may, under special circumstances, have some short-run benefits in terms of these goals, but as it undermines the dependability of government organizations it reduces government's capacity to respond to and control its environment and thus impedes political development and negatively affects the attainment of modernization goals.[16]

The Definition of Corruption

Not only is it difficult to find overall agreement on what the consequences of governmental corruption are likely to be, but there is little consensus on the very definition of the term. The task of definition has been made difficult by the normative connotations attaching to the concept of corruption, which give rise to problems

---

See *Report of the Commission of Enquiry into Irregularities and Malpractices in the Grant of Import Licenses* (Ollennu Report), (Accra, 1967), passim.

[16] It should be clear that I am not suggesting that increasing government capacity is *necessarily* related to economic development and modernization. These depend, among other things, on what is done with the capacity, on the commitments of political elites and the policies they decide to pursue.

of cultural ethnocentrism. Since corruption in its most general sense involves behavior that is a "perversion" of some preexisting standard, the question must inevitably arise as to whose standards behavior is to be measured against. Prior to the "behavioral revolution" in the social sciences the answer to this question was usually "the standards of the observer." In recent years, however, such a view has come to be seen as ethnocentric and of little use in empirical analysis, since the social unit being investigated might have standards of behavior quite different from those of the observer. One way to handle this problem is to hold the values or standards of the observer in abeyance and to define corruption in terms of the values and norms of the social system being investigated. Samuel Huntington defines corruption as "behavior of public officials which deviates from accepted norms in order to serve private ends."[17] The Huntington definition avoids problems of ethnocentrism by adopting whatever norms are generally accepted in a society as the standard against which corruption will be measured. While this definition avoids one problem it creates another, and analytically an equally serious one. It assumes that there is a general consensus on the definition of *public* and *private* and on the norms of behavior that relate to each. But such a consensus is a function of societal integration, a characteristic not likely to be common in countries undergoing changes associated with the process of modernization.[18] In a system lacking societal and political integration it is possible for accepted norms of behavior to be unrelated to "public ends," in the sense of goals that are attached to the contemporary state organization and its constituent political institutions.[19] In such a situation conformity to generally accepted norms may involve serving private ends, while serving "public" ends may entail behavior that deviates from these accepted standards.

A way out of the definitional dilemma posed by societal malintegration is to remove from the definition of corruption all consideration of *generally accepted* norms or standards of behavior. This can be done if governmental corruption is defined in organizational rather than societal terms, corrupt behavior being role behavior in political institutions which violates formally defined role obligations in favor of personal roles that are extraorganizational. Such a definition is offered by J. S. Nye: "Corruption is behavior which deviates from

[17] Huntington, *Political Order*, p. 59.

[18] Although Huntington explicitly takes account of this lack of integration, his definition is contradicted by this aspect of his analysis. See ibid., p. 60.

[19] I am suggesting, not that accepted norms are unrelated to "public" ends, but rather that the "public" that they relate to—lineage, village, tribe—is different than the one served by the political and administrative organizations of the contemporary state.

the formal duties of a public role because of private-regarding (personal, close family, private clique) pecuniary or status gains, or violates rules against the exercise of certain types of private-regarding influence."[20]

Nye's definition does not say whether the society in which the public institution is operating will view "private-regarding" behavior as a violation of accepted norms, as immoral, or as corrupt. This question is treated as an independent variable relating to the causes of organizational or institutional corruption, not as a matter of definition. It is possible that behavior that is corrupt from the vantage point of the organization will not be viewed as such by most actors in the social system; indeed the commonly accepted norms could, within the terms of this definition, judge behavior to be moral that from the organizational vantage point is corrupt. Note that within the Nye definition only those violations of rules that are motivated by private-regarding considerations are regarded as corrupt. This is an important distinction, because it is possible that a civil servant, for example, might violate some specific bureaucratic rule so as to further the efficient achievement of his organization's goals. Such a violation should be considered an act of initiative or innovation, not corruption.

It is not clear from the Nye definition whether all forms of private-regarding behavior in public organizations are to be considered corrupt, or only those forms that involve pecuniary gains for the public servant. That is, are all forms of particularistic behavior on the part of public officials—special consideration for relatives and friends or other forms of acquaintance, nepotism, and the like—to be regarded as corruption? Or is only particularistic behavior motivated at least in part by monetary considerations to be so regarded? I believe that the latter situation should hold. I would consider all forms of behavior in bureaucracy in which personal roles take precedence over organizational roles to constitute the problem of organizational control. Corruption could then be viewed as a subtype of this more general organizational problem.

The Basis for Administrative Corruption in a New State: Theoretical Perspective

This discussion of the problem of selecting an appropriate definition of corruption indicates the relevance of the theoretical framework

[20] J. S. Nye, "Corruption and Political Development: A Cost-Benefit Analysis," p. 419.

I have adopted in this study to an understanding of the causes of widespread bureaucratic corruption in transitional-type polities. However, the basis of corrupt behavior by public bureaucrats differs somewhat from that which exists in the forms of particularism we have been concerned with thus far. In the latter case the universalistic norms of the formal organizational role-set are violated because of a social tie, direct or indirect, between a public bureaucrat and some individual or group, while in the case of corruption universalistic standards are violated because of considerations of monetary gain on the part of the civil servant.[21] Despite this difference, the analytic framework utilized thus far is helpful to an understanding of administrative corruption.

Two aspects of the contemporary Ghanaian social system—elements of what can be termed institutional malintegration—are relevant to this discussion. The first has already received considerable attention. A social system in which a large proportion of social actors define identity and obligation primarily in terms of corporate kinship groups, which I have argued is true in Ghana, creates a type of systemic situation that is highly conducive to bureaucratic corruption. As I have suggested, in this type of system the families of public bureaucrats will tend to view the official positions of their members as possessions of the corporate descent group, to be used for the group's benefit. It has already been shown that such "possession" creates expectations on the part of family members for particularistic treatment by government agencies. But such power to grant special consideration is only a portion of the exploitable resources of many official positions. For example, influence associated with a bureaucratic position can be used to obtain jobs for relatives, and special consideration can be sold to "strangers," creating largess that can enhance the family's economic and social standing. When role compartmentalization is not a common feature of the socio-cultural environment, it is likely that public bureaucrats will be expected by their families to fully exploit the resource potential of their positions. Not to do so, on the basis of upholding one's "public trust,"

[21] James Scott suggests a distinction between "parochial" and "market" corruption. "As ideal types, 'parochial' corruption represents a situation where only ties of kinship, affection, caste, and so forth determine access to the favors of power-holders while 'market' corruption signifies a virtually impersonal process in which influence is accorded those who can 'pay' the most, regardless of who they are." Although I concur that the distinction is a necessary and important one, I feel that discourse is made less confusing if the term *corruption* is dropped completely from the first phenomenon. In the common "lay" usage the term *corruption* usually makes reference to behavior involving monetary malfeasance of some type. See James C. Scott, "The Analysis of Corruption in Developing Nations," p. 330.

would constitute ignoring one's primary social obligation to family in the name of a "public" that does not exist in social reality.[22] The important thing is that, in such a socio-cultural environment, giving aid and showing generosity to one's relatives and others to whom one has a personal tie is a primary social virtue. The man who does so receives great prestige and social esteem.[23] Thus, from the social vantage point of the civil servant, not only does his position within his extended family depend on his full exploitation of the resources of his office, but how well he does for his family will also greatly affect his standing in the larger community. Thus when bureaucratic organizations are embedded in a socio-cultural system in which roles are not differentiated and in which primary social value adheres in the family role-set, there exists an environment in which corruption—the appropriation of public office for private use[24]—is likely to find social support.

But the socio-cultural system of contemporary Ghana does more than create a receptive environment for corruption; in many cases it virtually demands corruption from its public servants. To understand this we must briefly examine another aspect of institutional malintegration in contemporary Ghana: an imbalance between the material obligations placed on civil servants by their "significant others" and the material resources available to them through their salaries. If the expectations placed on a public bureaucrat by those he cares about outdistance his ability to meet them with his legitimate income, then these expectations will create a motivation to supplement income through corrupt means. I shall presently argue and attempt to demonstrate empirically that such a situation exists in Ghana today as a significant aspect of her colonial legacy.

[22] I am suggesting, not that a public in the sense of community does not exist within the territory of Ghana, but rather that the "public" associated with the contemporary state is more formal than real.

[23] The social anthropologist P. C. Lloyd, writing about the Yoruba of Nigeria, notes that, in the attribution of high social status, generosity is stressed as a major value. He notes: "Although the rich man certainly enjoys to the full the benefit of his wealth, both material and non-material advantages accrue to his supporters—his descent group members, other kin, and his followers." Impressionistic evidence strongly suggests that the same can be said of the attribution of prestige and esteem among the peoples of Ghana. See P. C. Lloyd, "Class Consciousness Among the Yoruba," p. 332.

[24] In this context "private" refers not to the individual but rather to behavior directed toward extraorganizational goals. In discussions of corruption in transitional societies the contrast between "public" and "private" is unfortunate, since, as I am attempting to demonstrate, corruption really stems from a conflict over relevant publics. The social pressure placed on civil servants is directed, not to the service of "private" ends, but rather toward "publics"—family, lineage, tribe, and so forth—that differ in their definition from the formal "public" which the civil service bureaucracy supposedly serves.

The phenomenon of institutional emulation that, I have argued, is a significant aspect of the colonial heritage includes not only structural emulation—the adoption of bureaucracy introduced from Europe—but social emulation. This involves adopting as appropriate to positions in the new postcolonial civil service, the exalted status that attached to the Europeans who previously staffed the colonial administration. And exalted status brings great obligations. Numerous observers, including many African novelists, have noted that the acquisition of a "European post"—a post in the senior civil service—brings with it greatly increased influence, obligation, and responsibility within one's extended family.[25] These obligations and responsibilities carry a heavy material burden. Not only will the African civil servant be expected to provide financial assistance to his family in the form of periodic contributions befitting one in his "station"—school fees for young relatives, subsistence and housing for those less fortunate, and the like—but, as I will try to demonstrate, he is also likely to be expected to maintain the material aspects of a European "life-style." A Mercedes-Benz or Jaguar car, a Western-style house (preferably more than one story high), imported European clothing, and so forth have become the new symbols of exalted social position in African society—of "big man" status in Ghana.[26] For the civil servant the acquisition of such status symbols becomes not only a personal act but a duty to his extended family.[27] Since he is viewed as a representative of his corporate descent group, the appearance he presents to the community can affect the social position of the entire extended family. If he displays the status attributes of a "big man," his group will bask in his achievements; on the other hand, a failure to acquire the appropriate status symbols will be tantamount to undermining its social position. In sum, then, part of the colonial

[25] In particular see three novels: Chinua Achebe, *No Longer at Ease* (New York, 1962); and *A Man of the People* (New York, 1967); and Ayi Kwei Armah, *Fragments* (Boston, 1970). See also Lloyd, "Class Consciousness Among the Yoruba," p. 329; and K. E. DeGraft-Johnson, "The Evolution of Elites in Ghana," pp. 110-111; and also Stanislav Andreski, *The African Predicament*, p. 102.

[26] Note this description of "social emulation" in Ghana by Ghanaian sociologist K. E. DeGraft-Johnson. Discussing the emergence of a Ghanaian social elite after World War II, he writes: "To have had part of one's education in Europe or America, or even merely to have visited carried the prestige label 'been-to.' To live in a bungalow (however small) in the European residential area carried prestige. A senior civil service post was designated a 'European appointment' and was rated high. Eating European dishes frequently was prestigeful" ("Evolution of Elites in Ghana," p. 110).

[27] Thus, according to DeGraft-Johnson, "Not to conform to certain social expectations and use certain elite symbols was to lose face with friends and relatives. The newly arrived 'been-to' was often expected by his relatives to wear woolen suits. . . . As the standard of living rose, he was expected to own a car, a refrigerator, a radiogram, etc." (ibid., pp. 110-111).

legacy has been a form of social emulation that has meant, for an individual acquiring a post in the civil service, an obligation to maintain the outward appearance of a European life-style through the acquisition of a variety of consumer goods, many of which are imported. This obligation, especially when combined with his other financial obligations to the extended family, will entail great expense and will tend to outdistance what is financially available to the civil servant through his salary. One would expect that the lower a civil servant's rank the fewer would be the demands made upon him. But, of course, his salary would be smaller too. Consequently, one would expect that personnel at all levels of the service find themselves squeezed between the expectations of their significant others and the size of their salaries.

Many observers of postindependence African states have been highly critical of government bureaucracies and the personnel who make them up, for the share of scarce resources that they consume.[28] They have correctly pointed out that, relative to the rest of the population in African states, civil servants have inordinately high incomes, and that recurrent expenditures for government administrative organizations constitute a very large proportion of meager state revenue. Few observers, however, have pointed out the irony in this situation. Taken as an aggregate and compared with the rest of the population, civil servants are overpaid; when viewed as individual social actors, public bureaucrats receive salaries that are insufficient to meet the demands of their social environment. These salaries have in many cases been pegged to the salaries of the Europeans who were being replaced, but the high duties that many African governments have placed on imported consumer goods have made the symbols of status that are "socially appropriate" to civil service posts two to three times more expensive than they were when Europeans occupied these positions.

Up to this point we have been concerned with aspects of the social environment in postcolonial states that motivate public servants to use their official positions for monetary gain; the same environment also makes it likely that individuals will be willing to offer monetary considerations to civil servants. As we saw in chapter 5, in a socio-cultural environment in which clients do not perceive occupational and personal roles in a compartmentalized fashion, those who need services from public bureaucracy will expect the civil servant to treat his office as a personal possession, and if the civil servant is not personally obligated to them, they are likely to expect to pay for

[28] See, especially, Rene Dumont, *False Start in Africa*, pp. 78-87.

any services he renders them. Consequently, the civil servant, motivated to supplement his income by the social context in which he finds himself, is likely to be continually exposed to individuals willing to offer financial consideration for a wide variety of services. Thus both the motivation and opportunity for bureaucratic corruption can be said to have a systemic base in the socio-cultural environment within which administrative organizations are embedded.

There are three basic propositions that constitute the skeleton of the foregoing argument, and for which supporting evidence from the Ghanaian surveys will be provided: (1) material demands are made on the incumbents of civil service positions that their salaries are inadequate to meet; (2) the social position of civil servants will be affected by their ability to satisfy these demands; and (3) the satisfaction of these demands even by organizationally corrupt means will find general approval in the social environment.

The Basis for Administrative Corruption in a New State: The Data

The Status-Salary Gap

Data were presented in chapter 3 that revealed most civil servants to be under a substantial financial burden from obligations to their extended families.[29] It will be recalled that 80 percent of the civil servants interviewed said they were providing financial assistance to relatives other than wives and children, and that nearly one-third of them were supporting three or more such dependents. At this point let us turn to another aspect of the civil servant's financial burden—the gap between the status demands of his occupational position and the salary provided by that position.

To test the proposition that a civil service post brings with it a socially defined life-style involving the acquisition of various "European" consumer goods, the civil servant respondents were given a list of consumer items and were asked "Which of the items ... do you think a person in your position should be able to own?" The items, appearing on a card that was handed to each respondent, were the following: (a) quality automobile, (b) record player, (c) wireless, (d) house, (e) imported suits, (f) any other; (g) there is nothing in particular a person in my position should be able to own.

Note that the civil servants were asked what a person in their position *should* own. I did not seek to discover what types of things

[29] See pp. 61-62.

they actually possessed, nor were they asked what, in the abstract, they desired, but rather what they thought was *appropriate* for a person in their social and occupational position.

The first striking result of this item was the finding that almost without exception civil servants believe that the ownership of certain types of consumer goods should go along with positions like their own. Only 18 out of the 434 civil servants interviewed chose alternative (g)—"There is nothing in particular a person in my position should be able to own." All of the rest specified one or a combination of items from the list.[30] One-fifth (20.2 percent) of them stated that a person in their position should own all the items; approximately 40 percent specified a house, 33 percent an automobile, and 51 percent mentioned at least one of the smaller consumer goods (wireless, imported suits, record player).

As one would expect if consumer goods are viewed as symbols appropriate to the status of positions in the civil service, the judgments of the respondents about which items were appropriate to their positions varied with rank in the bureaucratic hierarchy. The consumption aspirations of senior officials tend to be more ambitious than those of junior personnel. This can be observed in table 28, in which a four-point index of consumption aspirations is cross-tabulated with rank in the civil service. The consumption aspiration index was constructed by combining the respondents' answers to the consumer item series so that point (1) on the index locates those respondents who felt a person in their position should own *all* the items in the series, and point (4) locates those who stated that a person in their position should own nothing in particular. Intermediate point (2) on the index is occupied by those who felt they should own either an automobile or a house, and by those who mentioned also some of the smaller consumer goods. Finally, intermediate point (3) locates those who mentioned as items appropriate to their position only one or more of the smaller, less costly, consumer goods (imported suits, wireless, record player, television). The table makes it clear that those in the higher ranks are far more likely than those in the lower ranks to aspire to owning all of the items presented, and also to obtaining the larger consumer items (auto and house), while those of lower rank are far more likely to limit their aspirations to the less costly type of consumer items. The major break in the pattern of aspirations is between what are termed the medium high and

[30] Roughly 10 percent of the respondents added furniture, television, or refrigerator to the items specified.

Table 28

Consumption Aspiration Index and Rank
in the Civil Service

		Rank		
Index	High	Medium High	Medium Low	Low
1. All items	37.9%	39.4%	10.0%	2.8%
2. Auto or house plus miscellaneous consumer goods; or auto; or house	39.4	40.4	15.4	14.7
3. Only miscellaneous consumer goods (no auto or house)	19.7	19.2	71.5	73.4
4. Nothing in particular	3.0	1.0	3.1	9.1
☐ Total	100.0	100.0	100.0	100.0
	(N=66)	(N=104)	(N=130)	(N=109)

NOTE: Chi Square for table significant at or below .001 level.

medium low ranks, with those in the ranks of senior executive officer and above tending to cluster at the high end of the consumption aspiration scale, and those with the rank of clerical officer through higher executive officer tending to fall at the lower end. This differentiation coincides with what in Ghana is informally termed the junior and senior service, a distinction that carries with it important status as well as other considerations.

The full import of the consumption aspirations of Ghanaian civil servants to an understanding of the genesis of corruption can only be obtained by relating the salaries of the civil servants to the cost of the things aspired to. All of the items on the list presented to the respondents are imported into Ghana as finished manufactured goods or, if made in Ghana, are the products of "last-stage" assembly plants.[31] In either case, the cost of shipping and the extremely high customs duties and purchase taxes that the government of Ghana applies to imports make these items extremely expensive for a

[31] "Last-stage" assembly plants are those industrial establishments that put together a finished product from imported semifinished parts. The finished products of such industries thus have a very high import component.

Ghanaian to own.[32] For example, at the time the interviews in this study were conducted, there was a 40 percent ad valorem purchase tax on automobiles valued at between $2,000 and $2,500,[33] a 65 percent ad valorem tax on those valued at between $2,500 and $3,500, and a levy of 200 percent on automobiles whose value exceeded $5,700.[34] This meant that, at the time, the purchase price of a small and nonprestigious automobile like a Volkswagen was more than $3,000, and a luxury auto such as a Mercedes or Jaguar could cost well over $10,000.[35] Imported clothing, household appliances, radios, phonographs, televisions, and so forth were also assessed customs duties at very high rates,[36] and thus their price to the Ghanaian purchaser was also substantially higher than their price in the country of origin. A suit that could be purchased in England for $50 would, after the addition of transportation costs and a 75 percent ad valorem customs duty, be likely to carry a price in Ghana of well over $100; a refrigerator or phonograph originally costing about $200 would in Ghana carry a price of over $400, and similar types of costs attached to the other consumer purchases deemed necessary by the respondents.

These prices achieve significance for this discussion through their relationship to the salaries paid to Ghanaian civil servants. Table

[32] In Ghana imported manufactured goods are usually strongly preferred to any substitute that might be made within the country. It is common in Ghana to hear locally made goods spoken of in a derogatory fashion as "made-in-here." The military regime that came to power in 1972 is attempting to change this orientation through public exhortation.

[33] The basic Ghanaian unit of monetary exchange was the New Cedi (NC). One New Cedi exchanged with the U.S. dollar at roughly the rate of 1:1. For clarity I will refer to the monetary cost of objects in dollars rather than New Cedis.

[34] This purchase tax was in addition to a 30 percent ad valorem customs duty, and was calculated on the value of the vehicle plus the amount of the customs levy. See Purchase Tax (Amendment) Decree, 1968, N.L.C. Decree 263, in *Ghana Business Guide, 1968*, p. 233. This decree took effect from July 16, 1968. Prior to that time the purchase tax was slightly lower on expensive automobiles and slightly higher on the cheaper ones.

[35] Despite this, imports into Ghana of Mercedes-Benz cars for private use were almost as numerous as those of any other manufacturer during the two years that preceded this study. During these years, the number of new Mercedes registered in Ghana exceeded that of cheaper makes such as Volkswagen, Datsun, Fiat, and Toyota, and were exceeded only by English Ford in 1966, and by Opel and Peugeot in 1967, and then by only a slight amount. The importance of the luxury automobile as a symbol of status apparently outweighed its seemingly prohibitive cost. For statistics on new motor vehicle registrations, see Ghana, Central Bureau of Statistics, *Monthly News Letter* (Accra).

[36] Import duty on selected items (in percent ad valorem): Wearing apparel (jackets, trousers, and slacks), 75 percent; pocket watches, wrist watches, 100; furniture, 150; radios, 75; refrigerators, 66 2/3; television sets, 75; phonograph records and recording tapes, 100. Sources: Customs and Excise Tariff, 1966 (as amended, 1967), First Schedule, Part A; and Customs and Excise Tariff Regulations, 1966 (L.I. 504) (Amendment) Decree, 1968. Published in *Ghana Business Guide*, pp. 175-176, and p. 229.

29 presents approximate salary ranges for civil servants (at the time the interviews were conducted) within the fourfold breakdown of ranks utilized throughout this study. When these salary ranges are

Table 29

Salary Ranges in the Ghana Civil Service

Rank	Salary Ranges (Approximate) Per Annum
High	$2,000 to $4,000
Medium High	1,300 to 2,000
Medium Low	550 to 1,300
Low	350 to 550

SOURCE: *Report of the Commission on the Structure and Remuneration of the Public Services in Ghana* (Accra, Ministry of Information, 1967), pp. 66-69.

compared with the cost of the consumer items that the respondents believe are appropriate to their positions, it becomes apparent that civil servants are unlikely to be able to satisfy their consumer aspirations on their official incomes. This becomes even more obvious with some finer salary breakdowns. For example, of those respondents in the high and medium high ranks who say a person in their position should own all of the items listed—house, quality auto, and an assortment of smaller consumer goods—86 percent are receiving salaries of between $1,300 and 2,600. Thus the purchase of a "quality" auto would consume well over an entire year's salary, and in many cases the salary of two and three years. When this is added to the cost of building or buying a house (for which much of the material is imported), to the price of the assorted smaller consumer goods thought appropriate, and to the other family-related financial obligations of these civil servants (living expenses for themselves, their parents, wives, and children; assistance to the wider extended family in the form of school fees for children; housing and subsistence for the economically less fortunate; contributions at funerals, outdoorings, and festivals), the gap between their consumption aspirations and the income provided by their salaries becomes clearly apparent. Those civil servants in the lower ranks, whose aspirations are lower and whose family obligations are fewer, are really no better off, since their salaried income is so much smaller. The clerical officer earning $400 annually is likely to find the purchase of his imported suits, record player, refrigerator, and so forth, as difficult as the administrative officer earning $2,500 finds the purchase of his automobile and house. It is true that many civil servants have access to means which can lighten their financial burden: relatively low interest loans for the purchase of automobiles and homes are made available by the civil service, and Ghanaian wives usually have some independent source of income.[37] But, however much these types of mechanisms may ease their situation, for most civil servants a substantial gap between aspiration and income is still likely to exist. And this is indeed what the civil servant respondents reported. When asked whether their present salary allowed them to buy the kinds of things they think they should own, a full 83 percent said that it did not.[38] There is little difference between persons at various salary levels on this question; the junior clerical officer, the middle-ranking executive officer, and the senior officer in the administrative class in almost all instances concur in the perception that their salaries are inadequate to sustain the life-style that they believe appropriate to their social positions.

We can reasonably conclude on the basis of the data that Ghanaian civil servants aspire to own a range of highly expensive consumer goods, and that their salaries are generally insufficient to satisfy these aspirations easily. There is still the question of whether there is a social basis to these aspirations. Are the aspirations a personal matter? Or, on the other hand, are expensive consumer items symbols of status which people like these respondents are expected by their "significant others" to possess, and would the failure to obtain them be socially costly for the individual civil servant? Items in both the Clientele Survey and the Civil Servant Survey provide evidence on this point. The questions asked of the clientele sample sought to determine whether possession of the type of consumer goods discussed above was in fact generally linked to social status in contemporary Ghana. One item asked the respondents to agree or disagree with this statement: "If a rich man does not buy an expensive car and build a large house he will lose standing in the eyes of his relatives and friends." As was expected, a substantial majority of both clientele samples felt that social position was dependent on "conspicuous

[37] Again I am grateful to Jon Kraus for pointing this out in a personal communication.
[38] The survey item read: "Do you feel that your present salary allows you to buy the kinds of things you should have?"

consumption." Among the university student respondents a total of 63.4 percent agreed with the statement, and the largest proportion of responses—36 percent—fell into the "strongly agree" category.[39] A comparison with the responses of the comparison/clientele sample indicates that belief in the importance of conspicuous consumption for maintaining social status is even greater among more traditionally oriented groups. Thirty of the thirty-eight nonliterate respondents, or nearly 80 percent of the group, agreed that if a rich man does not buy an expensive car and build a large house he will lose standing in the eyes of his relatives and friends.

A second item that indicates a link between conspicuous consumption and social status described seven different types of men and asked the respondents to pick the man they thought likely to be the *most respected* by people in Ghana.[40] Each of the survey instruments contained this item. In all three samples there was little consensus on which of the seven men would be most respected, none of the seven receiving a majority of the choices from any of the samples. However, in each case the man described as having "all the good things in life, a good car, a big house, fine clothing, etc." was considered likely to be the most respected by a relatively large proportion of the respondents. In the student sample such a man ranked first in the proportion of respondents choosing him as most respected; among the civil servants he ranked second; and among the comparison/clientele sample, third.

If, as impressionistic observations suggest and the data indicate, social standing in Ghana is related to the display of conspicuous consumption, and if the argument that individuals are perceived as extensions of their corporate group is correct, then Ghanaian civil servants should find themselves under social pressure from their significant others to obtain those consumer items that they themselves feel are appropriate to their positions. Direct evidence for this was sought from the civil servant respondents. Following the consumer item series the civil servants were asked: "What about your relatives and friends? Are they likely to expect you to own things of this sort?" The answers to this question revealed greater unanimity

---

[39] Four response categories were offered to the respondents: strongly agree, agree, disagree, strongly disagree.

[40] The seven descriptions are as follows: (1) He earns a high salary. (2) He is liked by the people with whom he works. (3) He is able to take care of his relatives and friends should they be in need. (4) He has all the good things in life: a good car, a big house, fine clothing, etc. (5) He is better at his job than anyone else. (6) He holds a position in which he has many subordinates. (7) He makes a contribution to the development of Ghana.

than practically any other item in the survey—a full 90 percent of the sample responded that yes, relatives and friends would expect them to own expensive consumer goods like the seven that appeared on the list presented to them. Thus the civil servants interviewed overwhelmingly perceived their significant others as expecting them to purchase status symbols for which in their own judgment their present salaries were inadequate.

I am not suggesting here that the practice of conspicuous consumption and its relationship to social status is unique to transitional societies like Ghana. What demands special notice in such societies is that the existence of the practice coincides with the emulation of the material symbols of a life-style that is indigenous to more affluent industrialized societies. In consequence there is a disjunction between the desire and demand for conspicuous consumption and the economic structure of a country like Ghana. The result is a general inability of public bureaucrats to "legitimately" obtain the financial wherewithal to live up to what is socially expected of them, and this can reasonably be expected to create widespread motivation for bureaucratic corruption.

Social Acceptance of Administrative Corruption

The phenomenon of a gap between social demands and salaried income creates a motive for corruption; it does not, however, provide social approval for it. This is produced by another aspect of institutional malintegration, the lack of role compartmentalization and consequent expectation that bureaucratic offices will be appropriated by the descent group of their incumbents. My hypothesis is that at the level of individual social actor institutional malintegration creates a situation in which the civil servant who engages in organizationally corrupt behavior so as to satisfy the demands of his significant others will be socially rewarded. He will be more highly esteemed, deemed more moral and worthy, than the civil servant who is unable to satisfy social expectations because of his commitment to the "morality" of the public organization in which he happens to work.

To test this hypothesis the following item was constructed for the clientele surveys. Respondents were told:

Here are descriptions of two senior government officials. Please tell me which one you think is the *better* man.

Official One: He has used his official position to "chop"[41] a great deal

[41] "To chop" is a pidgen English expression that, among other things, refers to the appropriation of public resources for "personal" use. See chapter 5, p. 120.

of money, but he has shown great generosity, coming to the aid of any of his people who are in need.

Official Two: He follows all rules and regulations of his office and has not "chopped" money, but as a result, although he would like to show generosity, he constantly refuses to help any of his people who are in need.

The question concerning which of the officials the respondent considered the better man was followed by two related questions:

Which of the two officials do you think most Ghanaians would consider the better man? Which of the two would you prefer to have as a relative?

An overwhelming number of the respondents in the university student sample expressed a personal preference for the noncorrupt civil servant, and almost as large a majority also perceived this preference as deviant within Ghanaian society. Only 27, or 7 percent, of these respondents felt that the corrupt official (he who "chopped" money) was the better of the two men, but 318, or 83 percent, of them believed that most Ghanaians would think he was. The accuracy of this last perception receives support from the responses of the comparison/clientele sample. While 7 percent of the university sample thought the corrupt official was the better man, 35 percent of the total comparison/clientele sample and a 62 percent majority of the nonliterate subset thought so. Also, of those respondents in the comparison/clientele sample who do not speak fluent English, 64 percent considered the corrupt official the better man of the two, and of those with no more than a primary school education 67 percent held this view. Thus, among those respondents whose social characteristics approximate most closely the norm within the Ghanaian population, the civil servant who observes the rules of his office and consequently finds it impossible to help his people is in the majority of cases held in lower esteem than the civil servant who appropriates the resources of his office for the benefit of his "people." Additionally, as was true of the university student sample, a large majority of the comparison/clientele sample believe that *most* Ghanaians will feel that the corrupt official is the better of the two men described.

Note that the question asked about what *most Ghanaians* would think, not about how the civil servant's family would feel. Therefore the findings can be interpreted as an assessment by the respondents of the social standing, respect, or esteem that two types of civil servants would enjoy in the general community. In short, there is a consensus among the respondents that of two civil servants—one that is corrupt and is therefore able to show generosity toward his family, and one that is uncorrupt and as a result lacks the resources to provide his people with assistance—the former will be more highly esteemed; he will be considered the better man by most people.

The figures presented above suggest again that personal commitment to the norms of public bureaucratic institutions is a product of acculturation through exposure to modernizing influences. I sought to test this further by breaking down the comparison/clientele sample by level of education. The findings are reported in table 30. Note

Table 30

Social Esteem and Organizational Corruption:
Effect of Education

Esteem	Level of Respondent's Educational Background		
	None or Primary	Middle School	Secondary School
Corrupt official seen as better man	66.6%	41.7%	18.2%
Uncorrupt official seen as better man	33.3	58.3	81.8
☐ Total	99.9 (N=18)	100 (N=24)	100 (N=33)

NOTE: Chi Square for table significant at or below .001 level.

that although some of the cells in the matrix are extremely small, the results obtained can be considered statistically significant at the .001 level. The results in table 30 show quite clearly that level of education affects the way an individual engaged in bureaucratic corruption will be perceived. The predominant view of those with little or no formal education is that the official who acts corruptly, and who as a result is able to show generosity to his kinsmen, is a "better" man than the official who is uncorrupt. The reverse is true among the most highly educated individuals. If we compare the responses of the university students with those of the comparison/clientele sample, we can see that university-educated people are less likely than those with secondary school backgrounds to esteem the organizationally corrupt official, and the latter are less likely to do so than those with middle school backgrounds, who in turn are less likely than those with primary education to approve of corrupt behavior.

Since it is common for respondents in survey research to affirm abstract principles in a manner that represents formalism more than a true reflection of attitudes that are likely to inspire action, the respondents were asked which of the two officials described would they prefer to have as a relative. It was reasoned that responses to this question would more accurately reflect attitudes that were likely to find social expression than the request that respondents reveal their personal belief about which of the two officials was the better man. Within both clientele samples a higher proportion of respondents said they would prefer the "corrupt" official for a relative than indicated that such an official was a better man; that is, in each case a portion of the respondents who had said the uncorrupt official was the better man actually preferred the corrupt official for a relative. In the university sample, one-fifth (19.2 percent) of the respondents said that, of the two officials, they would prefer to have the corrupt one as a relative, although only 7 percent said that he was the better man. Of the respondents in the comparison/clientele sample, nearly one-half (47 percent) preferred the corrupt official as a relative, although only 35 percent had said they thought him the better man. Thus, these findings indicate that the respondents are more likely to give social approval to administrative corruption, at least when it involves a member of their family, than was indicated by the original query about which official they would consider the better man.

Whether a person will prefer the corrupt or the uncorrupt civil servant as a kinsman is also affected by exposure to "modernizing influences," with those experiencing a great deal of exposure favoring the uncorrupt official and those with minimal exposure showing a predominate preference for the official who acts corruptly in order to show generosity. For example, within the comparison/clientele sample 68.4 percent of the nonliterates prefer the corrupt official compared with 24.3 percent of the literates; 70 percent of those who cannot speak English prefer such a man for a relative, compared with 56.6 percent of those who speak English haltingly, and only 5.6 percent of those who speak it fluently; 73.7 percent of those who have no postprimary formal education prefer the corrupt official for a relative, compared with 52 percent of those at the middle-school level, and 30 percent of those who have attended secondary school. In the sample of university students we find that the longer the respondent has been exposed to the environment of the University of Ghana campus the less likely he or she is to prefer the corrupt official as a relative. Nearly one-third (28.9 percent) of the first-year students expressed a preference to have the corrupt official as their relative, compared with 16.2 percent of the second-year students, 15.5 percent of the third-year students, and 13.6 percent of those in their fourth year.

These results thus add additional support to the contention that social approval for bureaucratic corruption has its basis in the persistence of a traditional understanding of role obligations. The data suggest that only those Ghanaians whose life experience has *intensively* introduced them into nontraditional forms of social organization are likely to personally accept an "organizational morality" which separates formal bureaucratic roles from family roles and in certain circumstances gives them precedence. At the same time, even those respondents who under certain circumstances accept the validity of organizational over family "morality" are under the impression that theirs is a deviant point of view, that most Ghanaians would approve of organizational corruption when it is used to aid the family. And this assessment appears to be borne out by the data, which show those respondents who are most typical of the majority of the Ghanaian population to be highly likely to esteem a corrupt civil servant who aids his family, over one who is uncorrupt and who therefore lacks the resources to offer such assistance.

It seems reasonable to conclude that the civil servant who fails to utilize his office so as to bridge the gap between his salary and the financial cost of the familial responsibilities that attach to one in his position will suffer socially, while the civil servant who appropriates the resources of his office so as to meet these demands—who engages in the conspicuous consumption expected of him, aids his kinsmen in their educational, housing, and welfare needs, and in general builds up the position of the family—will receive social approval, being appreciated not only by his family, but esteemed and respected in the larger community as well.

Discussion

There are two approaches in the contemporary social science literature that offer explanations different than those presented here for the prevalence of bureaucratic corruption in transitional polities such as Ghana. While I have adopted an essentially sociological approach,[42] others have suggested that corruption in societies under-going "early-stage modernization" can be attributed to economic and political factors. Those who adopt the economic approach argue essentially that corruption is a function of scarcity. They assert that because the demand for governmentally dispensed values is greater than the supply, the "market" price for these goods will be above their "official" price. Individuals who desire these scarce values will then be willing to buy them at their market price if they cannot obtain all they want at the official price.[43] The political approach to corruption has been cogently presented by James C. Scott.[44] He argues that bureaucratic corruption is an informal means to exert influence at the enforcement stage of the political process, and that it will be prevalent when channels to influence policy outcome at the input stage of the political process are for some reason unavailable.

Although the three approaches to bureaucratic corrup-tion—sociological, economic, and political—are not mutually exclusive, and thus the factors suggested by each may operate simultaneously, I find the economic and political approaches deficient in ways that only the sociological approach can overcome.

The economic approach is better at explaining the motives of the clients of public bureaucracy than it is in helping us to understand the behavior of bureaucrats. To use the economic terminology, the "market" price of official goods is determined not only by scarcity—supply and demand—but also by the willingness of the bureaucrat to sell official goods. This willingness is a function of his commitment to his bureaucratic role—the higher his commitment the higher the price necessary to overcome it. At a certain point the commitment of public bureaucrats to their roles could be so high that the prices necessary to overcome it would make the "market" purchase of official goods uneconomic from the point of view of the client, and thus corruption would decline. The problem, of course, is that economic factors do not help us to understand the relative commitments of

---

[42] Similar reliance on an essentially sociological approach can be found in Lloyd Fallers, *Bantu Bureaucracy*, chap. 10, passim; Huntington, *Political Order in Changing Societies*, pp. 60-61; and M. McMullan, "A Theory of Corruption."

[43] See, especially, Robert O. Tilman, "Emergence of Black-Market Bureaucracy: Administration, Development, and Corruption in the New States." Tilman argues: "Corruption involves a shift from a mandatory pricing model to a free-market model. The centralized allocative mechanism, which is the ideal of modern bureaucracy, may break down in the face of serious disequilibrium between supply and demand. Clients may decide that it is worthwhile to risk the known sanctions and pay the higher costs in order to be assured of receiving the desired benefits" (p. 440).

[44] James C. Scott, "The Analysis of Corruption in Developing Nations," p. 340.

public bureaucrats to their roles; the type of approach in this study seems more relevant for that.

The political approach suggested by Scott is valuable in that it directs our attention to corruption as a political resource affecting public policy, and therefore it must receive attention in any discussion of interest articulation and political influence in polities where corruption is pervasive. However, the explanation for corruption that emerges from this approach is incomplete, because it relies too heavily on the existence of formal structures as the independent variable. Formal structures that allow for political influence at the input stage of the political process may exist, but unless political actors know about them, understand how they operate, and have positive expectations about their use, they are unlikely to use them, and will attempt to avoid negative consequences of public policy by corruption at the output or enforcement stage of the political process. Conversely, political structures may allow for no real input of political influence from certain segments of the population, but if these segments believe that influence is possible, or at least more so than at the enforcement stage, corruption is not likely to occur. We cannot understand the relationship of political structures to corruption unless we understand the role orientations of citizens in relation to these structures. And these, of course, are a product of a socio-cultural environment. Finally, the political explanation of corruption, like the economic one, does not deal at all with the factors that affect the willingness of the bureaucrat to participate in the phenomenon. Even if the absence of open channels for exercise of political influence leads individuals and groups to seek to alter government policy at the enforcement stage, we are left without an understanding of when and why bureaucrats are motivated to cooperate with them. Administrative corruption is a two-sided relational phenomenon, and, I would argue, the analytic framework offered here, unlike the economic and political approaches, provides an understanding of both sides of the relationship.

VII

Organizational Commitment and Organizational Character: The Civil Servant's Role Orientation

Organizational Commitment and Organizational Performance

The last four chapters have focused on how, in Ghana, social pressure externally generated in the environment of the civil service tends to undermine one behavioral requisite of organizational effectiveness—the dependability of role performance. The difficulties faced by "transplant" organizations that involve social pressure from external role-sets—that is, the problem of boundary maintenance—were conceptualized as relating to the process of integration between organization and "host" society. There is, however, another dimension to institutional transfer that will influence operational effectiveness, and I have termed it *institutionalization*. Here I have in mind the way organizational members view the organization they work in and the roles they occupy—the extent and the content of their organizational commitment. For the influence of external role-sets on the behavior of the members of bureaucratic organizations is in part determined by the members' own commitments to the organization. If pressures generated by an external role-set conflict with the demands of the formal organizational role, then intense commitment to the organization can act as a counterweight, preserving organizationally dependable role performance. Furthermore, "institutionalization" can contribute to organizational effectiveness in another area, providing members with the motivation for spontaneous innovative behavior in the pursuit of organizational goals.[1]

Although most of the literature dealing with commitment to an organization has been concerned with the level of intensity, its content is equally important for the analysis of organizational performance. Individuals can identify with an organization in any number of ways, and these will fundamentally affect the way they behave. Earlier we discussed how organizational positions could be thought of as consisting analytically of two components: a role component—formally and informally prescribed behaviors relating to performance in the pursuit of organizational goals, and a status component—the esteem and prestige conferred on an individual by virtue of his occupation of a given position.[2] Now if commitment involves identification with role aspects of organizational membership, then behavior is likely to differ from the situation in which commitment is primarily to its status aspects. The former type of commitment would lead the incumbent to resist extraorganizational pressures that conflict with organizational performance, and to utilize behavioral decision criteria that reflect a concern for organizational goal achievement. In contrast, an organizational commitment that was of the same intensity but was directed primarily to status concerns would produce such behavior *only* in circumstances when failure to so behave would threaten the maintenance of the status perquisites of organizational position.

The behavioral consequences of this distinction between status and role relate to the difference between instrumentally and expressively based commitment.[3] Instrumental commitment is calculative, based on an assessment of material or status utility. Organizational commitment or identification that is predominately instrumental may or may not be positively related to eufunctional role performance, depending on how the organization handles the extrinsic satisfactions at its disposal. Thus a commitment of members to an organization on the basis of monetary rewards or career mobility will be related to effective role performance *only* to the extent that salary increases

[1] Cf. Chester I. Barnard, "The Theory of Formal Organization," in Robert T. Golembiewski et al., eds., *Public Administration: Readings in Institutions, Processes, and Behavior* (Chicago, 1966), pp. 33-39; see also Daniel Katz and Robert Kahn, *The Social Psychology of Organizations*, pp. 336-389; and Rensis Likert, "Measuring Organizational Performance," p. 41-50; Herbert A. Simon, *Administrative Behavior*, pp. 11-13, 198-199, and 218-219; H. A. Simon and J. G. March, *Organizations*, pp. 65-67.

[2] See pp. 14-15.

[3] See Katz and Kahn, *Social Psychology of Organizations*, p. 119.

and promotions are tied to such performance.[4] In contrast to the calculative nature of instrumental commitment, expressive commitment is consummatory; its basis is either enjoyment from role performance itself or identification with the goals to which one's role is contributing. When commitment is expressive, organizational activity is "instrinsically rewarding, it is directly expressive of the needs and values of the individuals involved."[5] As such, organizational commitment of the expressive type is likely to have a greater relationship to high levels of role performance—that is, to the investment of energy in role behavior and the utilization of organizational objectives as the basis of decisional criteria—than is commitment of the instrumental variety.[6]

Organizational Commitment and Organizational Character

In the study of administrative performance it is important to go beyond the assessment of the content of organizational commitment at the general level as predominately either instrumental or expressive, and to specify what particular goals, values, and methods constitute that content. Philip Selznick has pointed out that the set of perspectives on aims and methods that personnel come to share as they develop their identification with an organization create a virtual "organizational character."[7] In administrative organizations this means that a certain policy orientation is "built into" the organization through the values that members share and through their commonly held predispositions to certain methods and styles of operation.[8] When character is appropriate to, or congruent with, the current goals of an administrative organization, the result will be "increased reliability in the execution and elaboration of policy," with implementation oriented toward "its spirit as well as its letter."[9] But since goals can change, existing organizational character, based

[4] Cf. Victor H. Vroom, "Some Psychological Aspects of Organizational Control," pp. 75-77.

[5] Katz and Kahn, p. 119.

[6] Note that the distinction between expressive and instrumental commitment is similar in both definition and attributed consequences to the distinction made by David Easton between diffuse and specific support for a political system. It is also similar to Amitai Etzioni's distinction between normative and utilitarian compliance structures. See David Easton, *A Systems Analysis of Political Life*, pp. 153-230; and Amitai Etzioni, *A Comparative Analysis of Complex Organizations*, pp. 3-22.

[7] See Philip Selznick, *Leadership in Administration*, pp. 41.

[8] "The task of [organizational] leadership is not only to make policy but to build it into the organization's social structure. . . . This means shaping the 'character' of the organization, sensitizing it to ways of thinking and responding" (ibid., p. 63).

[9] Ibid.

on prior historical conditions, may also be inappropriate, hindering effective policy implementation. Thus in an analysis of public bureaucracy, an appreciation of the content of organizational commitment as it contributes to organizational "character" permits an assessment of the relationship between that "character" and the tasks assigned to the administrative organization by the government of which it is a part.

This has particular significance for low-income or "developing" countries like Ghana because of their special needs. In such countries, a heavy burden is placed on public administrative agencies as governments of new states seek increased rates of economic growth and greater social welfare. The policies enunciated to obtain these goals inevitably involve major departures in terms both of the social structures of these societies and of the conventional ways of doing things, since the conditions in which these changes are being made have often not been duplicated elsewhere. Further, these policies must be implemented within severe time and financial constraints. Time is at a premium because needs are often desperate, demands from an increasingly politically conscious populace are impatient, and a rapidly growing population often makes solutions at a later period far more difficult and costly. Furthermore, the relative poverty of the so-called developing countries means that they must "do more with less" if they are to achieve their goals. Thus, really effective administrative performance under such conditions will entail discovering financially cheaper ways of doing things than in the more economically advanced countries, so that more things can be done. Because of these needs and the constraints within which they must be met, effective administrative performance demands organizations with a character that entails high human energy inputs and self-sacrifice in the service of national development, and an orientation toward risk-taking, experimentation, and innovation—that is, an emphasis on goals rather than on rules.

The literature on public bureaucracy in Africa generally, and in Ghana particularly, offers little that could be called "hard" evidence on the level and content of organizational commitment, or the character of organizational identification. However, impressionistic observations on these subjects abound. There is a virtual consensus that the level of commitment to civil service roles or careers is high—a function of their relationship to political influence, material perquisites, and occupational mobility. However, since the high level of commitment to civil service posts is seen as a function of the monopoly on modern careers that the service held during the colonial era, the increased availability of alternative careers during the era of political independence is likely to complicate the picture considerably.

When we move from the area of intensity of commitment to the question of the content of organizational commitment and the "character" that it imparts to civil service organizations we find less consensus. One commonly held view is that, along with an intense commitment to the civil service, there is, especially at the senior ranks, a professional esprit de corps that incorporates values of public service and involves a commitment to national development and modernization. The civil service is seen as a dynamic institution in the African state, and civil servants are counted as an important segment of the "modernizing elite." Difficulties encountered by the public administrative agencies are related, in this view, not to the role orientations of its personnel but to deficiencies in technical skill, shortages of money, and interference by unsophisticated and venal politicians. In contrast, the impression that the civil services of African states—especially those in Commonwealth Africa—have made on other observers is of organizations dominated by a colonial character ("mentality") oriented more toward stability than change, more toward routine than innovation. And recently scholars with a neo-Marxist orientation have presented civil servants as members of a venal upper-class elite, whose commitment to their civil service roles is primarily in terms of the material privileges associated with their official positions and is unrelated to any commitment to national development.

The data generated by the surveys in this study provide an opportunity to assess these various views in light of empirical evidence, at least as far as Ghana is concerned.

Strength of Commitment to Civil Service Roles

Two items in the Civil Servant Survey indicate the extent or level of commitment that Ghanaian civil servants have to the civil service organization and their roles within it. Respondents were asked to suppose that they were advising an intelligent young man on his career, and to indicate what sort of career they would advise him to follow. When they had answered this question, they were asked, "What do you think of a civil service career for an intelligent young man?" It was reasoned that those respondents with a strong commitment to the civil service, those who valued their careers highly, would spontaneously recommend it as a career for an intelligent young man; that those who, when specifically asked about recommending a civil

service career, said it was a poor idea were weakly committed; and
that those whose recommendation of such a career came only after
the subject had been raised by the interviewer had a level of
commitment falling somewhere in between.

Table 31 gives a percentage breakdown of the careers spontaneously
recommended by the respondents. It can be seen that only 9 percent

Table 31

Career Recommended by Civil Servant Respondents

	Percent	**(N)**
Civil Service[a]	9.2	(40)
Professional (lawyer, doctor, engineer)	36.4	(158)
Accounting	5.3	(23)
Business	15.0	(65)
Skilled technician	12.8	(55)
Agriculturalist (modern farmer)	7.6	(33)
Teacher[b]	5.1	(22)
Military	.9	(4)
Not answered	7.7	(34)
☐ Total	100.0	(434)

[a] In Ghana it is possible for a person to be a doctor, lawyer, technician, etc., and also to be a civil servant. Answers that described this type of career were coded in the civil service category, while answers coded professional, technical, and the like, were those that implied dominant emphasis on the specialized career independent of any tie to government employment.

[b] In Ghana teachers are technically part of the public service, but not the regular civil service.

of the 434 civil servants interviewed spontaneously recommended the
civil service as a career. When those respondents who had not
mentioned the civil service were asked what they thought of it as
a career, an additional 30 percent said that it would be a good idea,
but 48 percent categorically stated that they would not recommend
it. Another 13 percent were unable to answer one way or the other.
In summary, only a minority, 39 percent, of the Ghanaian civil

servants interviewed seemed to be committed to, or placed a high value on, their civil service careers; as many as 48 percent suggested that the civil service was not worth the efforts of an intelligent young man. The responses to this interview item suggest that at least in Ghana the civil service career may not be nearly as highly valued as it is generally believed to be in Africa. Other items in the questionnaire corroborate the evidence obtained from the "career recommendation" series.

For example, one indication of the loyalty and commitment of members to an organization is their willingness to maintain their membership in the face of appeals from other competing organizations. Accordingly, the Ghanaian civil servants were asked, "Would you leave the public service if you were offered a job by a large and well-established private business firm under any of the following conditions: at a lower salary, at the same salary, at a higher salary."[10] While very few respondents said they would leave the civil service if offered a lower or the same salary, 72 percent stated they would leave if offered more money than they were making in the civil service. Only 27 percent evidenced a level of organizational commitment sufficient for them to state that they would not leave the service even if offered a higher salary by an outside organization.

It might be argued that the relatively small proportion of highly committed civil servants in the above figures resulted from the fact that the senior officers were not distinguished from clerks and other junior personnel. It is true that observers who speak of highly committed civil servants in the African countries are usually referring to those occupying the senior ranks. The data from Ghana do not support this proposition. When we break the sample down by rank we discover that high-ranking officers are no less likely to manifest weak commitment and no more likely to indicate strong commitment than are clerical officers. Table 32 shows this lack of relationship between rank and commitment to the civil service. The data reported are from the career recommendation series, and the strong, medium, and weak classifications correspond to those that were described earlier. A majority of all ranks said they would not recommend a civil service career to an intelligent young man. Practically the same proportion (almost 60 percent) of individuals manifest weak commitment to their roles among senior administrative personnel as among clerical officers. When it comes to strong commitments, the clerical

---

[10] This is an adaptation of a questionnaire item used by Alvin Gouldner to measure organizational commitment or loyalty in the United States. See his "Cosmopolitans and Locals: Toward an Analysis of Latent Social Roles—I."

Table 32

Respondent's Rank and the Strength of His Commitment to the Civil Service

Organizational Commitment	Rank			
	Low	Medium Low	Medium High	High
Weak[a]	58.5%	51.3%	52.1%	57.4%
Medium[b]	31.9	38.5	32.3	36.1
Strong[c]	9.6	10.2	15.6	6.5
☐ Total	100 (N=94)	100 (N=117)	100 (N=96)	100 (N=61)

NOTE: Only subjects who responded to the career recommendation series are included.

[a] Respondents who specifically said they would not recommend a civil service career to an intelligent young man.

[b] Respondents who said they would recommend a civil service career, but only after interviewer had raised the question of such a career.

[c] Respondents who spontaneously mentioned a civil service career when asked an unstructured question about what career they would recommend to an intelligent young man.

officers show, if anything, a slightly greater likelihood to manifest such commitment than do those in the top ranks.

A common finding in studies of organizational commitment is that length of tenure within an organization tends to increase the strength of commitment manifested by personnel.[11] These survey data indicate, however, that in Ghana the relationship between seniority and strength of commitment is ambiguous. Table 33 presents this relationship. First, it can clearly be seen that, on the basis of the operational index of organizational commitment that we have been using, the majority of civil servants at all seniority levels reveal weak commitment to their civil service careers, stating that they would not recommend such a career to an intelligent young man. However, the data suggest that weak commitment is more likely to be found among new entrants than among those who have spent some years within the service. But the effect of seniority so revealed is far from dramatic. The largest proportion of strongly committed civil servants

[11] For a discussion of this see Michael Crozier, *The Bureaucratic Phenonmenon*, p. 33; see also Simon and March, *Organizations*, pp. 73-75.

Table 33

Seniority and Strength of Commitment to the Civil Service

Organizational Commitment	Number of Years in the Civil Service		
	Under 4	5-10	Over 11
Weak	58.6%	52.0%	53.8%
Medium	27.6	36.3	38.6
Strong	13.8	11.7	7.6
☐ Total	100 (N=116)	100 (N=102)	100 (N=158)

NOTE: Only subjects who responded to the career recommendation series are included.

is also found in this group of new entrants. This suggests that while a large proportion (nearly 60 percent) of new entrants come with little positive affect toward the civil service and their careers in it, there is a small group, approximately 14 percent, that does enter with a highly positive orientation. The fact that the proportion of respondents manifesting strong commitment declines with level of seniority suggests that experience within the organization dampens the enthusiasm of some newcomers.

The finding that Ghanaian civil servants are on the whole not highly committed to the civil service, that they do not greatly value the civil service as an organization within which to pursue a career, raises a question about the sources of this low commitment. One plausible hypothesis is that, within contemporary Ghanaian society generally, the occupation of civil servant is less highly valued than competing occupations that carry more monetary or status benefits, and therefore for many civil servants current employment represents frustrated aspirations. The survey data provide some supporting evidence for this proposition.

If the hypothesis is correct, then we would expect those who are in the best position to qualify for alternative occupations and careers to be most likely to identify weakly with the civil service. Since formal education is the major source of career skills, we should find that those with the most education are the most likely to manifest a weak commitment to their civil service careers. And indeed this is the case. Although the relationship is not very powerful, the university-educated civil servants in the sample were somewhat more likely to say that they would not recommend a civil service career than were those with secondary-school, or only middle-school backgrounds. This can be seen in table 34. The main Clientele Survey provides

Table 34

Educational Background and Commitment to the Civil Service

Organizational Commitment	Educational Background		
	Middle School	Secondary School	University
Weak	53.7%	52.8%	61.0%
Medium	41.2	33.1	26.0
Strong	5.1	14.1	13.0
□ Total	100 (N=136)	100 (N=163)	100 (N=77)

NOTE: Chi Square level of significance for table is .05. Only subjects who responded to the career recommendation series are included.

further evidence in support of the hypothesis. Since the University of Ghana students who constitute the sample for this survey are among the most highly qualified in their society, their career aspirations are likely to be a good reflection of the relative value placed on various occupations by Ghanaian society generally. That is, since these respondents possess the requisite resources, they are likely to seek the careers that are most highly esteemed. Also, since the Ghanaian Civil Service recruits most of its new officers for the administrative class from the University of Ghana, the responses of this sample give a good indication of the orientations prevalent in the manpower pool from which the future top public administrators in Ghana will be drawn.

The University of Ghana student respondents were asked what career they would follow if they had a free choice, and were presented with a list of twelve occupations and space to add any additional ones. Table 35 presents the responses to this item, with occupations listed in the order of the frequency with which they were mentioned by the respondents. The evidence clearly does not support the general assumption that African students are particularly oriented to high-level administrative posts in the civil service. On the contrary, a civil

Table 35

Career Choices of University of Ghana Students

Career	Number of Respondents Choosing	Proportion of Respondents Choosing
Medicine	62	18.7%
University lecturer	57	17.2
Law	45	13.6
Business	35	10.5
Secondary school teaching	27	8.1
Management (private)	24	7.2
Civil service	22	6.6
Military	14	4.2
Politics	12	3.6
Farming	12	3.6
Police	11	3.3
Engineering	6	1.8
Other	5	1.6
☐ Total	332	100.0%
☐ No response	53	

The first three proportions (18.7, 17.2, 13.6) are bracketed together with the figure **49.5**.

service career ranked only seventh in the frequency with which it was chosen, representing the career aspiration of 6.6 percent of the 332 students who answered. The aspirations of Ghanaian university students are preponderantly toward the liberal professions of medicine, law, and university teaching, with medicine being most desired, receiving the choice of almost one-fifth (18.7 percent) of the respondents. Business and secondary-school teaching, generally believed to be held in low esteem as careers in African societies, both outrank the civil service as objects of career aspiration.

The lack of enthusiasm for a civil service career is not merely a function of predicted higher monetary rewards in alternative careers. This can be seen from the findings on another item in the survey questionnaire. The student respondents were presented with a list of four institutions—the civil service, a state-owned corporation, an expatriate (European or American) business firm, and a private Ghanaian business establishment—and were asked which they would most like to work for *if salaries were the same in all four*. Only 30 percent of the university students said they would prefer the civil service. Practically an equal number responded that they would most like to work in the American or European business firm, and the smallest proportion, 16 percent, said they would prefer the private Ghanaian business firm. Thus, even in this forced-choice situation, in which the professional careers that are most desired are not available, and in which pay among career options is equalized, there is no preponderate interest in civil service membership. These findings are consistent with those of Philip Foster, who studied secondary school students in Ghana. He, too, found that the desire for a civil service career was less widespread than is generally contended, with only 6.3 percent of his secondary school sample indicating a preference for a career in public administration.[12] Foster concludes his findings with a statement applicable to this sample as well: "Quite obviously these students do not conform to the familiar stereotype of a group oriented primarily to administrative . . . or bureaucratic-type occupations."[13]

In summary, the survey findings on the extent of organizational commitment in the Ghana Civil Service show that low levels of commitment are widespread throughout the service, and that these low levels of commitment tend to increase with increases in skill and qualification due to formal education. The findings obtained from

[12] Philip Foster, *Education and Social Change in Ghana*, p. 276.

[13] Ibid., p. 279. The availability of newly developed career options should not be seen as the only reason for the relatively low esteem in which civil service jobs in Ghana are held. In Ghana there is an historical basis to the contemporary occupational prestige ranking. The intensive and extensive commercial contact with the West experienced by the peoples resident on Ghana's Atlantic coast during the eighteenth and nineteenth centuries led to the development of an indigenous commercial strata of wealth and education. With the advent of colonialism, careers in the commercial sector (outside of petty trade) were made difficult for Africans to pursue, and so the younger members of the indigenous commercial "bourgeoisie" sought careers in the liberal professions of law and medicine. Consequently, in Ghana such professional careers were the most esteemed as far as the indigenous population was concerned, while in colonies without an indigenous commercial strata financially capable of seeking legal and medical careers, the civil service became the only avenue for career-status mobility.

the university student sample, as well as those of Foster for secondary school students, strongly suggest that the low level of commitment to the service displayed by civil servants is at least in part a product of an orientation that is generally characteristic of the social environment of the civil service organization. The civil service appears to be an organization that people enter because they have not been able for some reason to pursue some other, more highly valued career. Thus, for example, when the student respondents were asked which career they felt they would *actually pursue*, rather than which one they would choose, the proportion of respondents indicating a civil service career increased to 15.3 percent from the original 6.6 percent. Obviously a large portion of these Ghanaian university students who expect to enter the civil service would have preferred to do something else. This is consistent, of course, with the finding that the newest members of the service demonstrated the least identification and commitment, as measured by the career recommendation survey item.

Simply because a large proportion of civil servants place a low relative value on their careers, it cannot be inferred that they do not wish to maintain their positions, nor that there is a large turnover of personnel. These consequences are dependent on the availability of positions in the alternative, more highly valued types of organization. But since economic development in Ghana has not been great enough to expand the job market in relation to the growing manpower pool, these alternative positions do not in fact exist for the majority of dissatisfied civil servants. Thus 72 percent of the civil servant respondents said they would leave the service if offered a higher paying job outside, yet they remain inside, which indicates that such offers are scarce. Indeed, given the extraordinary growth in unemployment rates during the past few years, and the emerging potential of unemployment even for the highly educated stratum,[14] most civil servants can count themselves fortunate in having a job at all. Therefore, although the intensity of commitment to the civil service may be low for a majority of civil servants, this dissatisfied personnel is likely to remain "bottled up" within the organization and, paradoxically, highly concerned with protecting their positions.

Organizational Commitment: Content

At the beginning of this chapter I noted that in a study of the performance capacity of an organization the content of organizational

[14] See "Unemployment Has Become a Major National Problem," *Legon Observer*, July 16-29, 1971, p. 1.

commitment is important, as well as its strength or intensity. Intensity of commitment plays a significant part in determining the level of energy and motivation an individual is likely to direct to his role performance, and, should role conflict exist, it influences whether or not organizational role requirements will be placed above those of the other role-set. The content or nature of commitment, whatever its intensity, determines in what direction—to what ends—the energy invested in role performance is utilized. I have noted that the content of commitment can be conceptualized as either instrumental or expressive, with only the latter involving internal commitment on the part of personnel to organizational goals or role performance. I argued further that the nature of organizational commitment, because it involves personal identification with certain aims and methods, creates a particular organizational "character" and predisposes administrative agencies to certain types of policy and modes of operation. The Civil Servant Survey instrument contained items that bear on these aspects of the Ghanaian Civil Service.

To discover the nature of the respondents' organizational commitment, I simply asked them what in particular they liked about government work. In this way the reasons for any positive orientation toward the civil service that the respondents might have could be assessed. Table 36 clearly reveals that at the time of the interviews the content of the organizational commitment manifested by Ghanaian civil servants was almost entirely instrumental in nature. At the very most, 5.8 percent of the respondents gave reasons for liking civil service employment that indicated an expressive commitment.[15] Only 15 of the 434 civil servants interviewed liked their role because of some intrinsic job satisfaction, only 7 because it provided them an opportunity to help develop Ghana; only 3 saw the civil service as a way to serve people. In contrast, 322 respondents (74.2 percent of the total sample) liked government work particularly because it guaranteed them security. Concerning the security value of their civil service positions, most respondents had specific things in mind. The existence of a pension and the improbability of layoffs or dismissals were the most frequently given reasons for liking government work; pension was mentioned by 142 of the respondents, and "security of tenure" by 117. Another frequently mentioned security aspect of civil service employment is the "regularity" with which salaries are paid. Sixty-one respondents particularly like the fact that there was no

[15] The proportion may in fact be smaller than this, since the respondents were permitted to voice multiple reasons. Thus a respondent mentioning both job satisfaction and service would figure in the proportions corresponding to each category. Adding up the categories therefore may result in "double counting."

Table 36

Reasons Offered by Respondent for Why
He Likes Government Employment

Reasons	Percentage of Respondents (N=434)
Instrumental	
Provides security	74.2
Provides material benefits	15.2
Provides opportunity for upward mobility	4.4
Expressive	
Provides intrinsic job satisfaction	3.5
Provides opportunity to help develop Ghana	1.6
Provides services for people	0.7
Respondent likes nothing	15.2

NOTE: Percentage totals more than 100.0 because multiple reasons were permitted.

ambiguity or uncertainty as to the amount of money one would receive and when one would receive it. Respondents often combined all three types of security orientation in their answers. The content of organizational commitment revealed by this item varies not at all with rank, and only slightly with seniority. Thus 72 percent of the high-level officers in the administrative class said they liked government work because of the security it provides, as did 73 percent of the clerical officers. Turning to seniority, we find, not surprisingly, that officers nearing the end of their careers are more preoccupied with matters of personal security than are those just starting. What is surprising is the large proportion of juniors who resemble their seniors in the nature of their organizational commitment. Of those officers who have spent more than sixteen years in the service, 80 percent are security oriented, as are 70 percent of those with less than five years experience.

The organizational "commitment profile" that is revealed in table 36 is corroborated by the responses to other relevant items in the interview schedule. In the discussion of the strength of organizational commitment we noted that 72 percent of the respondents said that they would leave the civil service if offered a higher salary by a large and well-established private business firm. These responses, in addition to indicating a limited commitment to the civil service organization, indicate that at least approximately three-fourths of the civil servants interviewed have an instrumental commitment to the service, being willing to leave simply on the basis of a calculated monetary gain. In fact, this item shows the proportion of civil servants with a predominately instrumental commitment to be even larger. When the 117 respondents who said they wouldn't leave the service were asked why they would stay on, only 8 of these 117 provided a rationale with an expressive component—4 said that civil service work affords them an opportunity to make a contribution to Ghana's development, and another 4 answered that they found the type of work they were doing interesting, exciting, or well suited to them. Of the remaining 109 respondents—those whose reasons for remaining within the service are instrumental—all but 6 stress security considerations in their desire to remain within the civil service organization. In other words, of the 117 respondents who indicate that they would stay on in the service even if offered higher pay outside, a full 88 percent would do so primarily for considerations of security. Again, for this subset of respondents job security and pension are the main attractions, but this time job security appears of greater concern, being mentioned by 63 percent of the security-minded group, while pension rights are noted by 42 percent. Indeed, many of the responses to this question are striking for the extreme contrast between the feeling of job security within the service and perceptions of great uncertainty and vulnerability outside of it. Many respondents felt it unwise to move to a private business firm, no matter how large and well established, and no matter how high the salary, because in their view such an establishment might at any time collapse, with a consequent loss of employment, while the civil service would continue forever. The following examples are typical of such responses:

Higher executive officer, twenty-two years of service: "Generally, government never dies, but a big firm would one day collapse and an employee's future would be crippled. Thus there is much security in government employment."

Administrative officer, two years of service: "In the private business there is no guarantee that you would be employed permanently. Therefore if for any reason that business happens to collapse, all the employees would be laid off. On the other hand, if this situation confronts the civil service, arrangements could be effected to transfer or second such employees to other establishments in the same service, thus fulfilling their status as pensionable established officers."

Higher executive officer, three years of service: "Because a private firm could easily dismiss me at any time, whereas it is not easy to dismiss me in the public service. Moreover, a private firm could be dissolved when there is a slump and every employee would lose his job."

Administrative officer, one year of service: "I have the impression that the firms do not provide security and can collapse at any time. I feel there is greater security for me in the public service."

Not only do the survey data reveal that Ghanaian civil servants are oriented toward the civil service organization primarily in terms of the security it affords them, but they also indicate that those civil servants who are most strongly committed to the organization are also those who are most likely to be security conscious. This can be seen if, as before, we use the career recommendation question as a measure of organizational commitment and compare what strongly committed respondents (those who spontaneously recommended a civil service career) and weakly committed respondents (those who would not recommend a career in the civil service) say about why they like government work. Table 37 shows that civil servants who are strongly committed to their careers are more likely to be oriented toward them in security terms than those whose career and organizational commitment is weak. The difference between those who manifest strong and weak commitment is not very great, but it is statistically significant at the .001 level.

Table 37

*Strength of Commitment to the Civil Service
and Orientation Toward Security*

Security Orientation	Strength of Commitment	
	Weak	Strong
Mentions security as reason for liking civil service	69.9%	79.4%
Does not mention security as reason for liking civil service	30.1	20.6
☐ Total	100 (N=206)	100 (N=170)

NOTE: Chi Square for table significant at .001 level.

Results that corroborate the above are obtained if the relationship between commitment to the service and security orientation is examined in a different manner. Again take the career recommendation question as the measure of organizational commitment, but this time view those respondents whose recommendation of a civil service career comes only after an interviewer probe as less strongly committed than those who recommend it spontaneously. The latter group are found to be almost three times more likely to mention security in connection with their career choice—37.5 percent of those who mentioned the civil service spontaneously gave security considerations as their reason, and only 14.6 percent of those who recommended the civil service only after it had been mentioned by the interviewer.

Several interview items have been utilized to tap in different ways the content of the respondents' commitment to the civil service and their roles within it. Each of these has strongly corroborated the findings based on the other, and two conclusions seem warranted by the data: (1) Ghanaian civil servants, insofar as they are represented in the survey sample, are overwhelmingly committed to the civil service in an instrumental sense; only a small portion manifest a commitment based on an identification with the goals which the organization could and allegedly does seek, such as the development of Ghana and public service, or on satisfactions that are intrinsic to the role they are called on to perform. (2) The particular value that civil servants identify with the civil service and their role in it is that of personal and economic security.

Another striking aspect of these findings is how few respondents saw values such as national development, public service, modernization, and the like as related to occupational roles. When considering a career to recommend to an intelligent young man, only 19 percent of the respondents mentioned values of this sort as being relevant to such a choice.[16] While such findings cannot be considered conclusive

[16] One caveat must be kept in mind in assessing these results. As was noted in chapter 1, adherence to political ideology can affect the intensity and content of organizational commitments, and nationalist ideology can be an important aspect of commitment to public bureaucracy. The results just reported could have been modified after the military coup of 1972, which brought to power a group that increased the use of nationalist rhetoric and seemed to strike a responsive chord in some sectors of the Ghanaian population. It is by no means clear, however, that the post-1972 regime has actually produced enduring changes in the orientations of the Ghanaian populace. Note that the civil servants in this study were interviewed within just a few years after the fall of one of the most self-consciously ideological and nationalist governments in Africa, a government that had been in power for fourteen years. It seems far from certain that the present rulers have accomplished in two years what the Nkrumah government apparently was unsuccessful in accomplishing over a much longer period of time.

on the subject, they do open the question of whether the category "modernizing elite," often used for civil servants in low-income countries, is appropriate to civil servants in Ghana.[17]

The security orientation manifested by the respondents is suggestive of the types of role behavior they are likely to engage in, and of the sort of organizational character that will emerge from the combination of these behaviors. However, as I have argued elsewhere, personal orientations are only one in a number of vectors that shape human behavior. This is particularly true in bureaucratic organizations in which membership involves an occupational career, since the organization has at its disposal powerful rewards and punishments that can make some role behaviors either more beneficial or more costly than others, regardless of the individual actor's personal orientation. It is necessary, then, to look at the structure of rewards that is operative within the Ghanaian Civil Service before commenting on its organizational character.

Civil Service Incentive System

As I pointed out in the introduction to this chapter, an absence of performance goals in the role orientation of administrative personnel can be counteracted by an internal incentive system that is structured to encourage output. If personnel are instrumentally committed to the organization, then the incentive system can lead them to perform at high levels in their own utilitarian interests. Thus, within the Ghanaian Civil Service if maintenance of one's position and steady promotion depended on "productivity," then a security orientation would not preclude a motivation toward performance; indeed, it would come to depend on performance. But such an organization would be highly unlikely to be attractive to its members on the basis of the security it provides, because in fact it would provide little. Consequently, the fact that so many of the survey respondents see the virtue of the Ghanaian Civil Service as lying primarily in the security it offers is strong indication that the distribution of internal rewards has little to do with role performance. A brief glance at the structure of rewards will show that this is so, that the internal incentive system reinforces the lack of performance orientation manifested by its personnel.

[17] Findings strikingly similar to these, for Egypt, India, and Malaysia, indicate that placing civil servants in the category of "modernizing elite" may be of dubious validity. See Morroe Berger, *Bureaucracy and Society in Modern Egypt*, p. 74; Richard Taub, *Bureaucrats Under Stress*, pp. 75-76; and James C. Scott, *Political Ideology in Malaysia*, p. 138.

Simon and March have pointed out two important aspects of the relationship between reward systems and levels of productivity or performance.[18] First, the greater the dependence of organizational mobility on individual performance, the more likely personnel are to be motivated to perform well in their roles. Second, and very important, "the greater the subjective operationality of criteria used in promotion decisions, the greater the effect of the promotion system on the perceived consequences of action," or put another way, "the effectiveness of a system of rewards based on a given performance standard depends on how precise (subjectively) the standard is."[19] In other words, performance standards will only affect behavior in the desired direction if personnel clearly comprehend the criteria on which they are being judged, and the precise manner in which their performance on these criteria is linked to their mobility within the organization.[20] Only then can organization members have stable expectations about the consequences for themselves of one type of performance as opposed to another.

An examination of the internal incentive system within the Ghanaian Civil Service reveals that it does not meet the criteria of March and Simon.[21] Formally, mobility within the Ghanaian system of public administration requires performance. The Ghanaian Civil Service regulations are explicit on this point. They state: "In determining an individual civil servant's claims to promotion, account may be taken of efficiency, qualifications, seniority, experience, sense of responsibility, initiative and general behavior and, where relevant, his powers of leadership and of expression."[22]

If, however, we examine the actual criteria used to determine promotion, we see that they either are unrelated to performance standards at all or are related in a manner that cannot be subjectively operationalized and linked to precise standards by the personnel who are subject to them.

There are three bases on which promotion appears to be made in the Ghanaian Civil Service and which are used independently or in combination: confidential reports and recommendations of supervisors; competitive examination or personal interview or both; and

---

[18] Simon and March, *Organizations*, pp. 61-65.

[19] Ibid., p. 63.

[20] Peter Blau, studying a government employment agency in Chicago, found that the introduction of statistical records of performance increased productive efficiency, facilitated administrative control, and improved the relations between officials and their immediate superiors. See *The Dynamics of Bureaucracy*, pp. 36-56.

[21] This may be a characteristic of civil service organizations generally. However, Blau's research, described in n. 20, indicates that there are exceptions.

[22] Ghana, *Civil Service (Interim) Regulations, 1960), Article 36, Section 2, p. 14*.

seniority. The only one of the three that is in any way linked to performance is the confidential report of the civil servant's supervisory officer. Such reports can and obviously are supposed to take into account considerations of performance. But this method for regulating organizational mobility does not meet the Simon and March criteria, since the contents of these reports consist primarily of the subjective judgments of the supervisory officer. Consequently, those personnel being supervised cannot readily perceive operationalized standards of performance, that is, have stable expectations about precisely how their performance will affect their mobility. Many civil servants that were interviewed felt that the way to get a good confidential report was to maintain "smooth" relations with one's superior, and smooth relations were seen to be dependent more on "not being too outspoken" and showing proper respect and deference than on demonstrations of initiative or other forms of behavior related to high performance levels.[23]

Competitive examinations are administered to determine promotion between civil service classes—for example, for those in the executive class seeking entry into the administrative class—and between certain specialized grades within classes. Although the substantive content of these written examinations is unrelated to past performance, a departmental nomination is necessary if one is to sit for the test, and so performance criteria could hypothetically determine eligibility to enter the competition for promotion.[24] However, our comments about the confidential reports are applicable here as well. In some cases examinations are followed by personal interviews before the Civil Service Commission. Since the purpose of these is to determine the "personal qualities" of a candidate, they, too, cannot be said to provide an operationalized link between promotion criteria and past performance.[25]

Although seniority is only one of nine criteria listed in the *Civil Service Regulations* to determine eligibility for promotion, it appears to be in fact the major criterion utilized in the Ghanaian Civil Service. Data indicate that it is practically a necessary condition for promotion, if not a sufficient one. Table 38 presents a cross-tabulation of rank and seniority for all officers in the administrative class who hold university degrees. If performance were a major criterion used

[23] This probably explains in part the fact that almost 70 percent of the respondents interviewed said they would hesitate at least a little before disagreeing with a supervisor, and only 28 percent said they often told their superiors when they did not like some procedure on the job. Approximately 16 percent said they *never* expressed disagreement or complained to a supervisor.

[24] Interview with Secretary to the Civil Service Commission, January 5, 1969.

[25] For a description of the purpose of personal interviews see Gold Coast, *Report of the Commission on the Civil Service of the Gold Coast, 1950-51*, Vol. I, p. 24.

Table 38

Rank and Seniority: *The Administrative Class, 1968*
(Civil Servants Holding University Degrees Only)

Years of Service	Rank				
	Administrative Officer – Grade IV	Administrative Officer – Grade III	Administrative Officer – Grade II	Administrative Officer – Grade I	Principal Secretary
	% No.	% No.	% No.	% No.	% No.
Less than 5	96.4 (53)	0	0	0	3.4 (1)
5 to 9	3.6 (2)	100.0 (22)	0	0	3.4 (1)
10 to 12	0	0	84.6 (11)	0	0
12½ to 16	0	0	7.7 (1)	74.0 (17)	3.4 (1)
Over 16	0	0	7.7 (1)	26.0 (6)	89.8 (26)
□ Totals	100.0 (55)	100.0 (22)	100.0 (13)	100.0 (23)	100.0 (29)

SOURCE: Ghana, *Civil Service Staff List, 1967-1968.*

to determine eligibility for advancement, we should expect to find a considerable number of cases in which individuals have been promoted "out of turn," that is, hold ranks above most of the others who have entered the organization with them. Table 38 shows that this does not occur, at least in the more senior positions in the service. Out of a total of 142 cases, only 3, all principal secretaries, hold positions in advance of others who have spent similar amounts of time within the organization.[26] On the basis of the tabulation in table 38 it would appear that it is very rare for a civil servant to advance in rank until he has the requisite seniority. It can be inferred, then, that the promotional scheme of the Ghana Civil Service rewards seniority rather than performance. Of course, although seniority may be a necessary condition for promotion, it may not be sufficient. Poor performance could result in a failure to obtain the promotion for which a civil servant is made eligible by his seniority. If this were true, then we should expect to find a considerable number of individuals at ranks below others with whom they entered the service. Table 38 reveals that this phenomenon is rare also. In this case only 10, or 7 percent, of the 142 higher administrative personnel are in ranks below the majority of persons they entered the service with, which indicates that poor performance probably does not retard an individual's mobility within the organization. Other evidence would have to be available before any firm inference could be drawn from these figures (those who are not promoted may leave the service and therefore not show up in the statistics), but they do suggest that seniority is not only a necessary condition for promotion but a sufficient one as well. In summary, if performance rather than seniority is rewarded, a sizable proportion of individuals will hold ranks above and below others with whom they entered the organization. The Ghana Civil Service, however, as table 38 reveals, is practically "age-graded," each rank representing a homogeneous "seniority cohort."

Since these data are related only to officers in the administrative class, a similar tabulation has been made of rank and seniority for

[26] And these three were probably promoted more because of political influence stemming from former President Nkrumah than because of any exceptional performance on their part. Two of them were, during the early 1960s, prominent members of NASSO, the ideological "wing" of the Convention People's Party. (Cf. *Legon Observer*, August 2-15, 1968, pp. 4-6.) The third individual was also known to have political connections and was appointed directly to the position of principal secretary after having been turned down four years earlier for appointment at administrative secretary rank by the civil service commission. None of this indicates that these officers performed poorly. On the contrary, they may have been outstanding administrators. The point simply is that their promotions were probably not based on their administrative talent.

officers holding specialized posts in the Ministry of Education.[27] Here
we are dealing with a promotion ladder with three rungs—education
officer, senior education officer, and principal education officer. The
findings, presented in table 39, reveal the same pattern that was
apparent for officers in the administrative class—ranks are equivalent
to "age grades." Out of ninety-seven officers, not a single one is in
a rank more advanced than is appropriate to his seniority, and only
four are ranked below the other members of their "seniority cohort."

Table 39

Rank and Seniority: Education Officers (Institutional)

| Years in Service | Rank | | |
	Education Officer	Senior Education Officer	Principal Education Officer
	% **No.**	% **No.**	% **No.**
Less than 6	91.1 (41)	0	0
6 to 10	6.7 (3)	100.0 (38)	0
11 to 15	2.2 (1)	0	64.3 (9)
16 to 20	0	0	35.7 (5)
☐ Totals	100.0 (45)	100.0 (38)	100.0 (14)

SOURCE: Ghana, *Civil Service Staff List,* 1967-1968.

If this analysis is at all accurate, and performance is only marginally
related to mobility within the Ghanaian Civil Service, then we should
expect the respondents in the Civil Servant Survey to reflect this
in their thinking about the organization. In order to tap this dimension
of their role orientations I presented them with a description of two
civil servants, and asked which they thought would be promoted
first. One of these civil servants had what I would call a performance
orientation, shaping his behavior in ways that related to the achievement of organizational goals, while the second had a "ritualistic"
approach to organizational role behavior, strictly following rules in
every situation, regardless of the consequences for goal attainment.
The exact format of this item was the following:

[27] I considered only officers with university degrees, since the scheme of service, and
thus the established career pattern, is different for degree and nondegree officers.

Now suppose there are two civil servants in a department such as your own. The first follows regulations exactly in every situation. The second violates regulations in those situations where he feels the achievement of the department's goals requires it. Which of the two do you think is likely to be promoted sooner, the first or the second, or do you think they both have an equal chance?

In response to this question, only 99 (22.8 percent) of the 434 civil servants interviewed said that behavior oriented to achievement of organizational goals would be rewarded by more rapid promotion, and a full 76.4 percent of the sample expressed the belief that a civil servant behaving in a ritualistic, rule-dominated fashion would receive a promotion at least as rapidly. Of this group, 67.2 percent, or 51.2 percent of the total sample, felt that goal-oriented behavior would be negatively sanctioned—that the ritualistically oriented civil servant would be promoted sooner than the goal-oriented one. Not surprisingly, these perceptions are closely related to the respondents' understanding of which of the two types of bureaucrats their supervisors would think is the better civil servant. Sixty percent of the sample think that the rule-oriented or ritualistic bureaucrat would be favored by their superiors over a civil servant who was goal, or performance, oriented. If we remember that one criterion for promotion is the confidential report written by supervisors, and that departmental nominations are necessary to establish eligibility for promotion into certain ranks, we can see the clear relationship between these perceptions and the understanding that a rule orientation pays off in terms of mobility.[28]

This analysis of the incentive system in the Ghanaian Civil Service seems to indicate that the structure of rewards within the organization will not counteract, but indeed will reinforce, the general lack of a developmental or service orientation manifested by civil servants. Promotion appears to be based more often on seniority than on performance, and civil servants perceive role behavior that is ritualistic as being rewarded and that which is innovative and goal directed as being punished. When a primary concern with security on the part of personnel is placed in the context of such a reward structure,

[28] Civil servants in the higher ranks are somewhat more likely than those in the lower ranks to view a goal or performance orientation as positively related to promotion: while only 12 percent of the clerical officers thought the goal-oriented civil servant would be promoted first, 30 percent of the officers in the administrative grades thought so. At the same time, 70 percent of this latter group thought that goal orientation would be of no help in obtaining promotion, and one-half of this 70 percent thought it would actually harm the civil servant's chances.

it can be inferred that the organizational character of the Ghana Civil Service is not likely to be conducive to high levels of administrative performance in the pursuit of developmental goals. This combination of role orientations and reward structure is likely to produce a highly conservative posture toward policy and method—a preference for the routine, a reluctance to adopt practices that have not been tried in the past, a fear of the new and the risky, an overweening concern for rules and regulations. Furthermore, given the nature of the incentive system, the absence of any substantial expressive commitment to the organization indicates that not much energy is likely to be extended for the achievement of developmental and service goals. In sum, the orientation of Ghanaian civil servants toward their roles, in combination with the incentive system that is operative within the service, is hardly likely to produce that high level of human energy input and self-sacrifice, that willingness to experiment, innovate, and take risks that, as I argued earlier, are necessary for truly effective administrative performance under the constraints of scarce resources and limited time that exist in low income countries.

Security Orientations and Organizational Environment

The security orientation manifested by Ghanainan civil servants is not unusual for public bureaucrats in the so-called developing countries. Scholars concerned with the civil service organization in a number of different new states have all commented on the magnitude and prevalence of the phenomenon. Berger, in his study of Egyptian bureaucracy, found that only 7 percent of his sample said they entered the government service so that they could serve the community or out of some desire to perform a public service, while a majority entered for reasons relating to security.[29] Similar findings are reported by Richard P. Taub for the Indian Administrative Service and by James Scott for the civil service in Malaysia.[30] If findings have been similar, explanations have varied. Three types of explanations stand out: psychological, social structural, and ecological. The first mode of explanation stresses either personality variables or variables involving psychic disorientation. In the first instance socialization under colonial aegis is said to produce personality types

[29] Berger, *Bureaucracy and Society in Modern Egypt*, p. 74.
[30] Taub, *Bureaucrats Under Stress*, pp. 75-76; Scott, *Political Ideology in Malaysia*, pp. 138-144.

oriented toward security and bureaucratic ritualism.[31] The second type of psychological explanation views an orientation toward security, risk avoidance, and short-term goals as the consequence of a type of anomie induced by social change.[32] With old values destroyed by contact with the West, and the new values introduced by the West not yet internalized, the civil servant, this line of argument would contend, is set adrift without firmly rooted long-term values and goals, and so, to orient his behavior, he turns to the protection of short-term private and personal interests.

In sharp contrast to the psychologically oriented school are those scholars who seek an explanation for the security "mindedness" of "transitional" bureaucrats in social structural factors.[33] Here class-related variables are stressed. In this view the civil servants are an incipient ruling class in the new states—privileged, powerful, and set apart socially and economically from the mass of the population. From this perspective civil servants are not oriented toward development or service goals, simply because they have little identification with the new national unit or the "people" that inhabit it, except of course in terms of exploitation; their interests are class, not national. A security orientation is said to be the most effective way to serve this class interest because the ruling class in the new state has no independent economic base, and therefore it must depend for its well-being on the perquisites accompanying neocolonial domination by foreign business interests. The fact that many postcolonial civil servants received their training under the aegis of the colonial power is a second and reinforcing thread to this argument. Civil servants are viewed as having accepted the values of order and stability that are widely believed to have formed the character of the colonial administrative services, and as a result they manifest hostility toward policies and methods directed toward change and involving innovation and risk.[34]

The third mode of explanation for the dominant security orientation of public servants in low-income countries—the ecological approach—is associated with the work of James Scott on Malaysia. Scott argues that a security orientation is a rational response to existential

[31] See Lucian Pye, "Bureaucratic Development and the Psychology of Institutionalization," pp. 400-426.

[32] See Hahn-Been Lee, "Developmentalist Time and Leadership in Developing Countries."

[33] See, especially, Franz Fanon, *Wretched of the Earth*, pp. 119-164; also Rene Dumont, *False Start in Africa*; and Giovanni Arrighi and John S. Saul, "Socialism and Economic Development in Tropical Africa."

[34] See, especially, Geoffrey Bing, *Reap the Whirlwind*, p. 386.

reality in transitional polities: "Uncertainty about the future and instability are facts of life in transitional society and attempts to realize largely short-term personal goals represent a rational strategy against this background."[35] To Scott, transitional bureaucrats are committed to short-term gains and to narrow and personal goals because the uncertainties of the economic and political environment make commitment to long-term goals, such as development, too costly and hazardous.

The ecological approach adopted in this study is similar to the position argued by Scott in that I have constantly tried to show that civil servant behavior in Ghana is not the result of irrationality, ambivalence, and confusion, but rather a "rational" response of individuals to their environment. But my approach differs from that of Scott in that I have stressed the social aspect rather than the economic or political aspects of that environment—viewing the behavior of bureaucrats as a "rational" response to the values honored and demands made within the social fabric in which they are enmeshed. This general approach would seem to be relevant to the subject of this chapter also. Given the data already presented on the financial burden imposed on civil servants by their extended families, it is not difficult to understand why they would attach such importance to the security aspects of their careers. The demographic data in the Civil Servant Survey suggest that the majority of Ghanaian civil servants come from relatively poor backgrounds, many from families at the subsistence level.[36] From this, and from our knowledge of the size of the demands being made on them, we can conclude that most civil servants would have little to fall back on, if their salaries should decline, be delayed, or become unavailable. A loss of employment, even for a short period of time, or a postponement of salary payment, would in all probability, therefore, render the civil servant unable to meet his responsibilities to the extended family. Security, then, is strategically important for the civil servant in meeting his familial obligations.

Evidence on the social importance of meeting the responsibilities to "one's people" has been presented throughout this study, and particularly in the last chapter. However, one item in the interview schedule, not yet fully reported, permits a comparison of the social

[35] Scott, *Political Ideology in Malaysia*, p. 144.

[36] Only one-third of the respondents have fathers with occupations that could be considered middle-class professional. The fathers of a similar proportion are traditional farmers and fishermen. The paternal occupation of the rest of the sample falls into the "petty bourgeois" category—drivers, traders, minor clerks, and the like.

values attributed to the various sorts of role commitments under discussion—commitments to organizational performance, to national development, and to the types of things that necessitate a security orientation. Midway in the interview the civil servant respondents were asked which of seven types of men described to them did they think would be the most respected by people in Ghana. Each description involved a different basic value or goal orientation. The seven descriptions and the responses to the question are presented in table 40.

Table 40

Civil Servants' Perceptions of Type of Man
Most Respected in Ghana

Description of Man	Percentage of Respondents Perceiving Type of Man as Most Respected
1. He earns a high salary	3.6
2. He is liked by the people with whom he works	8.6
3. He is able to take care of his relatives and friends should they be in need	24.2
4. He has all the good things in life; a good car, a big house, fine clothing, etc.	24.4
5. He is better at his job than anyone else	7.3
6. He holds a position in which he has many subordinates who must obey him	2.3
7. He makes a contribution to the development of Ghana	29.6
☐ Total	100 (N=385)
☐ No response	(49)

Less than one-third (29.6 percent) of those who answered think that the man who has a commitment to national development will be the most respected. He is closely rivaled in the competition for social esteem by the man whose primary commitment is to his relatives and friends (24.2 percent), and by those who can afford to engage in conspicuous consumption (24.4 percent). If the earlier analysis of the significance of conspicuous consumption for the descent group is accurate, then in fact both man number three and man number four can be considered to demonstrate a primary orientation toward the extended family and allied personal relations. If such is the case, a commitment to "one's people" would be seen by almost twice as many of the civil servant respondents (48.6 percent) to be more highly esteemed than commitment to the development of Ghana. Income by itself, apart from the use of that income to benefit one's significant others, is perceived by the respondents as receiving little social merit in contemporary Ghana. Only 3.6 percent of the respondents believe that the man who "earns a high salary" will be the most respected of the men described. It is thought that little social esteem is offered to the man who is performance or achievement oriented in his job—he who "is better at his job than anyone else." To review these findings: a majority of the survey respondents viewed the fulfillment of obligations to the extended family as primary in the granting of social esteem, more important than contributions to the development of their country, occupational achievement, or simple income. In this context, the security of tenure and the regularity of salary payment, characteristic of the civil service, provide a permanent core of resources to meet familial responsibilities. As such, a security orientation is a rational "strategy" under the circumstances.

Recruitment Patterns and Organizational Character

If security is a rational strategy for the meeting of familial obligations, it is only one such strategy. A mobility orientation, for example, with its desire for rapid promotion and concomitant salary increases, would constitute another reasonable strategy for fulfilling responsibilities to the extended family. Also, the responses presented in table 40 suggest that there are a considerable number of individuals in Ghana who value a development orientation or an orientation toward job performance above commitment to one's relatives and friends. This raises the question of selective recruitment. Perhaps the Ghana Civil Service has a dominant security orientation in part because it recruits into its ranks those individuals most concerned about security and loses to other institutions those whose commitments are in other directions—toward mobility, development, or service. In other words, perhaps selective recruitment is operating to maintain a conservative, non-development-oriented character for the Ghanaian Civil Service.

Since the University of Ghana represents the main manpower pool for recruitment to posts in the administrative class, the clientele sample offers an excellent opportunity to investigate this proposition. It is true that this will provide data on only those entering the higher ranks of the service, but since it is individuals in such positions that constitute the leadership stratum within the civil service organization, they can be considered a strategic group in the shaping of organizational character.

The data generated by the Clientele Survey clearly show that University of Ghana students see security as the major element in the organizational character of the Ghana Civil Service. Like the civil servants themselves, the value which the students most often associate with civil service positions is the security they offer their incumbents. Student respondents were asked whether there was anything they would particularly like about the civil service as a career. The responses to this question are presented in table 41. Of the 202 respondents who could think of anything at all they would like about going into the civil service, the largest number gave the reason that it affords economic and job security to its members. Security, as a reason for liking a civil service career, outranks ability to contribute to the development of Ghana by more than three to one, intrinsic job satisfaction by twelve to one, opportunities for upward mobility by eight to one, and material benefits by almost four to one. Even if we enlarge the "development of Ghana" category to include those who say they would like the opportunity to improve the conduct of government, security is still the most frequently offered reason for a positive orientation to the civil service, by a ratio of almost two to one.

The fact that the civil service is viewed predominantly in security terms by individuals who make up the primary recruiting pool for top-level personnel has important implications for the organization. If the image or "character" of the service is viewed from the outside as oriented primarily to the security of its personnel, then it is likely to attract those individuals who are most security conscious, while potential recruits who are achievement oriented, or are interested in upward mobility or job satisfaction or in contributing to national development goals, will look elsewhere when choosing an organization within which to pursue a career.

The data from the survey of University of Ghana students indeed suggest that such a process is operating. It will be recalled that

Table 41

What Respondents Particularly Like about Civil Service Careers

Aspects Mentioned	Percentage of Respondents Mentioning Aspect[a]
Security	53.5
Opportunity to improve conduct of government	15.8
Opportunity to contribute to development of Ghana	14.9
Material benefits	14.4
Easy work	8.9
Promotion opportunities	6.4
Status	5.4
Intrinsic job satisfaction	4.5
Other	5.9
☐ Total number	(202)[b]

[a] Percentage totals more than 100.0 since respondents were permitted multiple responses.

[b] One hundred forty-nine respondents, or 42.5 percent of those answering the item, stated they liked nothing about a civil service career. Thirty-four respondents gave no response to the item.

respondents were presented with a list of four types of organizations—Ghana Civil Service, Ghana state corporation, private expatriate business firm, and Ghanaian private business firm—and were asked which of the organizations they would most like to work for if the salary offered was the same in all four cases. Then the students were asked the reasons for their choices. Although the choice of an organization was limited by the structure of the question, the reasons were obtained in a completely open-ended fashion. Table 42 sets out the reasons given by the respondents for choosing a career in one of the four types of organization. If we infer that the reasons given for making a career choice are an indication of the type of personal orientation a respondent has toward occupational roles, then we can

Table 42

Respondents' Institutional Choice and Reasons for Preference

Reasons for Preference	Institution in which Respondent Prefers to Pursue a Career			
	Civil Service	State Corporation	Expatriate Business	Private Ghanaian Business
1. Provides security	42.3%	12.9%	6.7%	1.6%
2. Material benefits	3.8	17.2	17.3	4.9
3. Mobility (promotion)	5.8	12.9	22.1	13.1
4. Intrinsic job satisfaction	7.7	34.4	18.3	29.5
5. Better working atmosphere	4.8	18.3	53.8	16.3
6. Makes contribution to Ghanaian development	35.6	25.8	1.9	44.3
7. Provides opportunity to improve institutions	15.4	13.9	0	14.8
8. No reason	0	5.4	6.7	6.6
☐ Total number	(104)	(93)	(104)	(61)

NOTE: Respondents were permitted to give multiple reasons for their career choice.

see from the table that respondents who chose the civil service are far more likely to be concerned with security than are those who chose any of the alternative organizations. Of those who chose the civil service, 42.3 percent are security oriented, compared with 12.9 percent of those who chose a state-owned corporation, 6.7 percent of those who would prefer to work for a European or American business firm, and 1.6 percent of those preferring a private Ghanaian business establishment. While representing only 28.7 percent of the respondents who answered the question, those opting for the service account for 68.8 percent of those mentioning security as a reason for their choice. The image of the service that these security-minded respondents project through their comments to the open-ended question is strikingly parallel to that expressed by the many security-conscious civil servants that were interviewed. Compare, for example, the following typical comments made by students to explain their choice of the civil service with the statements of the civil servants that were reported earlier in this chapter:

Because the civil service is an established organ of government and is not likely to break down while any of the others can find itself bankrupt and so collapsing.

The civil service makes a person's position permanent and secured. Unlike the other institutions which can declare you redundant when the time arises. That is, due to unforeseen circumstances.

It [the civil service] affords maximum security. You are not likely to lose your job when the corporation or other bodies have to be liquidated due to financial losses and incapability.

It [the civil service] is a secured and permanent establishment of the government and one would not fear to lose his job providing one is of good behavior. It is unlike other establishments which could be abolished anytime.

While the civil service is the most likely of the four alternative organizations to be attractive to the security-minded individual, the survey data suggest that it is the least likely of the four to attract individuals who are oriented toward upward mobility or who are concerned with the satisfactions provided by the nature of the job itself. Those exhibiting an orientation toward contributing to the development of Ghana are found in greatest proportion within the ranks of respondents who opt for the Ghanaian private business firm. Particularly illuminating are the responses in category (5), "better working atmosphere." Respondents choosing a career in a private American or European business firm are most likely to offer responses falling in this category, with a majority of 54 percent doing so. These respondents for the most part express a desire to pursue a career in an organization that is concerned with performance, rewards achievement, and is little affected by corruption.[37] Their responses are too numerous to permit a complete verbatim presentation, and so I have selected a number of typical statements as illustrations.

First-year student, arts major: "In the private expatriate business firm there is no idleness and malingering. One of its aims is to make profit and not deficit. Therefore, only conscientious workers are required. This closes the door of 'whom you know and not what you know' as far as nepotism."

Third-year student, administration major: "My work [in a European or American company] would be much more appreciated by my employers. Fellow employees are likely to be more cooperative. These will make me enjoy the work more and that's what I want."

Second-year student, arts major: "The organization [an expatriate firm] allows for fairness and promotion depending on the individual's own efforts and output."

Second-year student, arts major: "Promotion and other rewards would surely be awarded as a result of merit—I believe, judging by present Ghanaian standards today, that the management of the foreign business firm would be less corrupt and is likely to be made up of competent people."

First-year student, agriculture major: "With a private [expatriate] firm, I won't have to 'do something' before earning a promotion. Firms conduct in-service training for staff, and advancement to higher grades depends on the experience and degree of interest."

First-year student, administration major: "The European or American business firm is by far the most honest sector of Ghanaian economy. Expatriates instill the spirit of hard work into an employee's mind."

First-year student, agriculture major: "Tribalism and nepotism don't exist here [expatriate firm]. One has opportunities for further training and promotion."

What is most interesting and striking about responses like these is that they are offered almost exclusively by respondents who express a preference for careers in European or American companies. That is, those who through their responses manifest an orientation toward performance, achievement criteria, and a corruption-free environment see their best hope of obtaining these in organizations that are insulated from the Ghanaian social environment, insofar as leadership and control in the organization is non-Ghanaian. Some respondents explicitly make the connection between the Ghanaian social environ-

[37] In contrast, those respondents mentioning aspects of working atmosphere to explain a preference for the civil service refer to things like its laxness and its nonperformance orientation. For example: Second-year science student: "In the civil service there is less work to be done, sometimes you just sit down doing nothing. Also, you can go out at any time." First-year law student: "There is much freedom from actual work [in the civil service]. One can slack and go about leisurely."

ment and the types of things they would avoid by careers in expatriate-controlled firms. Thus one respondent, a third-year student with a major in one of the social sciences, felt that "the expatriate businessman is more concerned about employing competent persons without having to worry his head about who is a relative or a friend, and who is not.... And also, when it comes to promotion the person entitled to it will get it no matter who he is or where he comes from." Another respondent, in explaining his preference for the expatriate company, alluded to social pressures that would force him to be corrupt unless he were insulated from them by outsiders: "There [in an expatriate firm] my boss would be a foreigner and so I shall have the fear when trying to do anything corrupt.... To avoid being dishonest I have to be under a foreigner." A third respondent made a similar point but in a somewhat different fashion: "With the expatriate business firm the main basis of judgment about your work is your ability and initiative.... With the remaining three [civil service, state-owned corporation, private Ghanaian business] there is bound to be some interference, either politically or socially."

If expatriate businesses are viewed as providing an organizational context in which performance is desired and encouraged and in which corruption is severely limited, the data also show that University of Ghana students in large numbers see the Ghanaian Civil Service in almost the opposite terms. When they were asked if there was anything they would particularly dislike about a career in the civil service, the largest category of responses (31 percent) specified that the "atmosphere" within the organization discouraged hard work and dedication and made corruption difficult to avoid. Typical of these are the following statements by six respondents:

Second-year student, agriculture major: "It seems those working in the civil service are not kept busy working; either they do not have enough work to keep them busy or they choose to be lazy. I would not like to waste my talent and get 'rotten' as it were, doing practically nothing."

Third-year student, science major: "I cannot work as I would like to if I enter the civil service. When one works hard, he or she is told to relax because government work is not performed with might."

First-year student, medicine: "I would dislike going into the service because people talk evil things about a civil servant who tries to do his work well and does not accept bribes to fix [sic] people."

Second-year student, medicine: "I would not like to be in the civil service because the officials are dishonest and corrupt. Again they are inefficient in helping the growth of Ghana's economy because of carefree attitude officials adopt in going about with their work."

First-year student, social sciences: "If by going in [the civil service] I would become corrupt, if my friends and relatives would influence me in order to be giving them favors, I better not go into the civil service."

Second-year student, arts: "[I dislike the civil service career] because I may be corrupted, or may invite hostility from others in the service who would not like my stand against corruption."

In sum, the survey data show that the members of the strategic manpower pool from which the Ghana Civil Service draws recruits to its senior ranks tend to view the civil service organization as maximizing values primarily associated with personal security, and that a large part of this group explicitly sees the civil service as generating corrupt practices on the part of personnel and encouraging a negative orientation toward work and dedication. Further, the data indicate that the civil service is likely to attract those individuals who are most concerned about security, and that those persons interested in upward mobility, national development, achievement, and the like are more likely, if the opportunities exist, to seek employment in other types of institutions. This suggests that the service's essentially "conservative" organizational character, created by a combination of its internal reward structure and the security orientations of its personnel, is reinforced and perpetuated by a process of recruit self-selection.[38] While security-conscious persons are attracted to the civil service, the types of individuals whose personal orientation is more appropriate to effective "development administration" are likely to seek careers outside of the civil service, and often outside of Ghanaian institutions altogether. The results of the student survey indicate that those individuals who are most concerned with performance and achievement, and who wish to avoid corruption, are attracted to employment in expatriate business firms, seeing in these organizations a barrier between themselves and aspects of the Ghanaian social environment that discourage organizational performance and necessitate corrupt practices.

Conclusion

Neither the intensity nor the content of the commitment to the civil service revealed by the survey respondents suggests that the

[38] A small subset—15 percent—of those who chose the civil service from among the four alternative institutions said they did so specifically to get the opportunity to change what they saw as the "conservative" and corrupt character of the organization. For example, a second-year student gave this reason for preferring a civil service career: "The Ghana Civil Service is where irresponsibility, bribery, and corruption attain their highest proportions. Revolutionary changes are urgently needed there."

extent and character of organizational role orientations is likely to lead Ghanaian civil servants to resist externally generated role pressures. The attachment of most civil servants in the survey sample to their careers appears to be relatively weak, which suggests that their organizational commitment is not likely to override loyalty to such competing external reference groups as extended families, home villages, and the like. Moreover, because of the nature of their attachment to the organization they are unlikely to invest much energy in the performance of their official roles, even in the absence of conflicting obligations, or to be motivated to innovate in the direction of organizational goals. If civil servants were personally committed to values intrinsic to their organization roles, that is, if they maintained an expressive commitment to national development, service, achievement, performance standards, and so forth—then they might be personally motivated not only to resist counterorganizational role pressure but to concern themselves with high levels of role performance when no extraorganizational demands are being made, and to engage in spontaneous and innovative behavior in nonroutine situations.

However, the survey data indicate that Ghanaian civil servants are not especially oriented toward such values, and do not view their civil service roles in terms of these values. They are primarily concerned with security, and view their relationship to the civil service in terms of security. Such an orientation could produce "quality" role performance, but only if the internal incentive system of the organization were set up to do so and high levels of role performance, in ways appropriate to organizational goals, were made the prerequisite for security. But this, as I pointed out, is a contradiction in terms—the civil service is valued for the security it affords its members precisely because its internal incentive system is structured so as not to permit the manipulation of sanctions that would make the poor performer insecure.

The dominant security orientation of civil servants in low-income countries like Ghana is of importance for the process of modernization, and thus is of considerably greater significance than a similar orientation of civil servants in industrialized countries. The low-income states differ from the highly industrialized nations of the West in the role of government in the effort toward economic development. Much of the activity that contributed to economic growth and development in the industrial states took place in autonomous spheres, outside of government administrative organizations. However, in Ghana and elsewhere in Africa and Asia, government is the main, often the only, indigenous agent with the potential to mobilize and control the level of human and material resources necessary to affect economic and social change. If governments lack the organizational capability to meet this potential, there are no indigenous social entities that can, now or in the future, do the job autonomously. Consequently, an organizational character dominated by security consciousness which undercuts that capability is of far more consequence in countries like Ghana than in countries which in a different historical era were able to industrialize with far less reliance on governmental administrative agencies.[39]

[39] For a discussion of changing political imperatives consequent upon efforts to industrialize in the second half of the twentieth century, see Karl de Schweinitz, Jr., *Industrialization and Democracy.*

VIII

Conclusion

It isn't even that things are slow. Nothing works. There are dozens of organizations, supposed to take care of this and that. But if you want anything done you have to go running all round these stupid organizations themselves. ... The organizations might just as well not exist.

From *Fragments*, a novel about contemporary Ghana, by Ghanaian writer Ayi Kwei Armah

Behavior is considered to be *organized* when it is characterized by patterned activity of a cooperative and interdependent nature. When we speak of formal organization we refer to a conscious effort to establish such a system of cooperative and interdependent behavior through the assignment of roles to organizational membership, so that some goal or goals can be attained. Provided that the organizational structure, or technology, is rationally related to its purposes, it follows logically that the efficiency and effectiveness of a formal organization in attaining its goals depends on the degree to which members will behave, in routine situations, in the manner prescribed for their organizational positions and, in nonroutine situations, in an innovative manner that is informed by organizational goals.[1] The central theoretical thrust of this study is that in new organizations the occurrence of such behavior in a dependable and sustained way is determined by the relationship between organization and society. New role arrangements must, without losing their integrity, come to be integrated with role arrangements in the existing social environment—that is, mechanisms for the avoidance of role conflict

[1] Daniel Katz and Robert Kahn, *The Social Psychology of Organizations* p. 338.

205

must exist; and the new roles must be institutionalized—that is, they must come to be "infused" with social value.

In this study I have attempted to show that in Ghana the relationship between public administrative organizations and their socio-cultural environment is such as to inhibit the fulfillment of the two behavioral requisites for organizational effectiveness. I have argued, and have presented survey data to so demonstrate, that the social pressure placed on Ghanaian civil servants is such that organizationally dependable role behavior is unlikely, and that the values and reference groups to which commitment is socially rewarded are such that spontaneous innovation toward the accomplishment of organizational goals is minimized. This analysis has been placed within an explanatory framework which I believe has broad relevance to transitional-type states in the contemporary world generally and to postcolonial states especially. At the most general level, I have proposed that administrative performance suffers in such polities because of institutional malintegration, the existence of structurally differentiated organizations in an unsupportive socio-cultural environment, the consequence of a period of historical emulation, whereby institutions associated with the highly industrial states have been transferred, in a least their formal aspects, to the preindustrial states of the "third world."

At a less abstract level, and focusing on Africa, I have argued that the corporate nature of social organization in traditional African societies, and the related but more general gemeinschaft orientation toward social interaction that predominates in such systems, do not provide cultural legitimacy for the compartmentalization of personal and official roles. In consequence, when formal bureaucratic organizations are transplanted to such societies, it is very difficult, from the point of view of social survival, for personnel in the performance of their bureaucratic roles to maintain the necessary universalistic posture and requisite commitment to national development and service goals. The social environment in which public servants are enmeshed demands commitment to other reference groups and the fulfillment of obligations to other, competing role-sets. Obtaining social approval and esteem necessitates the violation of the norms and requirements of the organizational role-set, so that precedence can be given to the obligations of some other personal role-set or tradition-oriented mode of social behavior. In such a situation organizational role performance is undependable, and organizational goals are not likely to mobilize a sufficient quotient of the membership's energy to produce spontaneous and innovative behavior in the pursuit of organizational achievement. In short, the vector of social pressures which social psychologists have found so important in the shaping of human behavior is directed against the needs of organizational effectiveness.

Status versus Role Institutionalization

Implicit in this discussion is a general model of institutional transfer under colonial auspices, applicable in principle to military bureaucracy, political parties, legislatures, universities, and the like, as well as to civil service organizations. In his seminal article on institutional transfer and social change, C. S. Whitaker argued for a "dysrhythmic" conceptualization of change.[2] Against the commonly held notion that "once the penetration [of modern patterns] has begun, the previous indigenous patterns always change, and they always change in the direction of some of the patterns of the relatively modernized society,"[3] he proposed that in fact a good deal of the structure and behavior of preexisting social systems (the "traditional" society) has sustained itself in the face of penetration by Western ("modern") institutional forms. Although I differ with Whitaker over the consequences of such a process of change, this study does support his description of the process as basically dysrhythmic.[4] I have sought an understanding of the process of dysrhythmic change through the concept of status versus role institutionalization.

[2] C. S. Whitaker, Jr., "A Dysrhythmic Process of Political Change"; see also, *The Politics of Tradition*, conclusion.

[3] Whitaker, "A Dysrhythmic Process," p. 215.

[4] He seems to be inferring functional compatibility between traditional and modern institutions from the fact that the introduction of a formally modern political party in Northern Nigeria did not undermine traditional political structures, and indeed in some ways strengthened them. But my reading of Whitaker's own evidence belies this inference. Whitaker's own presentation suggests a case in which a political party whose constitutional form, and early operation, included what he terms modern elements—universalism, egalitarianism, achievement criteria, political participation—was soon penetrated and in fact transformed by the traditional political system of the Hausa-Fulani emirates, leaving an organization that was modern in only the most formal sense, and traditional in the substance of its operation and behavior.' "Prior to 1952, when parliamentary government was established, the NPC was controlled by a majority whose occupations, traditional social status, and political attitudes placed them outside the sphere of traditional elite membership and loyalty. . . . After 1952, control of the party passed to persons loyal to and dependent upon the emirate bureaucracies. . . . The apparatus of the traditional bureaucracy double[d] as the organizational machinery for the party. Having gained control of the party, the new dominant faction voted in 1957 to 'freeze' the slate of elected party officers, and no further voting was ever held. Indeed, after 1957, no open congresses of the party were held. . . . After 1953, NPC party nominations for parliamentary seats were monitored by and subject to

As I see it, the process of structural emulation that is a part of the colonial legacy has involved the institutionalization of new forms of social organization more in their status than in their role aspects. The status perquisites that accompany the positions that make up these new social structures do not manifestly threaten existing forms of social organization. Rather, the emulative structures open up new channels whereby already existing ("traditional") social groups can compete for status and wealth. By itself, the status aspect of the new positions does not demand a redefinition of the basis of traditional social solidarity and customary behavior, and thus it can easily be accepted, without appearing, on the surface, to conflict with existing social forms. The role aspects of the new positions, in contrast, involve the introduction of new performance standards, behavioral norms, and goal orientations. Consequently, their social acceptance entails the adoption of new forms of identity, value commitment, and social obligation, which make the role aspects of emulative organizations fundamentally threatening to existing forms of social organization in the host society. Since the status aspects of the new structures can be incorporated into a traditional struggle for status and power, these structures come to be highly prized for the resources they can provide, before they are prized for the values, goals, and performance standards that constitute their roles. It is in this sense that we can say that colonially inherited structures have been institutionalized more in their status than in their role aspects.

The result of this type of institutionalization is organizational behavior characterized by a great deal of formalism. Role incumbents demonstrate an extreme concern for ritualistic expression—that is, they are concerned to publicly verify the status attributes of their positions—while they reveal comparatively little interest in performance, or in goal attainment. There will be a great deal of social support for behaviors that enhance and reflect on their status and by extension the status of those they are personally associated with, but little such support for behavior that demonstrates a commitment to role performance. Indeed, to the extent that such performance interferes with personal relationships, it will generate social disapproval.

---

the approval of the emir."

What this description suggests is the utilization of a new organization by a traditional group in order to maintain and enhance its own status, while at the same time the modern role orientations of the new organization are replaced by traditional ones. This type of adaptation can be said to be functional from the perspective of the traditional political system, but can it be said to represent compatibility between modernity and tradition? In what sense was the NPC, after 1952, a modern organization? See Whitaker, "A Dysrhythmic Process," pp. 109-210.

Social Change, Political Development, and Organization Building

If political development at its most basic level is viewed as the process whereby the institutions of societal decision-making acquire increased capacity to control their material and social environment, then the creation of effective governmental administrative organizations can be seen as central to the process. In the perspective developed during this study a major obstacle to this aspect of political development is an unsupportive socio-cultural environment. As I see it, the creation of social support for the behavioral requisites of administrative performance involves the creation of harmony between new organizational role-sets and role-sets existing in the extraorganizational social environment. There are two logical ways in which this harmony could be established. One is for the modern organizational role-set to merge with and dominate the traditional corporate role-set. In such a situation the organization itself becomes the corporate group, and its norms and goals are the expression of corporate group identity and solidarity. This solution may approximate the path to modernization traveled by Japan. The organizations that emerge differ greatly from the classical Weberian bureaucracies of the West, but a strong commitment to organizational goals and social support for organizational role performance provides the basis for administrative effectiveness. The Japanese solution may, however, be of limited applicability to other "transitional" societies because of the unique character of Japanese traditional social organization. Here the corporate kinship unit is of limited significance, and it is subordinated to another corporate membership group, the household or *ie*, which is based on *work* rather than on descent.

The kinship which is normally regarded as the primary basic human attachment seems to be compensated in Japan by personalized relation to a corporate group based on work, in which the major aspects of social and economic life are involved. . . . This is the basic principle on which Japanese society is built.[5]

The traditional household, or *ie*, then, is a group based not on consanguinity and affinity but rather on participation in an integrated productive or occupational activity. The role of the *ie* institution as the basic unit of society in premodern times is played in the contemporary period by the modern company or unit of employment —thus the use of the expression "one railway family" (*kokutetsu-ikka*),

[5] Chie Nakane, *Japanese Society* (Berkeley and Los Angeles, 1970), p. 7.

which signifies the Japanese National Railway.[6] With the unit of occupational activity defined as a total institution, a dominant corporate group that subsumes the relevant kinship unit, there is no conflict with family roles , and therfore no need for the mechanism of role compartmentalization. Marion J. Levy makes this clear in his discussion of the relationship between traditional family obligations and official positions in Japanese "feudal" administrative structures:

Family, friends, feudal loyalties, everything he [the traditional bureaucrat] had been taught to respect, all of them, in both fact and ideal required the maximum objective use of his talents in the roles for which he was selected. The conflict between the betterment of one's family and the proper fulfillment of office so common in China was not to nearly the same degree a problem here because one's family and one's office were combined in this case.[7]

In summary, the Japanese institution of the household, defined in terms of a work unit rather than as a kinship unit, provided a mechanism for traditional integration and administrative centralization, which, moreover, could be adapted to and made supportive of effective organizational behavior in the contemporary era.

The features of social organization that made possible the Japanese solution to role integration do not appear to exist widely elsewhere. In a country like Ghana the nature of traditional social organization is quite different. The new state is an amalgam of numerous peoples with separate identities, and these in turn are composed of many small and decentralized, indeed often autonomous, kin-based corporate groups. Although such an arrangement may permit the merger of small business enterprises with family corporate groups, it hardly permits the use of traditional corporate identities and forms of behavior to bolster large-scale economic and political organizations. The traditional social organization characteristic of Ghana would seem to preclude the Japanese approach and to make mandatory the second avenue to institutional integration. This involves, on the one hand, a process of nation building through which public bureaucracies and their component roles are legitimized as parts of a new and more extensive community, and, on the other hand, the development of a socio-cultural environment that permits the social com-

---

[6] Ibid.

[7] Levy, "Contrasting Factors in the Modernization of China and Japan," *Economic Development and Cultural Change*, October 1953, p. 180.

partmentalization of official and personal roles. This implies a fundamental change in traditional social organization: a shift away from
the corporate kinship group as the basis of social solidarity and
psychological identity, and movement toward the "autonomous"
individual and impersonal interdependence as the foundations of
identity and solidarity. In change of this type the extended family
as an interacting social unit is not necessarily destroyed, but there
is a basic redefinition of the nature of membership and obligation,
so that a social context exists in which behavior that is non-kin-relat-
ed, and is even in conflict with family interests, can be morally
acceptable under certain circumstances. Nor does this sort of change
require the glorification of individualism—the worshipping of interpersonal competition and "rugged individualism"—but it does entail
the conceptualization of the individual as, in principle, possessing
a social existence and worth of its own, without reference to any
particular group to which it happens to belong. In this way a path
is cleared for the social actor to stand outside of the groups to which
he belongs, and thus a socio-cultural mechanism is created that can
limit role conflict in situations of multiple group membership.

I have attempted to show in this study that change of this type
is of limited scope in contemporary Ghana, and that this limitation
is at the root of her problems with the performance of public
administrative bureaucracy. Modernizing social change has certainly
begun, a consequence of social arrangements introduced by colonialism, and of the exposure of Ghanaian society to the international
communications system. But these changes are neither as swift nor
as basic as they were thought to be at the beginning of the 1960s.
The involvement of individuals in cash crop production and wage
labor has not been incompatible with maintenance of the corporate
extended family, which continues to perform important functions
as a manpower pool for the farmer and a "social welfare agency"
for the laborer. Even in bureaucratic institutions, where the formal
aspects of organization conflict with kinship obligations, the operation
of the institution need not interfere with continued loyalty and
responsibility to kin-based corporate groups, as long as the organization's role requirements are not enforced by informal and formal
mechanisms. We have seen in this study that some individuals have
a greater personal commitment to modern role orientations than
others have—this is particularly true of individuals with extensive
and intensive exposure to Western-influenced higher education. But
these individuals do not make up the type of cohesive social group

that could offer social support for new forms of role behavior. Rather, they are tied into social networks of more traditionally oriented individuals who exert social pressure for the maintenance of behavior that is appropriate to traditional kin-based corporate groups. Since an integrated system of psychological commitments, role expectations, and social sanctions takes a long time to break down, it is reasonable to suppose that in most instances the emergence of a cultural system supportive of modern bureaucratic roles is a gradual and lengthy process.[8]

The period of time needed to overcome the malintegration of bureaucratic organizations and their environment can be dramatically shortened if the administrative structures of society come to be dominated by a "deviant" subcultural solidary whose system of norms and values is supportive of administrative role orientations. By virtue of membership in such a group, individuals are cut off from external social memberships and are thus more or less immune from role expectations and social pressure emanating from the larger society. At the same time, they will receive social support from other members of the deviant subculture for role behavior that is organizationally eufunctional. Weber's discussion of Calvinism suggests the historical role that one such deviant subculture played in the economic development and modernization of Western society. Morroe Berger has suggested that in the contemporary nonindustrial states public bureaucracy itself can become the basis for such a modernizing subculture. He argues that the development of a sense of civil service professionalism will lead to a situation in which bureaucrats provide each other with the social support that is needed to improve organizational role performance.[9] But, bureaucratic occupations do not provide the necessary isolation of members from the social pressures originating in an unsupportive social system; and professional civil service ideology does not usually reject the existing socio-cultural order sufficiently, nor draw sufficient emotional commitment, to encourage individuals to resist these culturally based social pressures. This certainly seems to be the picture that emerges from this study of Ghanaian civil servants, and studies of other

---

[8] On the development of bureaucracy in the West, Max Weber writes: "The modern organization of the civil service separates the bureau from the private domicile of the official, and, in general, bureaucracy segregates official activity as something distinct from the sphere of private life. . . . *The condition is everywhere the product of a long development . . . . The beginnings of this process are to be found as early as the Middle Ages*" . (Max Weber, "Bureaucracy," in Hans Gerth and C. Wright Mills, eds., *From Max Weber*, p. 197). Emphasis added.

[9] Morroe Berger, *Bureaucracy and Society in Modern Egypt*, p. 124.

societies give similar indications.[10] Civil servants often form interest groups that seek to further and protect the social, political, economic, and professional standing of their numbers. Interest groups, however, are not deviant subcultural solidaries; they differ from these in the two respects that are central to this discussion—in their relationship to the larger society and in the extent of their internal solidarity.

Another group that can be considered potentially able to act as a modernizing solidary is a military organization that seizes political power. A number of obvious features make such organizations likely candidates for such a role: characteristically the military is organized in a manner that isolates its personnel from the larger society, and it is an institution generally characterized by high levels of internal discipline. A variety of factors, however, make success in such a role highly problematic generally, and in African states particularly. First, experience indicates that the cohesiveness and discipline that characterize military organizations before they play political roles tend to be substantially undermined once the military assumes political power. Solidarity depends on the maintenance of the type of geographic and functional isolation from the larger civilian society that is rooted in specifically military activity.

Second, it is by no means clear that the organizational commitments and role orientations that are functional in a specifically military context are easily transformed into a generalized intense commitment to developmental goals and to role orientations that are functional within civilian bureaucracy. Will the social support that encourages role dependability in the officers' mess, in the barracks, and on the battlefield be necessarily transferred so as to encourage dependable role behavior from military personnel who are assigned to the Ministry of Trade? Third, even if such were the case, military organizations are limited in the manpower they can commit to civilian bureaucracy by the need to maintain a viable military organization. Fourth, and most generally, the very type of isolation from civilian society that characterizes the military, and the concommitant apolitical, indeed antipolitical, ideological orientation that most officer corps possess, raises questions about the general political leadership capability that the military as an organization can provide. The types of problems that military officers are socialized to deal with are not likely to be similar to those they will face in political roles, nor are the methods they have been taught necessarily relevant

---

[10] See Morroe Berger's own work on Egypt, passim; see also, Richard Taub, *Bureaucrats Under Stress*; see also, James C. Scott, *Political Ideology in Malaysia*.

to the solving of these new problems. Moreover, the very isolation that may make military personnel relatively immune from social pressures emanating from society may also mean that the military organization and its personnel are uninvolved with and sometimes contemptuous of civilian society, attitudes unlikely to facilitate successful political leadership.

In the contemporary nonindustrial world the clearest examples of "deviant" subcultural solidaries that have been able to dramatically reduce the dysfunctional relationship between bureaucracy and society are Leninist political parties. Like early Calvinism, a Leninist party is a self-conscious social movement whose system of belief includes a rejection of the existing socio-cultural order, and whose members, by virtue of belonging to a deviant group, tend to be cut off from involvement with and concommitant social pressure from the traditional society.[11] When such parties succeed in seizing political power, they can, to some extent, short-circuit the effects of the traditional socio-cultural environment on public bureaucracy by ensuring that their cadre dominate and control these institutions.

Of course, the postcolonial governing elites in Ghana, as well as elsewhere in Africa, have—for better or for worse—not been leading a disciplined revolutionary political party. Consequently, they are less likely to be able to short-sircuit the dysfunctional effect of society on the performance of public bureaucracy, and inadequate administrative effectiveness becomes an endemic problem. It is true that after 1960 in Ghana the Nkrumah regime can be said to have attempted a Leninist-type strategy. Ideally, the Convention People's Party was made the society's focal institution. Its ideological mission was upgraded, all other major institutions were "seeded" with its cadre, and all with the purpose of penetrating and transforming the society. But for reasons that go beyond the scope of this study, the aspiration to turn the CPP into a vanguard party never became a reality. In the final analysis, the society penetrated the party; the CPP came to reflect Ghanaian society, but in a far different sense than Nkrumah had intended when he coined the phrase "Ghana is the CPP; the CPP is Ghana." As a mechanism to control and upgrade

---

[11] Jerry F. Hough, in a highly illuminating study of the Soviet Communist Party, found that during the 1920s and 1930s there were repeated party purges which "often centered on members who found it difficult to break their ties with the past—who still retained an interest in family land, who visited their villages in a suspiciously frequent way, who tried to maintain some contact with religion, etc." ("The Prerequisites of Areal Deconcentration: The Soviet Experience," paper presented to the seminar on the spatial aspects of development administration, University of Pittsburgh (July 1965), pp. 31-32).

the performance of public bureaucracy, the party, therefore, was of little use.[12]

The thrust of this entire work points to the conclusion that, in the absence of a politically dominant "deviant" solidary, the ability of governing elites to create effective administrative organizations, no matter what their personal commitment, is severely limited. For the present leaders of Ghana, as well as for the leaders of most if not all African states, the arena of feasible and effective policy choice in this regard will remain somewhat constricted. But within this constricted arena there are a number of policies which either are being or could be pursued. First there are the technical solutions to the problem—organizational restructuring and staff training. Such policies, I would argue, will produce little effective reform, since the socio-cultural environment will continue to undermine effective role performance. Indeed, the experience of Ghana during the past twenty years is a testimonial to the failure of this type of reformism. Organizational restructuring—the redrawing of ministerial responsibilities, the shifting of departments from one part of the bureaucracy to another, the creation of new bureaucracies outside the civil service structure, and the like—has been a fairly ubiquitous feature of government policy during each of Ghana's political regimes. But the degree to which problems persist, and the fact that the same agencies —for example, the Ministry of Agriculture or the Cocoa Marketing Board—are repeatedly the targets of reform, indicate that little success has resulted from technical solutions to inadequate administrative performance.[13]

One way to insulate bureaucratic personnel from the organizationally dysfunctional effects of external social ties is to adopt a policy of assigning administrators to posts in areas that are far from their homes.[14] Such policies have indeed had wide historical application. The traditional Chinese bureaucracy, for example, explicitly utilized

[12] The Nkrumah experience may offer a general lesson for radical regimes that pursue state-directed modes of economic development. Unless they possess a vanguard organization that can perform the function of insulating public bureaucracy from its social environment, they are likely to find that their developmental strategy and public policies rapidly outrun their organizational capacity.

[13] See Ghana, *Annual Estimates, Ministry of Agriculture* (1961, 1962, and 1963 editions); see also, *West Africa*, No. 2937 (September 24, 1973), pp. 1327- 1328; and, "Hackman's Expanding Cocoa Empire," *African Development*, May 1972, pp. 6-7; "The Ghana's Government's Businesses," *West Africa*, No. 9528 (July 23, 1973), p. 985.

[14] The Civil Servant Survey indicates that at the time this study was undertaken no such practice was followed in Ghana. The ethnic composition of the four administrative centers from which the survey sample was drawn was reflected in the distribution of ethnic background among the respondents. In each case the indigenous ethnic group predominated among the civil servants posted at these centers.

such a policy—"the law of avoidance"—so as to limit the influence of kinship and village ties on the magistrate. This type of policy, however, has at least one significant negative feature: in a culturally plural state the effectiveness of an administrator may be hampered if he is unfamiliar with the language and customs of the area in which he is stationed.

Another way to increase the dependability of role performance is to establish incentive and disciplinary systems that are related to performance, and that can be manipulated so as to enhance organizational accomplishment. Since the status perquisites of organizational membership and mobility are highly prized by the official's traditional membership group, the social pressure that would normally undermine role performance will be directed toward the support of such performance, if it is clearly perceived that poor performance will lead to a loss of such perquisites. Incentives can be structured in such a way that high levels of administrative performance are necessary if the corporate kinship group is to obtain the benefits it desires. This paradoxical situation offers an important lever to policy makers interested in improving the effectiveness of public bureaucracy. However, it is far more difficult to grasp the lever than might be apparent at first.

To begin with, the establishment of an incentive and disciplinary system of this type requires the dismantling of inherited civil service rules and regulations that were designed to give personnel security by building in various layers of procedural protection against the wielding of sanctions by organizational leadership. It is doubtful whether the contemporary political leadership in Ghana, or elsewhere in Africa, would have sufficient political support to engage in a drastic restructuring of the existing "scheme of service" in public bureaucracy, even if it were so inclined.[15] Paradoxically, such a policy, although it would improve administrative performance and thus

---

[15] The Nkrumah government often threatened to introduce a new disciplinary system into the civil service, and it abolished the Civil Service Commission to gain greater control over the service; but the degree to which it actually modified customary procedures in recruitment, promotion, and discipline appears to be far less than the political rhetoric of the regime has suggested. The later Busia government "sacked" several hundred public servants shortly after it came to power, but these firings appear to most observers to have been motivated by political and ethnic concerns more than by considerations of faulty administrative performance. The present military regime has sanctioned the practice of "drilling," whereby an army officer who is displeased with the behavior of a public servant forces the official to publicly engage in a strenuous and humiliating display of calisthenics. Although such a "system" of discipline may well lower morale, it is not likely to create a general improvement in performance levels, since its use is based on chance and whimsy; it is not systematically related to the behavior of personnel.

enhance the legitimacy of the political regime over the long term,[16] will undermine political support for the regime in the short term because it threatens the interests of a politically and socially strategic group.

Beyond this, there is the problem of finding a cadre of supervisory personnel genuinely committed to the role aspects of their positions, and sufficiently insulated from social pressures to administer a system of rewards and punishments in a manner that would produce dependable role performance and create innovative behavior in the pursuit of policy goals. This study has shown that, at least in Ghana, it cannot be assumed that senior administrative staff will on the whole be so characterized. Rather they resemble more junior personnel in the kinds of role pressures to which they are subject. Here, again, solutions are confounded by the systemic aspects of the problem. A structure of incentives will enhance performance if it is dependably implemented. But if general administrative implementation is undermined by the existing social environment, why should not the implementation of the incentive system be similarly undermined?

This situation offers political leaders two broad types of choices. They can rely on technical assistance from the industrial states. Such a policy will bring to administrative agencies a leadership cadre that can wield sanctions effectively because it is outside of the indigenous social system and is thus free of the obligations and demands of the system. A number of African countries—Kenya, the Ivory Coast, Zaire, and Zambia—have opted for this solution, particularly in the important economic subsystem. Although apparently successful in producing administrative effectiveness in the short run, the reliance on expatriate personnel has significant potential long-term costs. For one thing, it may well represent administrative "growth without development," for when the expatriate personnel leaves, the organization will again be freely penetrated by its social environment, and the old problems will return. Moreover, the costs of such a policy in the areas of national autonomy, mobility and social structure, psychological security, and indigenous culture may be so high as to outweigh the short-term benefits of enhanced administrative performance.

The alternative is to devise policies aimed at recruiting and creating organizational leaders who will effectively implement a formal system of performance incentives. The design of the incentive system is a minor matter compared with what must be seen as a prior and more

[16] On the relationship between the performance of public bureaucracy and regime legitimacy, see the Introduction, pp. 2-3.

fundamental concern: the creation of what Philip Selznick terms the "institutional core," an administrative leadership stratum that reflects the basic needs, values, and goals of the new organization, and the new polity more generally, in its own outlook.[17] For a governing elite, core building involves two interrelated tasks. First, it must elaborate an ideology (a system of goals, values, and beliefs); one which is reflected in their own behavior, which strikes a responsive chord in the population, and which can serve to tie roles in public bureaucracy to transcendental values, thus making service to the nation in the pursuit of developmental goals a meaningful alternative to service to some different and less inclusive social entity. The second and related task involves a conscious policy of selective recruitment of personnel. Two criteria must be primary for recruitment into the leadership stratum of the public bureaucracy—personal ideological commitment and the social ability to act on that commitment. If there is validity in the perspective that has been argued here, then a governing elite in a transitional polity interested in creating more effective public bureaucracy should selectively recruit into positions of administrative leadership individuals who are personally committed to national development and have concomitant performance and service orientations and, especially important, who are alienated from, or at least cut off from, existing traditional forms of social organization, in particular their corporate kinship groups.

There is little probability that the contemporary governing elite in Ghana, and in most other African countries, will actually engage in such a core-building program. It is by no means clear, for one thing, that they perceive such basic forms of traditional social organization as the corporate family as a systemic threat to organizational effectiveness.[18] And even if, as an abstract notion, they were to so comprehend the situation, it is doubtful that their commitment to development goals is strong and confident enough to allow them to move ruthlessly against the fundamental aspects of existing social organization. This is especially true, since they themselves are for the most part tied into, and to some extent maintain an affective link with, traditional social structures. Also, an institutional core, however inappropriate, already exists in public bureaucracy and must

[17] Philip Selznick, *Leadership in Administration*, pp. 105-106.
[18] They obviously comprehended the threat to their political power represented by the traditional system of authority, especially when it involves a highly developed system of chieftancy. But here we are referring to a basic form of social organization whose "threat" is not directly manifest, as is that of chiefs toward "modern" political leaders.

be removed if a new core, with a character more relevant to the needs of development administration, is to be created. Such an operation demands a governing elite with a great deal of self-confidence and more political support than perhaps is available to the elites presently in power. For all these reasons it is highly doubtful that the contemporary Ghanaian political leadership would actually attempt to create the type of institutional core that might greatly enhance administrative performance.

In short, when the basic problems of organizations stem from the existing socio-cultural environment, a relevant program of rapid and conscious solution to these problems can be undertaken only by groups who in one way or another are insulated from that environment. It is possible that the economic and political stresses now being experienced by Ghana and other African countries will create large groups sufficiently alienated from existing social arrangements to sponsor and support such programs. But, at least in the immediate future, those political leaders who are highly committed to development goals will find themselves constrained by a socio-cultural system that offers them little support in the building of organizations equal to the tasks they wish to pursue.

Appendix A

CIVIL SERVANT INTERVIEW SCHEDULE

The questionnaire which I am about to administer to you is a survey about opinions of civil servants and the problems they face in doing their job. The study is an independent piece of research being conducted at the University of California, Berkeley, in the United States and at the University of Ghana.

The answers you give to our questions will in no way be identified with you personally. Because we are only interested in statistical aggregates—that is, the percentage of persons who feel one way or another about a given issue, rather than the responses of any one individual—you can remain completely anonymous.

The questions that I will ask concern opinions and not facts. Therefore there will be no such thing as a right or wrong answer. Our only request is that you be *as frank as you can* in your responses.

Now unless there are any questions we can begin.

To begin with I would like to ask you a number of questions about your background. Let me start with education.
  1. How far have you gone in school?
     a. middle school
     b. started secondary school
     c. finished secondary school
     d. started university
     e. finished university
     f. other (specify)
  [If middle school, skip to question 3]
  1A. Which secondary school did you attend?
  [If nonuniversity, skip to question 2]
  1B. Which university did you attend?
  2. From whom did you get the most financial assistance for your education?
  3. Could you tell me what year you were born in?

Now I would like to ask you a few things about your family.
  4. Where are your people from? [Designate town and region.]
  5. What tribe are you?

220

6. What is or was your father's occupation?
7. Is your father literate in English?
   a. yes
   b. no
   c. semiliterate
8. Is your mother literate in English?
   a. yes
   b. no
   c. semiliterate
9. If you have brothers, what work do they do?
10. Do you provide financial assistance for any relatives or friends, with the exception of wives and children you may have? If so, how many do you aid?

Now I would like to ask a few questions about any travel experience you may have had.
11. Have you spent any time abroad? [If no, skip to question 12.]
11A. Where was that, and in what capacity did you go?
11B. How long have you spent outside of Ghana?

Now I would like to turn to some questions about your job experience.
12. What is your present rank in the civil service?
13. In what year did you enter the civil service?
14. Do you find your job very interesting, somewhat interesting, or not very interesting?
   a. very interesting
   b. somewhat interesting
   c. not very interesting

Now I would like to ask your opinion on some things about work and careers.
15. Suppose you were asked to advise an intelligent young man on his career. What sort of a career would you advise him to follow, and why? [If civil service career is not mentioned in question 15, ask]
16. What do you think of a civil service career for an intelligent young man?
17. Some jobs require more work than others. Therefore some people feel that they are required to do too much work, while others feel they do not have enough to do. How about you? Do you feel that
   a. you are expected to do too much
   b. you are expected to do too little
   c. or that the amount of work expected of you is just about right
18. In government work there are many types of jobs. Some involve working in an office, while others involve field work, that is, visiting villages, homes, factories, etc. Which type of work do you prefer?
   a. office work
   b. field work
19. *Hand Card No. 1 to respondent.* Which of the items on this card do you think a person in your position should be able to own? Please tell

me the letter corresponding to the item. [Probe: Are there any other items you would add to this list?]

    a. quality automobile
    b. record player
    c. wireless
    d. house
    e. imported suits
    f. any other (please specify)
    g. there is nothing in particular a person in my position should be able to own

19A. What about your relatives and friends? Are they likely to expect you to own things of this sort?

20. Do you feel that your present salary allows you to buy the kinds of things you should have? [If yes, skip to question 21.]

20A. What about the future? Do you think that in five years you will be able to afford these things?

21. *Hand Card No. 2 to respondent.* Please read the description of an imaginary situation which is on this card. When you have finished, I will ask you a few question about the situation which is described.

(Imagine the following: A civil servant is officially informed that he is to be transferred from Accra to a new post in Tamale. The civil servant is from Accra. He speaks the local language, has all his friends and relatives there, and he is looking after his aged parents who are too old to move to the North with him. For all these reasons he does not want to be transferred to Tamale. He therefore goes to the head of his department, who happens to be his cousin, and asks to be kept in Accra.)

In this situation, would the head of department's relatives be likely to expect him to arrange to have his cousin stay in an Accra post? [If no, skip to question 21D.]

21A. Do you think the head of department's relatives have a *right* to expect him to help his cousin in this situation?

21B. What are the head of department's relatives likely to think of him if he refused to help his cousin stay in the Accra post?

21C. Could the feelings of his relatives have any actual consequences for the head of department? If so, what consequences?

21D. In view of the head of department's government and family positions, what do you think he is likely to do in this situation?

    a. refuse to help his cousin
    b. help his cousin

22. Now I would like you to compare employment in the civil service with other types of employment. Is there anything you particularly like about government work? Please explain.

23. Is there anything you particularly dislike about government employment?

24. Now suppose there are two civil servants in a department such as your own. The first follows regulations exactly in every situation. The second violates regulations in those situations where he feels the achievement of the department's goals require it. Which of the two do you believe is the better civil servant? The first or the second?

25. Which of the two do you think your supervisor would feel is the better civil servant? The first, who follows regulations in every situation, or the second, who sometimes violates regulations when he sees a need to do so?

26. Which of the two do you think is likely to be promoted sooner? The first or the second? Or do you think they both have an equal chance?

Now I would like you to compare employment in the public service with employment in the private sector.

27. Would you leave the public service if you were offered a job by a large and well established private business firm under any of the conditions listed on this card? [Hand Card No. 3 to respondent.] Please tell me the letter corresponding to the condition you choose.

    a. at a lower salary
    b. at the same salary
    c. at a higher salary
    d. wouldn't leave [If answer is "wouldn't leave," ask respondent]

27A. Could you tell me why you would stay on in the civil service even if you were offered a higher salary by a private firm?

28. I would like to know something about how promotions are made in the Ghana Civil Service. What are the things that help a person get promoted? [Wait for response, and afterward *probe* with]

28A. Does it help to know a "*big man*" in the service?

Now let me present another imaginary situation to you, and then ask you some questions about it.

29. Suppose a civil servant arrives at his office one morning and finds several people waiting to see him about routine business. One of these people is a relative of his. Would it be proper to keep this relative waiting because others have come before him?

29A. What do you think the *average* civil servant in Ghana would actually do in this situation? Would he receive his relative before the others?

29B. Now let us turn our attention to the relative in this imaginary situation. What do you think he would expect? Would he be likely to expect to be seen before the others, or would he expect to be seen only after those who came before him have taken care of their business?

30. Now let us change the imaginary situation slightly. This time the person who comes to the office is a friend of the civil servant, but not a relative. Would this make any difference? [If yes, respondent to explain.]

31. On this card there is another imaginary situation. After you read it, I'll ask you some questions about it. [Hand Card No. 4 to respondent.]

(A civil servant is assigned to factory insepction; his duty is to ensure that factories conform to safety laws. In one factory he sees a floor that looks as if it might give way under the weight of a machine. According to the usual procedure, he telephones his superior, the chief inspector, but he finds that he is away and will not return that day. Since the factory inspector believes the floor may collapse at any moment, he asks the factory owner to close down the factory until repairs are made. The factory owner refuses, showing him a certificate of approval, issued only two weeks before by the civil servant's superior, the chief inspector. But believing the danger

77

to be great, the civil servant orders the factory closed despite the approval so recently given by his superior.)

Do you think the civil servant's superior will discipline him for taking such a step if in fact the floor *does not* collapse?

32. If you were the superior would you discipline him for having taken the action he did?

33. Why? [Be ready to hand Card No. 5 to respondent.]

34. Here is another card. On it are listed characteristics of seven men. On the basis of the descriptions of the men provided on the card, could you tell me which two of them are likely to be most respected by people in Ghana? [Respondent need only give you the number.]

1. He earns a high salary.
2. He is liked by the people with whom he works.
3. He is able to take care of his relatives and friends should they be in need.
4. He has all the good things in life—a good car, a big house, fine clothing, etc.
5. He is better at his job than anyone else.
6. He holds a position in which he has many subordinates who must obey his orders.
7. He makes a contribution to the development of Ghana.
   [*Now ask*] Which of the two will be more respected?

Now I would like to turn to the work situation in your department (ministry) and ask you some questions about it.

35. Do you think that the department (Ministry of ———) is a good place to work?

36. Could you explain why:

37. Would you prefer to work in some other government department or agency? [If no, skip to question 38.]

37A. Where would you prefer to work and why would you prefer it?

38. What is the rank of the immediate superior to whom you report?

39. How often do you see him?
    a. at least once a day
    b. about every other day
    c. at least once a week
    d. at least once a month
    e. less than once a month

40. Do you know your superior personally, aside from your official capacity?

41. How often does he talk to you about your job?
    a. at least once a week (very often)
    b. at least once a month (just often)
    c. less than once a month (rarely)

42. How often do you talk to the head of your department?
    a. more than once a week
    b. at least once every two weeks
    c. about once a month
    d. never

43. I would like to ask you a question about how supervisors exercise their authority in this department (ministry).

In some organizations supervisors simply issue orders, without consultation with their subordinates. In other organizations supervisors seek out the advice of their subordinates before deciding on how things should be done. In general, which type of organization is this department? Do supervisors consult with their subordinates on how things should be done, or do they merely issue orders without any thought of their subordinates' opinions?

 a. consult with subordinates

 b. merely issue orders

44. Do you think there is any advantage to supervisors seeking out the advice of those under them? [If no, skip to question 45.]

44A. What are the advantages?

45. How free do you feel to disagree with your supervisor to his face? Which of the following descriptions best fits your own feelings about this?

 a. It's better not to disagree.

 b. I would hesitate some before disagreeing.

 c. I would hesitate, but only a little.

 d. I wouldn't hesitate at all to disagree to his face.

46. When you don't like some policy or procedure on the job, how often do you tell your opinion to one of your superiors: Would you say you do it:

 a. very rarely or never

 b. sometimes

 c. often

47. Is it useful to call upon your colleagues for assistance on problems which may arise in the course of your work: [If yes, skip to question 48.]

47A. Why is that so?

48. About how many of your colleagues at work are you tight with?

49. How often do you spend time with people in your department outside of working hours?

 a. every day

 b. at least once a week

 c. at least once a month

 d. never

50. How often do you take your lunch with any of the other people you work with?

 a. never

 b. only occasionally

 c. regularly

51. If someone asked you to describe yourself, and you could tell only one thing about yourself, which of the answers on this card would you be most likely to give? [Hand Card No. 6 to the respondent.] Please tell me the letter corresponding to the description you choose.

 a. I come from (hometown)

 b. I work at (name of department or ministry)

 c. I am a civil servant

 d. I am a (name of tribe)

 e. I am a graduate of (name of school)

f. any other (please specify)

52. If you could tell me two things about yourself, what on the list would you add?

53. Suppose that an ordinary citizen finds it necessary to go to a government official concerning ordinary official business. Which of the methods listed on this card would be the *most effective* for him to use in order to accomplish his purpose? [Hand Card No. 7 to respondent.]

      a. He should see a relative of his who is also a government official.

      b. He should go directly to the official's office and state his problem.

      c. He should see a friend who knows the government official.

[If respondent gives "b" as his answer, probe by saying, "I am concerned with the *most effective* method, not necessarily with the proper one.]

54. Which of the three methods do you think is the second most effective?

55. Which of the methods do you think the average Ghanaian would be likely to use first?

56. In a person's day-to-day activities he comes into contact with various groups of people. For example, relatives, friends, workmates, etc. Usually we desire to be admired by certain groups, while the opinions of others mean little to us. Now think for a moment about the groups of people you would most like to be admired by. Which are these? [If more than one group is mentioned, ask]

57. Now could you tell me which one of these groups you most want to be admired by?

58. Now let me present one last imaginary situation. Please read the description on this card. [Hand Card No. 8 to respondent.]

(X is a civil servant whose job it is to evaluate the records of secondary school graduates and recommend *one hundred* of them for scholarships to university. The final choice of some *seventy-five* awards will be made by a specially selected scholarship board, but before a name is presented to the board it must be approved by Mr. X. One of the students who has applied for a government scholarship is from X's hometown, and is the son of a man who helped X financially during the period of his own education. While the boy is a very good student, he does not rank among the top one hundred applicants.

A number of people from X's village, including the applicant's father and X's own brother, have come to Accra to beg X to recommend the boy for a scholarship. X, however, ignores the pleas of his relatives and friends, and does not include the hometown boy in the one hundred names he submits to the scholarship board.

How would this act by X affect his relations with his relatives and the other people in his village? [Probe: How would they feel about what he had done?]

59. How would the people X works with feel about what he had done? Would they think he was foolish to ignore the pleas of his family and friends? Would they think he had shown good judgment? Or would they be largely indifferent, not having an opinion one way or another?

60. Do you think that this imaginary situation is very realistic? Do you think it likely that such a situation would occur? Would a civil servant in X's position be likely to find himself under pressure from relatives and friends?

Now we come to the last set of questions. I will read several short statements to you, and I would like you to tell me whether you strongly agree, agree, disagree, or strongly disagree with each of them.

61. A civil servant should not allow his personal affairs to interfere with the carrying out of his duties.

62. Merit has little to do with promotions in the Ghana Civil Service.

63. The harder a person works the more he will be respected by his colleagues.

64. A civil servant should give equal treatment to all members of the public with whom he deals.

65. Most people around here are helpful and cooperative, and try hard to do their jobs well.

66. A civil servant's job is to observe the regulations in every situation.

67. Civil servants are fortunate because people do not bother them for special consideration, but rather expect equal treatment.

The interview is now over. Thank you very much for kindly giving us so much of your time.

Appendix B

CLIENTELE QUESTIONNAIRE

Instructions for Completing Questionnaire

Most questions can be answered by simply ticking the appropriate blank next to the alternative that is provided. In those cases where alternative answers are not presented, your answer can be written in the space provided.

Please do not sign your name or otherwise identify yourself as a respondent. In this way the confidential nature of your answers is completely assured.

Please fill the questionnaire out by yourself. You can discuss the questions after you have filled it out, but in order to satisfy scientific criteria please do not do so prior to giving your answers.

When you have finished completing the questionnaire, detach the name card and place both questionnaire and name card in the box provided at your hall porter's desk. This method will allow me to determine who has returned the questionnaire, while removing any connection between your name and your answers.

To begin with we would like to know some things about your background. This will allow us to compare the answers of different types of people, e.g., young versus old, male versus female, etc.
  1. Sex
  2. How old are you?
  3. What tribe are you?
  3. Where are your people from? (Designate town and region.)
  5. What is your religion?
  6. What is or was your father's occupation?
  7. How far did your father go in school?
     a. no school
     b. primary school
     c. middle school
     d. secondary school
     e. university
     f. postgraduate
     g. other (specify)
  8. How far did your mother go in school?
     a. no school

    b. primary school
    c. middle school
    d. secondary school
    e. university
    f. postgraduate
    g. other (specify)

9. Is your father literate in English?
    a. yes
    b. no
    c. semiliterate

10. Is your mother literate in English?
    a. yes
    b. no
    c. semiliterate

11. What is your father's approximate yearly income?
    a. below N¢200
    b. N¢200-N¢600
    c. N¢600-N¢1,000
    d. N¢1,000-N¢2,000
    e. N¢2,000-N¢4,000
    f. N¢4,000-N¢6,000
    g. N¢6,000
    h. N¢8,000-N¢10,000
    i. over N¢10,000

12. What secondary school did you attend?
    a. for "O" level
    b. for "A" level

13. Is this your first, second, third, fourth, or fifth year at the university?

14. What course of study are you pursuing for your University degree?
    a. arts
    b. social sciences
    c. natural sciences
    d. engineering
    e. medicine
    f. law
    g. education
    h. agriculture

15. Are you working towards a general or honors degree?

16. Have you spent any time outside of Ghana?
    a. Outside of Ghana in Africa?
    b. Outside of Ghana in Europe or America?
    c. Outside of Ghana in both Europe or America, and Africa?

17. When you begin to earn a salary, will you be under obligation to your family because of the assistance they gave you during the period of your own education and upbringing?

17A. If you answered "Yes," could you describe the form this obligation will take?

18. If you had a free choice of careers to follow, what type of career would you choose? (Pick one)
    a. medicine

    b. law
    c. university lecturer
    d. secondary school teacher
    e. civil service
    f. politics
    g. farming
    h. military
    i. police
    j. business
    k. management (private corporation)
    l. engineering
    m. other (please specify)

Now we would like to know which career you feel that you will actually pursue. (Put an X in the appropriate blank in the above table.)

19. Thinking for a moment about the civil service as a career, is there anything you would particularly *like* about going into the civil service?

20. Is there anything you would particularly *dislike* about going into the civil service?

21. If the pay were the same, which of the institutions listed below would you most like to work for? Pick the appropriate one.
    a. Ghana Civil Service
    b. state corporation
    c. private expatriate (European or American) business firm
    d. Ghanaian private business firm

22. Thinking of your answer to question 21, could you briefly state why you would prefer this type of employment.

Now we turn to the main part of the questionnaire, which deals with the relations of citizens to government departments, agencies, and ministries.

23. First, we are interested in the things that affect the treatment you will receive in dealing with government agencies. Each statement in the series below describes a civil servant with a particular characteristic. In each case assumè that you have gone to a government office and are dealing with a civil servant who has the given characteristic. For each one we would like to know if because of this characteristic you could expect to receive *better* treatment, *worse* treatment, or the *same* treatment from him compared to other people using the services of the government office.
    a. The civil servant is *from your hometown.* Compared to other people, could you expect better treatment, worse treatment, or the same treatment? [This question was repeated for each given characteristic.]
    b. The civil servant is *your close friend.*
    c. The civil servant is *your father's brother.*
    d. The civil servant is your *grandmother's sister's husband.*
    e. The civil servant is *your mother's cousin (your mother's mother's sister's son).*
    f. The civil servant is *the husband of your father's brother's wife's sister.*
    g. The civil servant is *your brother-in-law's brother.*
    h. The civil servant is *the brother of your father's brother's wife.*
    i. The civil servant is a *Ga.*

j. The civil servant is a *Fanti.*
k. The civil servant is an *Ashanti.*
l. The civil servant is an *Ewe.*
m. The civil servant is an *Akim.*
n. The civil servant is an *Akwapim.*
o. The civil servant is a *Northerner.*
p. The civil servant is *a good friend of your brother's.*
q. The civil servant is *an old school mate.*
r. Is there anything which is not mentioned in the above series (a-q) which you think would affect the treatment a person will receive from government agencies? If so, what are these things?

24. Suppose you go to a government office to take care of some routine business. The business should take only a few minutes to transact, but you find yourself waiting three hours. Then the government official calls you over and simply says "go and come."

What would be your likely reaction to this situation? (Pick the statement below that comes closest to your probable reaction.)

a. I would realize that "this is the way things are," that it is to be expected, and I would come back the next day.
b. I would become angry and demand an explanation from the civil servant.
c. Becoming angry, I would demand that the civil servant serve me, and if he did not I would go and see his superior or supervisor.
d. I would offer to "do something" if he would finish the business straight away.

25. We are interested in the most effective ways of getting things done at government offices in Ghana. Let us say you had some *routine* business with a government department or agency. Below are listed five alternative ways of getting your business done. Which of these would be the most effective, i.e., would get the business successfully completed in the shortest time?

a. You see a friend who knows the official with whom you must deal.
b. You go straight to the government office and state your business.
c. You visit the official in charge at his house prior to going to his office, and offer to "do something."
d. You find someone to "fix things" with the responsible official.
e. You go to the office and "dash" the official with whom you must deal.

26. Now let us suppose that the business you had to transact was urgent and demanded rapid attention. In this case would the most effective alternative be the same as in the previous question or would it be different?

27. If you answered "different," could you write down the number of the alternative which you believe is most effective in this case.

28A. Now we would like to know which of the alternatives you believe would be the *least* effective one to use. First in the case of routine business. (Write the number of the alternative in the space provided.)

28B. Now in the case of urgent business.

29. Here are descriptions of two senior government officials. Please pick the one you think is the better man.

a. Official One. He has used his official position to "chop" a great deal of money, but he has shown great generosity, coming to the aid of any of his people who are in need.

    b. Official Two. He follows all rules and regulations of his office and has not "chopped" money, but as a result, although he would like to show generosity, he constantly refuses to help any of his people who are in need.

30. Which of the two above officials do you think most Ghanaians would consider the better man?

31. Which of the two would you prefer to have as a relative?

32. Here is a short imaginary situation. Read it and then answer the question that follows.

A person finds that a civil servant with whom he is dealing does not do his job properly. As a result he goes to see a man's superior in order to make a complaint.

What would be the likely result of this action? Would the person be likely to have helped his cause, to have hurt his cause, or wouldn't his action be likely to make any difference?

33. If you found yourself in the situation described in question 32, would you insist on seeing the civil servant's superior or supervisor?

34. Now suppose that you were teaching a child how to deal with the government civil service. Which of these three ways would you tell him to use when approaching civil servants for help?

    a. As government employee he is your servant, and it is his job to give you prompt help. You should simply state what you want from him.

    b. He is in a position of authority and therefore you must show proper respect if you expect help from him.

    c. Although civil servants are employed to serve people like you, it is best to show respect if one wants some help from them.

35. Some people say that knowing a "big man" in government plays an important part in whether the government will help a private citizen with some problem he has; other people say that this is not so. In your opinion, does knowing a "big man" play an important part in whether the government will help a private citizen?

    a. Yes, a very important part.

    b. Yes, a somewhat important part.

    c. No, not a very important part.

    d. No, no part at all.

36. Below you will find an imaginary situation presented. Please read it carefully, and then answer the questions that follow.

Your father is a civil servant who is posted in Accra, and he has just got notice that he will be transferred to a new post in Tamale. Your entire family lives in Accra, and if your father must move your family life will be seriously disrupted. Now, your mother's sister is married to a man who is the head of your father's department, and therefore he has the power to arrange to have your father keep his Accra post.

Do you think it likely that your father or some other member of the family will ask your relative to fix things?

37. If he were asked, is it likely that your relative would arrange to have your father stay in the Accra post?

38. Do you think that you have a *right* to expect the husband of your mother's sister to arrange to have your father stay in Accra?

39. What would be the reaction of your family if your relative refused to fix things for your father? Would his refusal affect his relations with them? If so, how? (Please be specific.)

40. At present, do you think the national government is doing a *poor, fair*, or *good* job?
   a. very poor
   b. poor
   c. fair
   d. good
   e. very good
   f. excellent
   g. don't know

41. If you were asked to give an efficiency rating of the Ghanaian Civil Service, which of the following ratings would you give? Efficiency is:
   a. exceedingly low
   b. very low
   c. low
   d. average
   e. high
   f. very high
   g. exceedingly high

42. Now think ahead ten years. Do you think efficiency will have improved, stayed about the same, or gotten worse?
   a. improved
   b. stayed about the same
   c. gotten worse

43. About how many of the *high government officials* would you say are probably dishonest or corrupt—many of them, some of them, just a few of them, or none of them at all?

44. We would like to know what kinds of men are respected in Ghana. Descriptions of seven men are listed below. Please pick the one which you believe is likely to be most respected by people in Ghana.
   a. He earns a high salary.
   b. He is liked by the people with whom he works.
   c. He is able to take care of his relatives and friends should they be in need.
   d. He has all the good things in life: a good car, a big house, fine clothing, etc.
   e. He is better at his job than anyone else.
   f. He holds a position in which he has many subordinates who must obey his orders.
   g. He makes a contribution to the development of Ghana.

45. Now we would like to know which man would be the next most respected. Please indicate this by placing an "X" in the appropriate blank.

46. Now suppose you were attempting to carry out some routine business at a government office. You have visited the office *three* separate times, but each time the civil servant in charge says your forms are not ready and that you should "go and come." What would you conclude is the trouble?

a. The staff is overworked.
b. The staff is lazy.
c. The official is looking for a "dash."
d. The staff is incompetent.
e. The official is trying to show his importance.
f. Other (please specify).

Now we come to the final set of questions. Here are some kinds of things people tell me when I interview them. I would like to know whether you strongly agree, agree, disagree, or strongly disagree with them. Tick the appropriate answer after each statement.

47. Government officials in Ghana are cooperative and courteous.

48. I don't think public officials care much about what people like me think.

49. Government employees in Ghana are dedicated to serving the public and to the development of the country.

50. The government does very little to help a person like me.

51. It is best to have as little as possible to do with government officials.

52. In getting ahead in life ability means little; it is *who you know* that is really important.

53. A "big man" should not have to work hard, but should hire others to do the hard work for him.

54. If a rich man does not buy an expensive car and build a large house, he will lose standing in the eyes of his relatives and friends.

Appendix C

COMPARISON/CLIENTELE INTERVIEW

SCHEDULE

[Interviewer determines answers to questions 1 and 2]
1. Sex of respondent?
2. How well does respondent speak English?
   a. not at all
   b. a little
   c. fairly well
   d. fluently

First, I would like to know some things about your background: your job, your age, where you're from, things like that.
   3. What was your age at your last birthday?
   4A. Have you been to school?
   [If no, skip to question 5]
   4B. How far did yu go in school?
   5. Do you read English?
      a. not at all
      b. somewhat
      c. well
   6. What is your tribe?
   7. Where are your people from? [Designate town and region]
   8. Where are you living now?
   9. For how long have you lived in this area?
[If respondent lives outside of Accra, ask questions 9A and 9B. Otherwise skip to question 10.]
   9A. Have you ever lived in Accra?
   9B. How often do you go into Accra?
   10. What job do you do?
   11. What job did or does your father do?
   12. What religion are you?

Now we turn to the main part of the questionnaire, which deals with the relations of citizens to government departments, agencies, and ministries.
   13. First, we are interested in the things that affect the treatment you

will receive in dealing with government agencies. Each statement in the following series describes a civil servant with a particular characteristic. In each case assume that you have gone to a government agency and are dealing with a civil servant who has the given characteristic. For each one we would like to know if because of this characteristic you could expect to receive *better* treatment, *worse* treatment, or the *same* treatment from him compared to other people using the agency's services.

      a. The civil servant is *from your hometown*. Compared to other people, could you expect better treatment, worse treatment, or the same treatment? [This question was repeated for each particular characteristic.]

      b. The civil servant is *your close friend*.

      c. The civil servant is *your father's brother*.

      d. The civil servant is *your grandmother's sister's husband*.

      e. The civil servant is *your mother's cousin* (your mother's mother's sister's son).

      f. The civil servant is *the husband of your father's brother's wife's sister*.

      g. The civil servant is *your brother-in-law's brother* (your sister's husband's brother).

      h. The civil servant is *the brother of your father's brother's wife*.

      i. The civil servant is a *Ga*.

      j. The civil servant is a *Fanti*.

      k. The civil servant is an *Ashanti*.

      l. The civil servant is an *Ewe*.

      m. The civil servant is an *Akim*.

      n. The civil servant is an *Akwapim*.

      o. The civil servant is a *Northerner*.

      p. The civil servant is *a good friend of your brother's*.

      q. Is there anything which is not mentioned in questions I have just asked which you think would affect the treatment you will receive from civil servants? If so, what are these things?

14. Suppose you had to go to a government office to take care of some routine business. The business should take only a few minutes to transact, but you find yourself waiting three hours. Then the government official calls you over and simply says "go and come."

What would be your likely reaction to this situation? Tell me which of the following statements comes closest to your probable reaction.

      a. I would realize that "this is the way things are," that it is to be expected, and I would come back the next day.

      b. I would become angry and demand an explanation from the civil servant.

      c. Becoming angry, I would demand that the civil servant serve me, and if he did not I would insist on seeing his superior or supervisor.

      d. I would offer to "do something" if he would finish the business straight away.

15. Here are descriptions of two senior government officials. Please tell me which one you think is the better man.

      a. Official One. He has used his official position to "chop" a great deal of money, but he has shown great generosity, coming to the aid of any of his people who are in need.

    b. Official Two. He follows all rules and regulations of his office and has not "chopped" money, but as a result, although he would like to show generosity, he constantly refuses to help any of his people who are in need.

16. Which of the two do you think most Ghanaians would consider the better man?

17. Which of the two would you prefer to have as a relative?

18. We are interested in the most effective ways of getting things done at government offices in Ghana. Let us say you had business with some government department or agency. Below are listed alternative ways of getting your business done. Which of these would be the *most effective*, i.e., would get the business successfully completed in the shortest time?

    a. You see a friend who knows the official with whom you must deal.

    b. You go straight to the government office and state your business.

    c. You visit the official in charge at his house prior to going to his office, and offer to "do something."

    d. You find someone to "fix things" with the responsible official.

    e. You go to the office and dash the official with whom you must deal.

19. Now I am going to tell you a short story. When I have finished, I will ask you a question about it.

A government official gives special help to some people from his hometown. As a result they send a delegation to Accra to thank him, and they present him with twenty cedis "dash" in appreciation of what he has done. The official, however, gives back the "dash," explaining that he was doing his job when he helped them.

What do you think about this official's refusal to accept the gift from his people? Which of the following statements best describes your feelings about him?

    a. He is too proud.

    b. He is trying to be too independent of his people.

    c. He thinks the "dash" was too small and expects the delegation to return wth more.

    d. He is an honest man.

    e. He has insulted his people.

20. Here are three statements about how to deal with civil servants. Tell me which you think is the most correct one.

    a. As a government employee the civil servant is there to serve people like you, and it is his job to give prompt help. Therefore, when going to see a civil servant you should simply state what you want from him.

    b. A civil servant is in a position of authority and therefore you must show him proper respect if you expect help from him.

    c. Although civil servants are employed to serve people like you, it is best to show respect if one wants some help from them.

21. Now I will tell you a short story, and then ask you a question about it.

A person finds that a civil servant with whom he is dealing does not do his job properly. As a result he goes to see the man's superior in order to make a complaint.

What would be the likely result of this action? Would the person be likely to have helped his cause, to have hurt his cause, or wouldn't his action be likely to make any difference?

    a. He hurt his cause.
    b. He helped his cause.
    c. No difference.

If you were in the above situation, would you insist on seeing the civil servant's superior or supervisor?

22. Now suppose you were attempting to carry out some routine business at a government office. You have visited the office three separate times, but each time the civil servant in charge says your forms are not yet ready, and that you should "go and come." What would you conclude is the trouble?

    a. The staff has too much work to do.
    b. The staff is lazy.
    c. The official is looking for a "dash."
    d. The staff is incompetent.
    e. The official is trying to show his importance (that he is a "big man").
    f. Other (specify).

23. We would like to know what kinds of men are respected in Ghana. Here are descriptions of seven men. Please tell me which one you believe is likely to be *most* respected by people in Ghana.

    a. He earns a high salary.
    b. He is liked by the people with whom he works.
    c. He is able to take care of his relatives and friends should they be in need.
    d. He has all the good things in life: a good car, a big house, fine clothing, etc.
    e. He is better at his job than anyone else.
    f. He holds a position in which he has many subordinates who must obey his orders.
    g. He makes a contribution to the development of Ghana.

24. Which of the seven would be the next most respected?

25. Some people say that knowing a "big man" in government plays an important part in whether the government will help a private citizen with some problems he has; other people say that this is not so. In your opinion, does knowing a "big man" play an important part in whether the government will help a private citizen?

    a. Yes, a very important part.
    b. Yes, a somewhat important part.
    c. No, not a very important part.
    d. No, no part at all.

26. At present about how many of the high government officials would you say are probably dishonest or corrupt—many of them, some of them, just a few of them, or none of them at all?

27. Now what about the high government officials in the Nkrumah

government? About how many of them would you say were probably dishonest or corrupt—many, some, just a few, or none at all?

28. At present, do you think the national government is doing a poor, fair, good, or very good job?

29. Could you tell me whether or not you have ever been a member of a trade union?

30. Have you ever voted in an election?

31. Have you registered to vote during the current registration campaign?

Now here are some things people tell me when I interview them. Could you tell me whether you strongly agree, just agree, strongly disagree, or just disagree with them.

32. I don't think public officials care much about what people like me think.

33. Government officials in Ghana are cooperative and courteous.

34. Government employees in Ghana are dedicated to serving the public and to the development of the country.

35. The government does very little to help a person like me.

36. In getting ahead in life ability means little; it is *who you know* that is really important.

37. A "big man" should not have to work hard, but should hire others to do the hard work for him.

38. It is best to have as little as possible to do with government officials.

39. If a rich man does not buy an expensive car and build a big house he will lose standing in the eyes of his relatives and friends.

Appendix D

THE CIVIL SERVANT SAMPLE

Table A

Breakdown of Sample by Age of Respondents

Age	Number	Percentage
Under 30	184	42.4%
31-40	122	28.1
41-50	80	18.4
Over 50	28	6.5
N.A.	20	4.6
☐ Total	434	100.0

Table B

Breakdown of Sample by Location of Post

Location	Number	Percentage
Accra	177	40.8%
Koforidua	110	25.3
Ho	94	21.7
Cape Coast	51	11.8
☐ Total	432	99.6

Table C

Breakdown of Sample by Position in Bureaucratic Hierarchy

Position	Number	Percentage
Top level[a]	182	41.9%
Middle level[b]	141	32.5
Lower level	111	25.6
☐ Total	434	100.0

[a] Administrative Officer I, II, III, IV, Principal, and Senior Executive Officer.
[b] Higher Executive Officer, Executive Officer.
[c] Clerical.

Table D

Breakdown of Sample by Seniority of Respondents

Years in Service	Number	Percentage
Less than 2	61	14.1%
2 to 7	141	32.5
8 to 13	84	19.4
14 to 19	75	17.3
20 to 25	41	9.4
Over 25	32	7.3
☐ Total	434	100.0

Appendix E

THE CLIENTELE SAMPLE

Table E

Breakdown of Student Sample by Type of Community
Respondent's Family Resides In

Community Type and Size	Respondents	
	Number	Percentage
Urban (Accra — 700,000; Kumasi — 400,000)	52	13.5%
Semi-urban (10,000-50,000)	54	14.0
Town (2,000-9,999)	144	37.4
Village (less than 2,000)	90	23.4
N.A.	45	11.7
☐ Total	385	100.0

Table F

Breakdown of Student Sample by Literacy
of Respondent's Parents (in English)

Literacy of Parents	Respondents	
	Number	Percentage
Both parents literate	94	24.4%
One parent literate	153	39.7
Both nonliterate	132	34.3
N.A.	6	1.6
☐ Total	385	100.0

Table G

Breakdown of Student Sample by Paternal Occupation

Father's Occupation	Respondents	
	Number	Percentage
Senior civil servant	40	10.4%
Professional or managerial	17	4.4
Non-University teacher	27	7.0
Businessman	12	3.1
Clergyman	7	1.8
Clerk, salesman	36	9.4
Police or military	9	2.3
Skilled artisan	25	6.5
Trader	25	6.5
Traditional authority	9	2.3
Farmer or fisherman	147	38.2
Other	18	4.7
N.A.	13	3.4
☐ Total	385	100.0

Table H

Breakdown of Student Sample by Father's Level of Education

Father's Education Level	Respondents	
	Number	Percentage
No school	145	37.7%
Primary	22	5.7
Middle	118	30.7
Teacher training college	27	7.0
Secondary	47	12.2
University	20	5.2
N.A.	6	1.5
☐ Total	385	100.0

Selected Bibliography

Abegglen, J. C. *The Japanese Factory, Aspects of Its Social Organization.* Glencoe, Ill.: Free Press, 1958.

Abueva, Jose V. "Administrative Doctrines Diffused in Emerging States: The Filipino Response." *Political and Administrative Development.* Edited by R. Braibanti. Duke, N. C.: Duke University Press, 1969.

———. "The Contribution of Nepotism, Spoils, and Graft to Political Development." *East-West Center Review*, III (1966), 45-54.

Ackerman, Nathan. "Social Role and Total Personality." *American Journal of Orthopsychiatry*, XXI (1951), 1-17.

Adu, A. L. *The Civil Service in Commonwealth Africa.* London: George Allen & Unwin, 1969.

Almond, Gabriel, and Verba, Sidney. *The Civic Culture.* Princeton: Princeton University Press, 1963.

Almond, Gabriel, and Coleman, James, eds. *The Politics of the Developing Areas.* Princeton: Princeton University Press, 1960.

Amarteifio, G. W. *Tema Manhean.* Accra: Ghana University Press, 1966.

Andreski, Stanislav. *The African Predicament.* New York: Atherton Press, 1969.

Apter, David E. *Ghana in Transition.* New York: Atheneum Publishers, 1963.

———. *The Politics of Modernization.* Chicago: University of Chicago Press, 1965.

Arrighi, Giovanni, and Saul, John. "Socialism and Economic Development in Tropical Africa." *Journal of Modern African Studies*, VI (1968), 141-169.

Asch, Solomon E. "Effects of Group Pressure upon the Modification and Distortion of Judgments." *Basic Studies in Social Psychology.* Edited by H. Proshansky and B. Seidenberg. New York: Holt, Rinehart & Winston, 1965.

———. *Social Psychology.* Englewood Cliffs, N.J.: Prentice-Hall, 1952.

Austin, Dennis. *Politics in Ghana: 1946-1960.* London: Oxford University Press, 1964.

Back, Kurt W. "Influence Through Social Communication." *Journal of Abnormal and Social Psychology*, XLVI, 2 (January 1951), 9-23.

Banton, Michael. *Roles.* New York: Basic Books, 1965.

Barker, Ernest. *The Development of Public Service in Western Europe.* London: Oxford University Press, 1945.

Barnard, Chester I. "The Theory of Formal Organization." *Public Adminis-*

tration. Edited by T. Golembiewski et al. Chicago: Rand McNally & Co., 1966.

Bayley, David H. "The Effects of Corruption in a Developing Nation." *Western Political Quarterly,* XIX, 4 (December 1966), 719-732.

Bendix, Reinhard. "Tradition and Modernity Reconsidered." *Comparative Studies in Society and History,* IX, 3 (April 1967), 292-346.

Berg, Eliot. "Socialism and Economic Development in Tropical Africa." *Quarterly Journal of Economics,* LXXVIII, 4 (November 1964), 549-573.

Berger, Morroe. *Bureaucracy and Society in Modern Egypt.* Princeton: Princeton University Press, 1957.

———. "Bureaucracy East and West." *Administrative Science Quarterly,* 1957, 518-529.

Beyer, William C. "The Civil Service of the Ancient World." *Public Administration Review,* XIX (1959), 243-249.

Bing, Geoffrey. *Reap the Whirlwind.* London: MacGibbon & Kee, 1968.

Birmingham, W.; Neustadt, I.; and Omaboe, E. N., eds. *A Study of Contemporary Ghana.* Vol. I, London: George Allen & Unwin, 1966. Vol. II, Northwestern University Press, 1967.

Blau, Peter M. *Dynamics of Bureaucracy.* Chicago: University of Chicago Press, 1955.

Blau, Peter M., and Scott, W. Richard. *Formal Organizations.* San Francisco: Chandler Publishing Co., 1962.

Boateng, E. A. *A Geography of Ghana.* Cambridge: Cambridge University Press, 1966.

Bohannan, Paul. *African Homicide and Suicide.* Princeton: Princeton University Press, 1960.

———. *African Outline.* Middlesex, G.B.: Penguin, 1964.

Bottomore, T. B., ed. *Karl Marx.* New York: McGraw-Hill Book Co., Inc., 1964.

Brokensha, David. *Social Change at Larteh, Ghana.* Oxford: Oxford University Press, 1966.

Burke, Fred. "Public Administration in Africa." *Journal of Comparative Administration,* I, 3 (November 1969), 345-378.

Caldwell, J. C. *Population Growth and Family Change in Africa.* New York: Humanities Press, 1968.

Cameron, N. *The Psychology of Behavior Disorders.* Boston: Houghton Mifflin Co., 1947.

Caplow, Theodore. "The Criteria of Organizational Success." *Social Forces,* XXXII, 1 (October 1953), 1-9.

Card, Emily, and Callawy, Barbara. "Ghanaian Politics: The Elections and After." *Africa Report,* XV, 3 (March 1970), 10-15.

Clignet, Remi, and Foster, Philip. *The Fortunate Few.* Evanston: Northwestern University Press, 1966.

Cohen, Ronald. "Traditional Society in Africa." *The African Experience.* Vol. I. Edited by John Paden and Edward Soja. Evanston: Northwestern University Press, 1970.

Coleman, James, and Rosberg, Carl. *Political Parties and National Integration in Tropical Africa.* Berkeley and Los Angeles: University of California Press, 1964.

Colson, Elizabeth. "Competence and Incompetence in the Context of Independence." *Current Anthropology*, VIII, 1-2 (February-April 1967), 92-110.

Constas, Helen. "Max Weber's Two Conceptions of Bureaucracy." *American Journal of Sociology*, LII (January 1968), 400-409.

Converse, Philip E. "The Nature of Belief Systems in Mass Publics." *Ideology and Discontent*. Edited by D. E. Apter. Glencoe, Ill.: Free Press, 1964.

Crozier, Michael. *The Bureaucratic Phenomenon*. Chicago: University of Chicago Press, 1964.

Crutchfield, R. S. "Conformity and Character." *American Psychologist*, X, 5 (May 1955), 191-198.

Danquah, J. B. *The Akan Doctrine of God*. London: Frank Cass & Co., 1968.

de Graft-Johnson, K. E. "The Evolution of Elites in Ghana." *The New Elites of Tropical Africa*. Edited by P. C. Lloyd. Oxford: Oxford University Press, 1966.

de Schweinitz, Karl. *Industrialization and Democracy*. Glencoe, Ill.: Free Press, 1964.

Deutsch, Karl W. *Nationalism and Social Communication*. New York: M.I.T. Press and John Wiley & Sons (joint), 1953.

———. "Social Mobilization and Political Development." *American Political Science Review*, LV, 3 (September 1961), 493-514.

Dresang, Dennis. "Entrepreneurialism and Development Administration in Zambia," *African Review*, I, 3 (January 1972), 91-117.

Due, Jean M. "Agricultural Development in the Ivory Coast and Ghana." *Journal of Modern African Studies*, VII, 4 (December 1969), 637-660.

Dumont, Rene. *False Start in Africa*. New York: Frederick A. Praeger, 1966.

Durkheim, Emile. *Division of Labor in Society*. Glencoe, Ill.: Free Press, 1933.

Easton, David. *A Systems Analysis of Political Life*. New York: John Wiley & Sons, 1965.

Eisenstadt, S. N. *Essays on Comparative Institutions*. New York: John Wiley & Sons, 1965.

Eldersveld, S. J.; Jagannadham, V.; and Barnabas, A. P. *The Citizen and the Administrator in a Developing Democracy*. Glenview, Ill.: Scott, Foresman & Co., 1968.

Esman, Milton J. "The Ecological Style in Comparative Administration." *Public Administration Review*, XXVII (September 1967), 271-278.

Etzioni, Amatai. *A Comparative Analysis of Complex Organizations*. Glencoe, Ill.: Free Press, 1961.

Fainsod, Merle. "The Structure of Development Administration." *Development Administration: Concepts and Problems*. Edited by I. Swerdlow. Syracuse: Syracuse University Press, 1963.

Fallers, Lloyd A. *Bantu Bureaucracy*. Chicago: University of Chicago Press, 1965.

Fanon, Franz. *The Wretched of the Earth*. New York: Grove Press, 1965.

Festinger, Leon. "Informal Social Communication." *Psychological Review*, LVII, 5 (September 1950), 271-282.

Festinger, Leon; Schachter, Stanley; and Back, Kurt. *Social Pressures in Informal Groups*. Stanford: Stanford University Press, 1950.

Field, M. J. *Search for Security*. Evanston: Northwestern University Press, 1960.

———. *Social Organization of the Ga People*. London: Crown Publication, 1940.

Finer, S. E. "Patronage and the Public Service: Jeffersonian Bureaucracy and the British Tradition." *Public Administration Review*, XXX (1952), 329-358.

Fleming, William G. "Authority, Efficiency, and Role Stress." *Administrative Science Quarterly*, XI (December 1966), 386-404.

Forde, D., ed. *Social Implications of Industrialization and Urbanization in Africa South of the Sahara*. New York: U.N.E.S.C.O., 1956.

Foster, Philip. *Education and Social Change in Ghana*. Chicago: University of Chicago Press, 1965.

Georgeopoulos, S., and Tannenbaum, A. S. "A Study of Organizational Effectiveness." *American Sociological Review*, XXII, 5 (October 1957), 534-540.

Gerth, Hans, and Mills, C. W. *From Max Weber*. Oxford: Oxford University Press, 1958.

Getzels, J. W., and Guba, E. G. "Role, Role Conflict and Effectiveness." *American Sociological Review*, XIX (1954), 164-175.

Ghana Business Guide, 1968. Accra: Ringway Press, 1968.

Gouldner, Alvin W. "Cosmopolitans and Locals: Toward an Analysis of Latent Social Roles—I." *Administrative ScienceQuarterly*, II, 3 (December 1957), 281-306.

———. "The Norm of Reciprocity." *American Sociological Review*, XXV (1960), 161-178.

Greenstone, J. David. "Corruption and Self-Interest in Kampala and Nairobi." *Comparative Studies in Society and History*, VIII, 2 (January 1966), 199-210.

Gross, N. C.; Mason, W. S.; and McEachern, N. W. *Explorations in Role Analysis: Studies of the School Superintendency Role*. New York: John Wiley & Sons, 1958.

Gross, N. C.; McEachern, A.; and Mason, Ward S. "Role Conflict and Its Resolution." *Role Theory*. Edited by B. J. Biddle and E. J. Thomas. New York: John Wiley & Sons, 1966.

Gullahorn, John T. "Measuring Role Conflicts." *American Journal of Sociology*, LXI (January 1956), 299-301.

Gusfield, Joseph. "Tradition and Modernity: Misplaced Polarities in the Study of Social Change," *American Journal of Sociology*, LXII, 4 (January 1967), 351-362.

Hahn-Been, Lee. "Developmentalist Time and Leadership in Developing Countries." Occasional paper for Comparative Administration Group of American Society of Public Administration, 1966.

Hanna, William John. "Image-Making in Field Research: Some Tactical and Ethical Problems of Research in Tropical Africa." *American Behavioral Scientist*, IX (January 1965), 15-20.

Harris, Richard L. "The Effects of Political Change on the Role Set of the Senior Bureaucrats in Ghana and Nigeria." *Administrative Science Quarterly*, XIII, 3 (December 1968), 386-401.

Hill, Polly. *The Migrant Cocoa-Farmers of Southern Ghana*. Cambridge: Cambridge University Press, 1963.

Homans, George. *The Human Group*. New York: Harcourt Brace Jovanovich, 1950.

Huntington, Samuel P. *Political Order in Changing Societies*. New Haven: Yale University Press, 1968.

Hyden, Goran. "Social Structure, Beauracracy, and Development Administration in Kenya," *African Review* I, 3 (January 1972) 118-129.

Hyden, Goran; Jackson, Robert; and Okumu, John. *Development Administration, The Kenyan Experience*. Oxford: Oxford University Press, 1970.

Jackson, J. M., and Saltzstein, H. D. "The Effect of Person-Group Relationships and Conformity Processes." *Journal of Abnormal and Social Psychology*, LVII, 1 (July 1958), 17-24.

Jacobson, Eugene; Charters, W. W., Jr.; and Lieberman, Seymour. "The Use of the Role Concept in the Study of Complex Organizations." *Journal of Social Issues*, VII, 3 (1951), 18-27.

Jahoda, Gustav. "Love, Marriage and Social Change." *Africa*, XXIX, 2 (April 1959), 188-189.

———. "Social Aspirations, Magic and Witchcraft in Ghana: A Social Psychological Interpretation." *The New Elites of Tropical Africa*. Edited by P. C. Lloyd. Oxford: Oxford University Press, 1966.

———. *White Man*. London: Oxford University Press, 1961.

Janowitz, Morris; Wright, Dale; and Delany, William. *Public Administration and the Public Perspectives Toward Government in a Metropolitan Community*. Michigan Governmental Studies, No. 36. Ann Arbor: University of Michigan, 1958.

Kahn, Robert L., et al. *Organizational Stress*. New York: John Wiley & Sons, 1964.

Kasfir, Nelson. "Prismatic Theory and African Administration." *World Politics*, XXI, 2 (January 1969), 295-314.

———. "Towards the Construction of Theories of Administrative Behavior in Developing Countries," *African Review*, I, 3 (January 1972), 155-165.

Katz, Elihu and Eisenstadt, S. N. "Response of Israeli Organizations to New Immigrants." *Administrative Science Quarterly*, V 1 (June 1960), 113-133.

Katz, Daniel, and Kahn, Robert L. *The Social Psychology of Organizations*. New York: John Wiley & Sons, 1966.

Kelly, Harold H. "Salience of Membership and Resistance to Change of Group Anchored Attitudes." *Human Relations*, VIII, 3 (1955), 275-290.

Killian, Lewis M. "The Significance of Multiple-Group Memberships in Disaster." *American Journal of Sociology*, LVII, 4 (January 1952), 309-413.

Kilson, Martin. *Political Change in a West African State*. Cambridge: Harvard University Press, 1966.

Kimble, David. *A Political History of Ghana, 1850-1928*. London: Oxford University Press, 1963.

Kingsley, J. Donald. "Bureaucracy and Political Development, with Particular Reference to Nigeria." *Bureaucracy and Political Development.* Edited by J. La Palombara. Princeton: Princeton University Press, 1963.

Kothari, Rajni. "Tradition and Modernity Revisited," *Government and Opposition*, III, 3 (Summer 1968), 273-293.

Kwei, Ayi Armah. *Fragments.* Boston: Houghton Mifflin Co., 1970.

Landau, Martin. "Linkage, Coding, and Intermediary Organizations." *Journal of Comparative Administration*, II, 4 (February 1971), 401-429.

Leff, Nathaniel H. "Economic Development through Bureaucratic Corruption." *American Behavioral Scientist*, VIII, 3 (November 1964), 8-14.

Leighton, A. H. *Psychiatric Disorder Among the Yoruba*, Ithaca, N.Y.: Cornell University Press, 1963.

Lerner, Daniel. "Communication Systems and Social Systems. A Statistical Exploration in History and Policy." *Behavioral Science*, II, 4 (October 1957), 266-275.

LeVine, Robert A. "Personality and Change." *The African Experience.* Vol. I. Edited by J. N. Paden and E. W. Soja. Evanston: Northwestern University Press, 1970.

LeVine, Victor T. *Political Leadership in Africa.* Palo Alto: Hoover Institution on War, Revolution and Peace, 1967.

Leys, Colin, "What is This Problem About Corruption?" *Journal of Modern African Studies*, III, 2 (August 1965), 215-230.

Likert, Rensis. "Measuring Organizational Performance." *Harvard Business Review*, XXXVI, 2 (March-April 1958), 41-50.

Lloyd, P. C. *Africa in Social Change.* Baltimore: Penguin Books, 1967.

———. "Class Consciousness Among the Yoruba." *The New Elites of Tropical Africa.* Edited by P. C. Lloyd. Oxford: Oxford University Press, 1966.

Lofchie, Michael F., ed. *The State of the Nations.* Berkeley and Los Angeles: University of California Press, 1971.

McClosky, Herbert, et al. "Issue Conflict and Consensus among Party Leaders and Followers." *American Political Science Review*, LIV, 2 (June 1960), 406-427.

McClosky, Herbert, and Di Palma, Giuseppe. "Personality and Conformity: The Learning of Political Attitudes," *American Political Science Review*, LXIV, 4 (December 1970), 1054-1073.

McMullan, M. "A Theory of Corruption." *Sociological Review*, IX, 2 (July 1961), 181-200.

Magid, Alvin. "Dimension of Administrative Role and Conflict Resolution Among Local Officials in Northern Nigeria." *Administrative Science Quarterly*, XII (September 1967), 321-338.

Meadows, Paul. "Motivation for Change and Development Administration." *Development Administration: Concepts and Problems.* Edited by I. Swerdlow. Syracuse: Syracuse University Press, 1963.

Meillassoux, Claude. *Urbanization of an African Community.* Seattle: University of Washington Press, 1968.

Merton, Robert K. "Bureaucratic Structure and Personality." *Social Forces*, XVIII, (1940), 560-568.

———. "The Role-Set: Problems in Sociological Theory." *British Journal of sociology*, VIII (1957), 106-120.

———. *Social Theory and Social Structure.* Glencoe, Ill.: Free Press, 1956.

Miller, Delbert, and Schull, Fremont, Jr. "The Prediction of Administrative Role Conflict Resolution." *Administrative Science Quarterly*, VII (1962), 143-160.

Milne, R. S. "Mechanistic and Organic Models of Public Administration in Developing Countries." *Administrative Science Quarterly*, XV, 1 (March 1970), 57-68.

Morse, Nancy C.; Reimer, E.; and Tannenbaum, A. S. "Regulation and Control in Hierarchical Organization." *Journal of Social Issues*, VII, 3 (1951), 41-48.

Ness, Gayl D. *Bureaucracy and Rural Development in Malaysia*. Berkeley and Los Angeles: University of California Press, 1967.

Norris, Robert W. "On Inflation in Ghana." *Financing African Development*. Edited by T. J. Farer. Cambridge: M.I.T. Press, 1965.

Nye, J. S. "Corruption and Political Development: A Cost-Benefit Analysis." *American Political Science Review*, LXI, 2 (June 1967), 417-427.

Oduro, Kwame. "The Law and Corruption." *Legon Observer*, I, 9 (October 28, 1966), 18-20.

Ollennu, N. A. "Aspects of Land Tenure." *Some Aspects of Social Structure in Ghana: A Study of Contemporary Ghana*. Vol. II. Edited by W. Birmingham et al. Evanston: Northwestern University Press, 1967.

Omari, T. Peter. "Changing Attitudes of Students in West African Society Toward Marriage and Family Relationships." *British Journal of Sociology*, XI, 3 (September 1960), 197-203.

Ort, Robert S. "A Study of Role-Conflicts as Related to Class Level." *Journal of Abnormal and Social Psychology*, XLVII, 2 (April 1952), 425-432.

Page, Charles Hunt. "Bureaucracy's Other Face." *Social Forces*, XXV (October 1946), 88-94.

Parsons, Talcott. *The Social System*. Glencoe, Ill.: Free Press, 1951.

Parsons, Talcott, et al., eds. *Theories of Society*. Glencoe, Ill.: Free Press, 1965.

Parsons, Talcott, and Shils, Edward. eds. *Toward a General Theory of Action*. New York: Harper & Row, 1951.

Patchen, Martin. "Some Questionnaire Measures of Employee Motivation." Survey Research Center Monograph No. 41. Ann Arbor: University of Michigan, 1956.

Pauker, Guy. "The Role of the Military in Indonesia." *The Role of the Military in Underdeveloped Countries*. Edited by J. J. Johnson. Princeton: Princeton University Press, 1962.

———. "Southeast Asia as a Problem Area in the Next Decade." *World Politics*, XI, 3 (April 1959), 325-345.

Peasah, J. A. "Institutionalised Corruption." *Legon Observer*, XI, 4 (February 17-March 2, 1967), 11-13.

Peil, Margaret. *The Ghanaian Factory Worker*. Cambridge: Cambridge University Press, 1972.

Phillips, A. *Survey of African Marriage and Family Life*. London: Oxford University Press, 1953.

Plotnicov, Leonard. *Strangers to the City*. Pittsburgh: University of Pittsburgh Press, 1967.

Presthus, Robert. "The Social Bases of Bureaucratic Organization." *Social Forces*, XXXVIII, 2 (December 1959), 103-109.

———. "Weberian vs. Welfare Bureaucracy in Traditional Society." *Administrative Science Quarterly,* VI, 1 (June 1961), 1-24.

Price, Robert M. "Military Officers and Political Leadership." *Comparative Politics,* III, 3 (April 1971), 361-379.

———. "A Theoretical Approach to Military Rule in New States: Reference Group Theory and the Ghana Case." *World Politics,* XXIII, 3 (April 1971), 399-430.

Priestly, Margaret. *West African Trade and Coast Society.* London: Oxford University Press, 1969.

Prothro, James W., and Grigg, Charles M. "Fundamental Principles of Democracy." *Journal of Politics,* XXII (May 1960), 276-294.

Pye, Lucian. "Armies in the Process of Modernization." *The Role of the Military in Underdeveloped Countries.* Edited by J. J. Johnson. Princeton: Princeton University Press, 1962.

———. "The Army in Burmese Politics." *The Role of the Military in Underdeveloped Countries.* Edited by J. J. Johnson. Princeton: Princeton University Press, 1962.

———. *Aspects of Political Development.* Boston: Little, Brown & Co., 1966.

———. "Bureaucratic Development and the Psychology of Institutionalization." *Political and Administrative Development.* Edited by R. Braibanti. Durham, N.C.: Duke University Press, 1969.

———. *Politics, Personality and Nation Building: Burma's Search for Identity.* New Haven: Yale University Press, 1962.

Rake, Alan. "Zambia: Six Years After." *African Development* (Zambia Supplement), October 1970.

Rattray, R. S. *Ashanti Law and Constitution.* Oxford: Clarendon Press, 1929.

Reissman, Leonard. "A Study of Role Conceptions in Bureaucracy." *Social Forces,* XXVII, 3 (March 1949), 305-310.

Riggs, Fred W. *Administration in Developing Countries.* Boston: Houghton Mifflin Co., 1964.

———. "Bureaucrats and Political Development: A Paradoxical View." *Bureaucracy and Political Development.* Edited by J. La Palombara. Princeton: Princeton University Press, 1963.

———. *Thailand: The Modernization of a Bureaucratic Polity.* Honolulu: East-West Center, 1966.

Rimmer, Douglas. "The Crises in the Ghana Economy." *Journal of Modern African Studies,* IV, 1 (May 1966), 17-32.

Rothchild, Donald. "Ethnic Inequalities in Kenya." *Journal of Modern African Studies,* VII, 4 (December 1969), 689-712.

Rouch, Jean. "Migrations au Ghana." *Journal de la Société des Africanistes,* XXV, 19 (1956), 33-196.

Rudolph, L. I., and Rudolph, S. H. "The Political Role of India's Caste Associations, *Pacific Affairs,* XXXIII, 1 (March 1960), 5-22.

Ryan, Selwyn. "Socialism and the Ghanaian One-Party State." Unpublished paper, Department of Political Science, York University, Toronto, Canada, 1969.

Schachter, Stanley. "Deviation, Rejection, and Communication." *Journal of Abnormal and Social Psychology,* XLVI, 2 (April 1951), 190-207.

Schein, Edgar. *Coercive Persuasion.* New York: W. W. Norton & Co., 1961.

Schurmann, Franz. *Ideology and Organization in Communist China*. Berkeley and Los Angeles: University of California Press, 1968.

Schwab, William B. "Oshogbo—An Urban Community." *Urbanization and Migration in West Africa*. Edited by Hilda Kuper. Berkeley and Los Angeles: University of California Press, 1965.

Scott, James C. "The Analysis of Corruption in Developing Nations." *Comparative Studies in Society and History*, II, 3 (June 1969), 315-341.

———. "Corruption, Machine Politics, and Social Change." *American Political Science Review*, LXIII, 4 (December 1969), 1142-1158.

———. *Political Ideology in Malaysia*. New Haven: Yale University Press, 1968.

Seidman, Ann. "The Inherited Dual Economics of East Africa." Unpublished manuscript.

Selznick, Philip. *Leadership in Administration*. New York: Harper & Row, 1957.

Senghor, L. S. *On African Socialism*. New York: Frederick A. Praeger, 1964.

Sherif, Carolyn, and Sherif, M. *Attitude and Attitude Change: The Social Judgment-Involvement Approach*. Philadelphia: W. B. Saunders Co., 1965.

Sherif, Muzafir. "Integrating Field Work and Laboratory in Small Group Research." *American Sociological Review*, XIX, 6 (December 1954), 759-770.

———. *The Psychology of Social Norms*. New York: Harper & Row Publishers, Inc., 1936.

Sherif, Muzafir, and Sherif, Carolyn. *Groups in Harmony and Groups in Tension*. New York: Harper & Row, 1953.

Siegel, Alberta, and Siegel, Sidney. "Reference Groups, Membership Groups, and Attitude Change." *Journal of Abnormal and Social Psychology*, LV, 3 (November 1957), 360-364.

Siffen, William J. *The Thai Bureaucracy*. Honolulu: Eat-West Center Press, 1966.

Simon, Herbert A. *Administrative Behavior*. Glencoe, Ill.: Free Press, 1957.

Simon, Herbert A., and March, John. *Organizations*. New York: John Wiley & Sons, 1958.

Spiegel, John P. "The Resolution of Role Conflict Within the Family." *Psychiatry*, XX (February 1957), 1-16.

Stinchcombe, Arthur L. "Social Structure and Organizations." *Handbook of Organizations*. Edited by James G. March. Chicago: Rand McNally & Co., 1965.

Stouffer, S. A. "An Analysis of Conflicting Social Norms." *American Sociological Review*, XIV (1949), 707-717.

Stouffer, S. A., and Toby, J. "Role Conflict and Personality." *American Journal of Sociology*, LVI, 5 (March 1951), 395-406.

Stryker, Richard W. "Local Reform in the Ivory Coast: A Perspective on the 'Development Process.' " Paper presented to African Studies Colloquium on Decision-Making and the Development Process in Africa, University of California, April 3, 1968.

Sutcliffe, J. P., and Haberman, M. "Factors Influencing Choice in Role Conflict Situations." *American Sociological Review*, XXI (1956), 695-703.

Swerdlow, Irving. "Economics as Part of Development Administration." *Development Administration: Concepts and Problems.* Edited by I. Swerdlow. Syracuse: Syracuse University Press, 1963.

Tannenbaum, A. S. "Control and Effectiveness in a Voluntary Organization." *American Journal of Sociology,* LXVII, 1 (July 1961), 33-47.

Taub, Richard. *Bureaucrats Under Stress.* Berkeley and Los Angeles: University of California Press, 1969.

Tetteh, P. A. "Marriage, Family, and Household." *Some Aspects of Social Structure in Ghana (A Study of Contemporary Ghana).* Vol. II. Edited by W. Birmingham, I. Neustadt, and E. N. Omaboe. Evanston: Northwestern University Press, 1967.

Tiger, Lionel. "Bureaucracy in Ghana." Unpublished Ph.D. dissertation, University of London, 1963.

Tilman, Robert O. "Emergence of Black-Market Bureaucracy: Administration, Development, and Corruption in the New States." *Public Administration Review,* XXVIII, 5 (September-October 1968), 440-442.

Toby, Jackson. "Some Variables in Role Conflict Analysis." *Social Forces,* XXX, 3 (March 1952), 323-327.

Turner, Ralph H. "Moral Judgment: A Study in Roles." *American Sociological Review,* XVII (February 1952), 70-77.

———. "Role-Taking, Role Standpoint, and Reference-Group Behavior." *American Journal of Sociology,* LXI, 4 (January 1956), 316-328.

———. "Self and Other in Moral Judgment." *American Sociological Review,* XIX, 3 (June 1954), 249-259.

Udy, S. H., Jr. "Bureaucratic Elements in Organization." *American Sociological Review,* XXIII (1958), 415-418.

———. "Technical and Institutional Factors in Production Organization." *American Journal of Sociology,* LXVII (1961), 247-260.

United States Department of Agriculture, Economic Research Service. *Indices of Agricultural Production in 29 African Countries.* December 1965.

Uphoff, Norman T. "Ghana and Economic Assistance: Impetus and Ingredients for a Theory of Political Development." Paper delivered at the 66th Annual Meeting of the American Political Science Association, Los Angeles, September 8-12, 1970.

Vroom, Victor H. "Some Psychological Aspects of Organizational Control." *Perspectives in Organizational Research.* Edited by W. W. Cooper et al. New York: John Wiley & Sons, 1964.

Wahlke, John C., et al. *The Legislative System.* New York: John Wiley & Sons, 1962.

Wallerstein, Immanuel. "The Decline of the Party in Single-Party African States." *Political Parties and Political Development.* Edited by J. La Palombara. Princeton: Princeton University Press, 1966.

———. "Ethnicity and National Integration in West Africa." *Cahiers d'Etudes Africaines,* III (October 1960), 129-138.

Wardwell, Walter I. "The Reduction of Strain in a Marginal Social Role." *American Journal of Sociology,* LXI (1955), 16-25.

Warren, Roland L. "Social Disorganization and the Interrelationship of Cultural Roles." *American Sociological Review,* XIV, 1 (February 1949), 83-87.

Whitaker, C. S., Jr. "A Dysrhythmic Process of Political Change," *World Politics*, XIX, 2 (January 1967), 190-217.
———. *The Politics of Tradition*. Princeton: Princeton University Press, 1970.
Wraith, Ronald. "Administrative Change in the New Africa." *African Affairs*, LXVI (July 1967), 231-240.
Wraith, Ronald, and Simpkins, Edgar. *Corruption in Developing Countries*. London: George Allen & Unwin, 1963.
Young, Crawford. *Politics in the Congo*. Princeton: Princeton University Press, 1965.
Zolberg, Aristide. *Creating Political Order*. Chicago: Rand McNally & Co., 1966.
———. "The Strucutre of Political Conflict in the New States of Tropical Africa." *American Political Science Review*, LXII, 1 (March 1968), 70-87.

Government Documents

Ghana. Census Office *1960 Population Census of Ghana*. Vol. I. Accra: 1962.
———. *1960 Population Census of Ghana: Special Report "E"—Tribes of Ghana*. Accra: 1964.
Ghana. Central Bureau of Statistics. *Monthly News Letter*. Accra.
———. *Statistical Handbook, 1967*. Accra: 1967.
Ghana. The Civil Service. *A Handbook for New Entrants*. Accra: 1961.
———. *(Interim) Regulations, 1960). Accra*.
Ghana. Establishment Secretariat. Organization and Methods Bulletin. October 1963.
Ghana. *Report of the Commission Appointed to Enquire into the Manner of Operation of the State Housing Corporation*. Accra: 1968.
Ghana. *Report of the Commission of Enquiry into Alleged Irregularities and Malpractices in Connection With the Issue of Import Licences*. Accra: 1963.
Ghana. *Report of the Commission of Enquiry Into Irregularities and Malpractices of the Grant of Import Licences*. Accra: 1967.
Ghana. *Report on the Commission of Enquiry into Trade Malpractices in Ghana*. Accra: 1965.
Ghana. *Report of the Commission of the Structure and Remuneration of the Public Services in Ghana*. Accra: 1967.
Ghana. *Report of the Commission of Enquiry on the Local Purchasing of Cocoa*. Accra: 1968.
Gold Coast. *Report of the Commission on the Civil Service of the Gold Coast, 1950-51*. Accra.
Nigeria. Federal Ministry of Information. *The Adebo Commission: First Report of the Salaries and Wages Review Commission*. Lagos: 1970. [Quoted in *West Africa*, 2796 (January 9-15, 1971).]
Uganda. *The Common Man's Charter: First Steps for Uganda to Move to the Left*. Kampala: 1969.

Index

Abueva, Jose V., 132
Accra, 49, 50
Achebe, Chinua, 35
Adae Butu, 119n17
Adangbe peoples, 49, 50
Administrative performance: basic requirements of, 22–24, 56–59, 205, 206; and impersonality, 29, 30; and individualism, 31, 32, 211; and institutionalization, 32–42, 37, 38, 166–168; and integration of organization and society, 24–32, 205, 206; and ritualism, 35, 36, 189, 190; significance of ideology for, 33–36, 218; in United States, 57, 58. *See also* Administrative weakness; Civil Servant Survey; Clientele Survey; Client role orientation; Comparison/Clientele Survey; Organizational Performance
Administrative weakness: ecological explanation for, 8, 11–14; psychological explanation for, 8–11. *See also* Corruption; Dash
Adu, A. L., 44n4, 45
Africa: colonial legacy, 150–155, 170; contrasts with Western bureaucracies, 40–42; importance of government in, 1, 2, 145, 203, 204; military organizations in, 4, 207, 213, 214; morality and public roles, 34–36; research on bureaucracy in, 4; social change in, 107; social organization in, 13, 26–29, 206, 207
Akan peoples, place of family among, 60, 61
Akim, 50
Akwapim, 50

Almond, Gabriel, 90, 91
America. *See* United States
Armah, Ayi Kwai, 37n29, 205
Ashanti, place of family in, 59
Asia: China, 28n12, 210, 215, 216; India, 45, 191; Japan, 209–211; Malaysia, 191; Pakistan, 3n5
Attitude Surveys. *See* Civil Servant Survey; Clientele Survey; Comparison/Clientele Survey

Ballachey, E. L., 108, 109
Barnard, Chester I., 33
Behavior: effect of modernizing influences on, 84–86; nonconforming, 31, 32, 211; organized, 205–207. *See also* Administrative behavior; Role theory
Berger, Morroe, 46n10, 63n20, 64n21, 191, 212, 213
Bribery. *See* Corruption; Dash
Brokensha, David, 60, 61, 120n18
Bureaucracy. *See* Public bureaucracy; Civil service

Caldwell, J. C., 61, 62n18
Calvinism, 84, 212, 213
Cape Coast, 49, 50
Caplow, Theodore, 109
Careers, choice of, 170–178, 195–202
Carnes, J. A., 121
China: kinship group and Communist rule, 28n12; traditional kinship system, 210; "rule of avoidance" in classical bureaucracy, 215, 216
Civic Culture (Almond and Verba), 91, 92

257